Favourite Perennials for Atlantic Canada

How to choose plants and design your garden

ALSO PUBLISHED BY BOULDER PUBLICATIONS

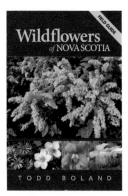

Wildflowers of
Nova Scotia

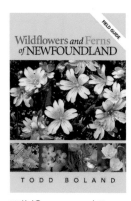

Wildflowers and Ferns
of Newfoundland

Wildflowers of
New Brunswick

Trees and Shrubs of
the Maritimes

Trees and Shrubs of
Newfoundland
and Labrador

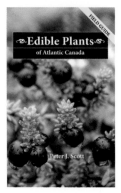

Edible Plants of
Atlantic Canada

Edible Plants of
Newfoundland
and Labrador

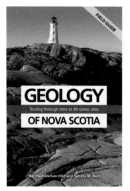

Geology of
Nova Scotia

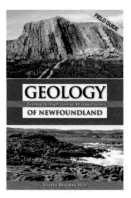

Geology of
Newfoundland

ATLANTIC BOTANIC COLLECTION

FAVOURITE PERENNIALS FOR ATLANTIC CANADA

How to choose plants and design your garden

TODD BOLAND

BOULDER PUBLICATIONS

Library and Archives Canada Cataloguing in Publication

Boland, Todd, author
        Favourite perennials for Atlantic Canada / Todd Boland.

(Atlantic botanic collection)
Includes bibliographical references and index.
ISBN 978-1-927099-96-4 (hardcover)

        1. Perennials--Atlantic Provinces--Identification.   2. Perennials--
Atlantic Provinces--Handbooks, manuals, etc.   I. Title.

SB434.B65 2018   635.9'3209715   C2018-900153-4

Published by Boulder Publications
Portugal Cove-St. Philip's, Newfoundland and Labrador
www.boulderpublications.ca

Design and layout: Todd Manning
Editor: Stephanie Porter
Copy editor: Iona Bulgin

Printed in Canada

We acknowledge the financial support of the Government of Newfoundland and Labrador through the Department of Tourism, Culture and Recreation.

CONTENTS

INTRODUCTION

I started gardening over 40 years ago. My parents and grandparents had a strong love of gardening, and I guess it was inevitable for that passion to be passed on to me. My earliest gardening experience was planting a flower bed under a large maple in our backyard. Our typical small city lot in St. John's, Newfoundland, was almost entirely devoted to growing vegetables. The only place I was allowed to grow a few flowers was in the fringe areas where vegetables could not be grown—the shady area under the maple. Like all gardeners, I quickly learned that growing plants in the shade is a challenge. I had my work cut out for me, and I was not yet a teenager. With many trials and errors, not to mention the death of many plants, I started to figure out what I could and could not grow.

As my parents aged, the care of the vegetable garden passed to me. By then, I was in university, pursuing a degree in plant ecology. At about this time I became an avid plant collector; I wanted one of every plant I could find. The offerings at our local plant nurseries were not enough, so I started combing through any seed and plant mail-order catalogue I could find. I joined our local horticultural society and then the North American Rock Garden Society, Alpine Garden Society, and Scottish Rock Garden Club. Alpine plants are my passion.

I didn't let my Canadian hardiness zone 5b limit me. I was determined to push the limits. Zone 6 and even zone 7 plants crept into my collection. The vegetables slowly gave way to flowers until my backyard garden became a miniature botanical garden.

As a career, I worked at a plant nursery, led botanical tours across Newfoundland exposing visitors to the diversity of native plants, taught horticulture at a community college, and finally landed my dream job of working at the Memorial University of Newfoundland (MUN) Botani-

Memorial University Botanical Garden

cal Garden. My passion for plant collecting grew in leaps and bounds, as the Botanical Garden became an extension of my own garden. Few people find a career that is also their hobby. I consider myself very fortunate.

My second hobby, photography, went hand in hand with gardening. I amassed a huge photograph library. Every plant I saw, native or ornamental, was suddenly a photographic subject. I saw familiar flowers in a new light. I like to share my photos, and social media offers me many ways to do that. Through specific gardening websites like Dave's Garden, various garden forums, Flickr, and Facebook, my photos made their rounds. Little did I know that this would result in my being invited to give talks to gardening groups across North America, where I had the opportunity to meet talented gardeners, several

of whom became my mentors. Ultimately, this love of plants and photography culminated in my being asked to write a series of field guides to the trees, shrubs, and wildflowers of Atlantic Canada for Boulder Publications. With that task completed, I was ready to move on to a new project—this book.

There is no shortage of books on the market describing popular garden plants, but they are either generic or specific to the United Kingdom or the United States. Few books are specific to the gardening conditions of Atlantic Canada. A plant that flourishes in the southern US or England may not necessarily do well in Atlantic Canada. With 40-plus years of gardening in this region and a love of photography, I had what I needed to fill this gap in gardening literature.

DOING THE LATIN DANCE

Have you ever noticed how different geographical regions have various names for the same plant? For example, the common names elephant's-ear, giant rockfoil, and pigsqueak all refer to the same plant, *Bergenia*. Purple loosestrife and yellow loosestrife might appear to be related on the basis of their common name, but they are not even closely related. Partridgeberry in Nova Scotia refers to the plant *Mitchella repens*; in Newfoundland, that common name refers to an unrelated plant, *Vaccinium vitis-idaea* (a blueberry relative), which also goes by the common names lingonberry, rock cranberry, or mountain cranberry. Confusing?

Botanists have long known that assigning common names to plants introduces problems when they have to communicate with those from other geographical regions, especially in different languages. Even gardeners from various regions have different common names for the same plant. That's why you often encounter scientific names when you look up information on a particular plant. As a student of botany, I embrace these scientific names, but I know many gardeners' eyes glaze over when they encounter them. As a rule, most botanical literature uses scientific names. These names are not difficult to understand once you get used to them. You probably already know more than you think you do—*Phlox*, *Delphinium*, *Astilbe*, and *Hosta* are scientific names that are also used as common names.

Scientific names for all living organisms follow a binomial nomenclature or two-name system. All names are written in Latin (the scientific name is informally called a Latin name). Latin was traditionally the language of scholars but is now considered a dead language (no nationality *speaks* Latin). The use of Latin to name plants—as well as all other species—is now a worldwide convention.

Bergenia, commonly known as pigsqueak, giant rockfoil, or elephant's-ear

The first part of the scientific name identifies the genus to which the organism belongs. Different plants belonging to the same genus are closely related to each other. The second part identifies a specific group of genetically similar individuals: the species within the genus. When written, the first letter of the genus is always capitalized, but that of the species is lowercased. Both words are italicized. For example, the genus *Campanula* is the scientific name used for most bellflowers of the world. As a gardener, you may know of many types of bellflowers—peach-leaved, great, milky, and Carpathian, to name a few. To distinguish the specific types, each is given its own species name. The peach-leaved bellflower is called *Campanula persicifolia*; the milky bellflower, *Campanula lactiflora*. The genus name *Campanula* denotes that they are related to each

Actaea rubra

Actaea rubra var. *neglecta*

other, but the species name identifies each type of bellflower. Scientific names, although difficult to pronounce, spell, and remember, make communication about living organisms more organized.

So why am I going on about scientific names? The perennials described in this book are listed alphabetically by their scientific names. Think of this as an introductory lesson in botany.

HYBRIDS, CULTIVARS, VARIETIES …

Because not every different plant is a distinct species, this book refers to varieties, hybrids, cultivars, and strains. Different *varieties* of plant species occur in nature; seedlings grown from a variety will have the same characteristics as the parent plant. For example, the scientific name of a white-fruited red baneberry found in the wild is *Actaea rubra* var. *neglecta*. If you were to germinate seed from this variety, most, if not all, of its offspring would also have white fruit. A variety name, usually designated by "var.," is italicized, as it is usually written in Latin. The term *plant type* usually refers to a plant variety.

A *cultivar* denotes a "cultivated variety." Culti-

vars are selected and cultivated by humans. Some cultivars originate as mutations on plants, others hybrids (crosses between two different species). If cultivars obtained from a hybrid are generally similar, but show some minor variation, such as flower colour, they are often referred to as a *strain*. *Named cultivars* are clones, which means that all are genetically identical to each other. A cultivar must be propagated through cuttings, grafting, or tissue culture. If grown from seed, the offspring may look quite different from the parent. A cultivar name is always enclosed in single quotation marks and often written in English rather than Latin. For example, *Doronicum orientale* 'Little Leo' is a dwarf cultivar of leopard's-bane. *Selection* is often interchangeable with cultivar. A cultivar *series* is a group of named cultivars which may have similar height and habit but may differ in flower or leaf colour. An example is the Spotlight series of hollyhock: all plants have the same height and growth habit but come in a variety of flower colours, each of which has a named cultivar, such as the yellow 'Spotlight Sunshine', bicoloured white and yellow 'Polarstar', and bright red 'Mars Magic'.

WHAT IS A PERENNIAL?

The ornamental plants that we grow in our gardens fall into two broad groups—the woody and the herbaceous. The woody plants make up the skeleton of the garden, providing structure, helping to define garden "rooms," and contributing to privacy or windbreaks. Such plants do not dieback to the ground in winter; rather, their woody stems remain year-round, generally becoming broader or taller with time. These are the trees, shrubs, and vines.

The herbaceous plants generally dieback to the ground in winter, re-sprouting from the base each spring. These plants are further divided into annuals, biennials, and perennials. Annuals, most often grown from seed each year, flower all summer and perish in winter, and are often referred to as bedding plants. Biennials germinate and produce a rosette of leaves in their first year, survive the winter, then send up flowering stems in their second summer; they generally die in their second winter. Perennials live for at least three years and, most times, grace our gardens for many years. Technically, trees, shrubs, and vines are woody perennials. The herbaceous perennials (those that dieback each winter) and, to a lesser degree, biennials are the focus of this book.

TODD BOLAND

Planning a garden

Planning a perennial garden, especially if gardening is new to you, can be a daunting task. Sketch out what you want. Look at the plant tag: not only does it provide the plant's scientific name but its light requirements, hardiness, and dimensions. Water requirements and blooming season may also be included. Such information is essential in planning your garden. Ideally, a garden should be attractive throughout the season; therefore, you need to grow a variety of perennials that bloom at various times.

Some things to consider when you are planning your perennial garden:

1. LOCATION AND SIZE OF PLANTING AREA

Where will the perennial garden be located? In front of a fence? Free-standing in the middle of a lawn? Along the side of a house or a driveway? Bordering a patio?

How large a planting area do you want? For ease of cultivating and weeding, many gardeners prefer a narrow border-style garden that is less than 4 feet wide. Others place stepping stones among the plants to access wider beds without trampling the plants. Some prefer round beds. A popular trend is for free-standing, irregularly curved "island" beds. If you are new to gardening, it is best to start small. You can always (and you likely will) expand the bed later.

BELOW: Island beds

A dry, sunny border

2. LIGHT

A critical factor, light can make or break a good garden display. Too often, new gardeners purchase a plant impulsively without realizing its light requirements. Usually, it is a sun-lover that ends up being planted in too much shade. Over time, the health of the plant deteriorates or it becomes very leafy with few flowers. As a rule, most plants grown for their impressive floral displays are sun-lovers, while those grown primarily for their attractive foliage are better in the shade. There are, however, exceptions on both sides.

Observe your potential planting area from sunrise to sunset to determine how much light it receives. Is it sunny all day or does it only get morning, midday, or late afternoon sun? If the area is most often shady, is the shade dense (like under evergreen trees and shrubs or along the north side of a house or solid fence) or is it dappled (such as under small-leaved deciduous trees)? If a neighbouring house or building is white, it may reflect light onto the north side of your house, providing bright shade. Perennials planted under deciduous trees often receive nearly full sun in spring.

3. SOIL MOISTURE

Next determine the moisture level in the soil of the planting area. Under trees and shrubs, the soil is likely to be dry, as the overhead canopy acts as an umbrella and the trees and shrubs absorb any soil moisture faster than the perennials. Sunny slopes are also apt to be dry, as are gravelly or sandy soils. In these locations, select drought-tolerant plants. If irrigation is not an issue, this is not critical, but as many municipalities practice water conservation, it is best to work with nature and grow drought-resistant plants in the dry areas.

Low-lying areas, on the other hand, may be quite moist if not downright soggy, especially in spring as the snow melts. It can be more challenging to overcome this issue: it is better to select plants that can tolerate such conditions. Perennials at a Glance (pages xxxv to xli) provide a reference list of plants for the driest and wettest sites.

4. HARDINESS

Agriculture Canada's hardiness rating system is based primarily on the minimum winter temperature. The US Department of Agriculture (USDA) has a similar system, although not as detailed as the Canadian system. In both systems, the ratings range from 0 to 10: 0, the High Arctic; 10, essentially tropical. The USDA system ratings are whole numbers, hence zones 4, 5, or 6. In Canada, the zones are subdivided into *a* or

Atlantic Canada plant hardiness zones

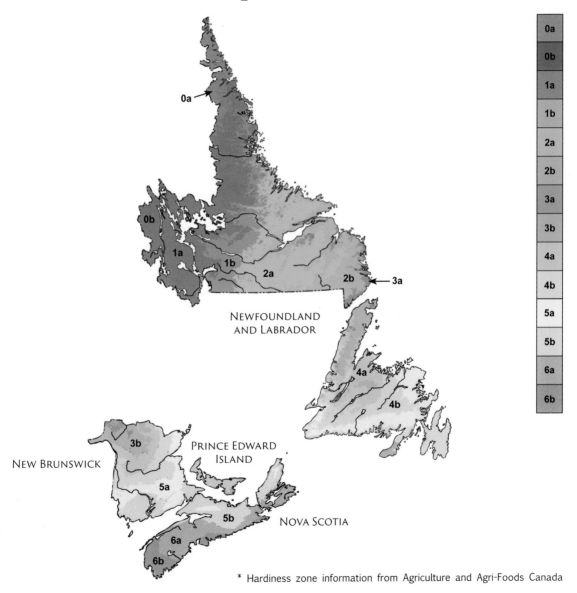

NEWFOUNDLAND AND LABRADOR

PRINCE EDWARD ISLAND

NEW BRUNSWICK

NOVA SCOTIA

| 0a |
| 0b |
| 1a |
| 1b |
| 2a |
| 2b |
| 3a |
| 3b |
| 4a |
| 4b |
| 5a |
| 5b |
| 6a |
| 6b |

* Hardiness zone information from Agriculture and Agri-Foods Canada

b. For example, you may be in zone 4a or zone 4b: *a* represents the colder end of zone 4, *b* the milder end. As noted earlier, plant tags usually indicate the hardiness zone. Once you know what zone you are in, you can select the proper plants. If you wish to err on the side of caution, select a plant that is rated for a zone lower than your growing zone (e.g., a zone 4 plant if you live in zone 5). However, as some gardens have milder microclimates than those assigned for that zone, you might be successful in growing a plant that is not rated hardy for your area, such as a zone 6 plant in zone 5. As you become more familiar with both plants and your zone, you may want to experiment to see what can survive in your area.

5. PLANT SIZE AND LAYOUT

Once you have determined the characteristics of the growing area and you know the size and shape of the bed you will create, you are ready to select the plants. Refer to the plant tags for the overall dimensions. How tall and wide will it be? If the flower bed is small, select a plant that is in scale with it. For example, a rayflower, *Ligularia stenocephala* 'The Rocket', would be out of place in a 1-metre-wide bed. But neither do you want all low-stature plants in a bed; variable heights add drama and interest.

If the bed is viewed only from one side, as in a border-style garden, keep the taller plants in the back, the shorter in the front. To help with this, the plant descriptions in this book include suggestions for the placement of a particular plant in a border. If the bed is island-style, keep taller plants in the middle and use the lower ones as edging.

Heuchera 'Miracle' is often grown for its foliage

6. THINK FOLIAGE

While it would be ideal if all perennials bloomed continuously through the season, like dwarf bleeding-heart (*Dicentra eximia*) and bloody cranesbill (*Geranium sanguineum*), most perennials only bloom for a short period. As a result, it is important to think about a plant's foliage. Some plants, like Siberian iris (*Iris siberica*), have narrow fine foliage which provides a vertical element in the garden. Others, like rayflower (*Ligularia dentata*) and rodgersia (*Rodgersia podophylla*), have large bold leaves. Still others, like astilbe, have soft-textured, fernlike foliage. Hosta, as well as the rash of new coralbells (*Heuchera*), are selected for their foliage rather than their flowers. And ferns and ornamental grasses are grown exclusively for their foliage. Some spectacular gardens are based primarily on leaves, with flowers simply a bonus. Gardening is all about mixing and matching and having fun in the process. If you don't like the location of a perennial, the plant can always be moved.

Some aspects of soil

WHAT IS SOIL?

Soil, the upper layer of earth, usually contains both inorganic and organic components. It anchors plants and provides water and nutrients. The inorganic or mineral component includes both the soil particles and, as many gardeners in our region realize, plenty of rocks. The larger soil particles are sand. Sandy soils are generally well drained but poor at retaining nutrients and prone to becoming dry. Clay particles are the smallest and result in dense, poorly drained but often nutrient-rich, soil. The size of silt particles is between that of sand and clay, and silty soils have the best qualities of sandy and clay soils.

How can you determine if your soil is sandy or clay? Roll some moist but not soggy soil between your fingers. If the texture is like sandpaper, it is sandy soil; if the soil rolls like putty, it is clay; if it has a silky feel, silt dominates. Gardening books often cite loam as the ultimate soil type. Loam is simply soil that contains nearly equal amounts of sand, silt, and clay and thus is reasonably fertile and well drained but holds some moisture.

Soil also has an organic component: plant particles and living organisms such as worms, beetles, fungus, and bacteria. All are essential to healthy soil. Gardeners can alter the organic plant-based component by adding organic material to the soil. Peat is perhaps the most popular soil amendment, but various composts, whether store-bought or home-made, are also ideal. Compost may add needed nutrients but peat does not. However, both improve the mineral quality of the soil. When added to a sandy soil, the organic material helps the resulting soil to retain moisture and nutrients; added to a clay soil, it helps loosen the soil structure and improve drainage.

Willow gentian thrives in acidic soil

SOIL DEPTH

One of the most critical factors to creating a good perennial bed is soil depth. Ideally, a perennial bed should have 30 centimetres of good-quality soil. This can be challenging if you live in a typical city lot where the topsoil has been scraped away prior to house construction, with just 15 centimetres of often poor-quality soil brought back for laying the prescribed landscape sods before the house is sold. Shallow, poor-quality soil results in weak plants that are prone to drying out. Good-quality soil of the proper depth is key to a healthy perennial bed. If the planting area is simply too rocky to create a soil bed that is 30 centimetres deep, use raised beds filled with soil.

SOIL PH

Gardening books often state that "this plant prefers acidic soil" or "this plant prefers alkaline soil." Sometimes specific pH ranges are given; for example, rhododendrons prefer a soil pH of 4.5 to 6. Soil pH is the measure of its acidity or alkalinity. The pH ranges from 0 to 14, with 0 being very acidic and 14 very alkaline; pH 7 is neutral. Lemon juice, which is acidic, has a pH of about 2. Bleach is alkaline, with a pH of 12.6. Soils of the world usually range from pH 3.5 to 9. Generally, areas with a high rainfall have acidic soil; dry regions have alkaline soil. In Atlantic Canada, which is relatively wet, most soil ranges from pH 4.5 to 6, which is on the acidic side; consequently, it is ideal for rhododendrons, heaths, and heathers. As a rule, most plants prefer soil with a pH of 5.5 to 7.5.

If a plant prefers acidic soil but is exposed to a higher pH, it will likely have difficulty in absorbing iron, a needed micronutrient. The leaves become chlorotic, turning yellow but often retaining green veins. On the other hand, if a plant prefers neutral to alkaline soil and is exposed to acidic soil, aluminium toxicity can kill the active root tips, leading to stunted growth with cupped or wrinkled leaves.

Ideally, ascertain your soil pH; kits are available for doing this. If your soil pH is 5.5 or higher, you should be able to grow almost all of the perennials described in this book. If it is below 5.5, a copious dusting of lime each year helps to raise the pH to suitable levels; alternatively, select perennials which tolerate acidic soil. Check Perennials at a Glance (page xxxv) to determine which plants are most tolerant to highly acidic soil. Plants listed as preferring neutral to alkaline soil should be annually dusted with lime, unless it is above pH 7.

PROPAGATING PERENNIALS

Perennials can be started from seed, cuttings, and divisions or by purchasing potted plants. The latter is usually the most efficient and simplest but also the most expensive. A sure sign of spring is when a local nursery or big-box store starts to sell potted plants, whether they are annual bedding plants, perennials, trees, or shrubs. I can spend a day wandering from nursery to nursery, seeing what new plant varieties have appeared for the current season. There is nothing more satisfying than purchasing a new plant and returning home to lovingly add it to the garden. A potted plant provides instant impact and satisfaction. But they can be pricey—some of the newer peony or hosta varieties cost $20 or more.

Some perennials are offered earlier in the season as bagged or boxed roots or bulbs. Lilies, blazing star, bleeding-heart, and peonies are of-

Pulsatilla thrive in alkaline soil

TODD BOLAND

ten sold this way. They are often less pricey than plants sold already growing in pots. Keep in mind that these bagged or boxed plants are often sold too early for direct planting outdoors. If you decide to wait to buy them until it is safe to plant them directly outside, they often become leggy or spindly. When this happens, they rarely develop into satisfactory plants. It is better to pot them and grow them indoors in a sunny, cool window until the risk of frost has passed.

You could also talk to a friend who already has that special plant—he or she may be willing to give you a slip. The slip may be a cutting, but, more than likely, it will be a division from the plant. Many of our perennials are easily propa-

Rudbeckia and *Helenium* are easily grown from seed

gated by digging and dividing. They may be dug in spring just as they emerge and, with a spade, trowel, or knife, cut into two or more smaller portions. If it is a spring-blooming plant like lungwort, leopard's-bane, or primrose, you can also divide them in mid-late summer. The exceptions are plants that have one or several main taproots rather than a fibrous mass of roots. Perennials with taproots, which include columbine, pasqueflower, peony, and balloon flower, are either difficult or impossible to divide.

Some perennials benefit from being dug and divided regularly. Beebalm, Shasta daisy, and yellow loosestrife grow so rapidly that, after a few years, their centres die out and the only vigorous portions are those located around the perimeters. When this happens, dig the plant, divide it into several pieces, replant the outer portions, and discard the weaker inner parts.

Another popular way to propagate perennials is by seed. Start them indoors to get a jump-start on the season or directly sow them in the garden. Seeds may be from plants in your own garden or purchased at nurseries or big-box stores. Remember: if you collect your own seeds and the parent plant is a hybrid, the offspring may not necessarily look like the parent.

Starting perennials from seed is the cheapest way to obtain new plants, but it is challenging. If you have an unheated greenhouse, you can start sowing seeds in early April. If they are started in cool conditions, most perennial seedlings will tolerate a light frost during a cold April night. If they are started indoors, you need a sunny but cool window. If conditions are too warm indoors, the seedlings may become thin and weak and perform poorly when planted outside. Unlike bedding plants and vegetables, many perennial seeds need a cold period, below 4°C, to break their seed dormancy. This cold, which simulates a winter period, is called a stratifica-

Ligularia, Astrantia, and *Crocosmia* are easily propagated by division

tion period. It ranges from four to 12 weeks depending on the plant species. Other perennials need their seeds scraped, a process called scarification. Some need light to germinate, others darkness. Some germinate best when temperatures are below 10°C; others prefer over 20°C. Yet others must be sown as soon as the seeds are ripe. A good internet reference site for determining how to germinate a particular perennial seed is provided by the Ontario Rock Garden and Hardy Plant Society (http://www.onrockgarden.com/germination-guide/plants). If you wish to grow perennials from seed, those that are sown like standard bedding plants are baby's breath, bellflowers, catmint, any "daisies," bergenia, hollyhock, poppies, soapwort, and thyme.

When sowing seeds indoors, a few rules are essential. Start with clean pots and sterilized soil. Failure to do so may result in damping-off disease, which is due to a fungus that kills the seedlings within days of germination. Fill the clean

pots with soil, then water before sowing the seeds. If the seeds are dustlike, simply sprinkle them on the damp soil surface. If larger, cover them with a thin layer of soil, then gently water again. In both cases it is often helpful to cover the pot with cellophane to maintain a high humidity until the seeds sprout. Soil that becomes too dry just as the seeds start to send out roots can result in failed seed germination. Keep the pots in bright light but not full sun, as cellophane-covered soil can cook emerging plants. Within a few days of germination, remove the cellophane and place the pots in full sun, preferably in a cool window. Seedlings will be sturdier if grown in cool conditions.

Another factor to keep in mind: plants should never be taken from indoor or greenhouse conditions and planted directly outside. This also applies to annual bedding plants. Plants should be slowly exposed to outdoor conditions in a process called hardening-off. A week or so before plant-

ing outside, place the potted plants in a sheltered shady spot outside for the day, and bring them inside at night. Do this for about three days, then place them where they get morning sun but afternoon shade. You can now leave them outside at night. After another three or so days, they are ready for permanent life outside.

If you have seeds that need stratification, you have two choices. Mix the seeds with damp sand and place the seed-sand mix in a small bottle (such as a pill bottle) kept in the refrigerator for the prescribed number of weeks. Then sow the seed-sand mix in spring as above. Alternatively, sow the seeds in pots in the autumn, leaving them in an unheated garage or a sheltered spot outside. The seeds should start to germinate in May. Having been grown outside from the start, they do not need a hardening-off process before being planted in their permanent locations.

Garden maintenance

WATERING

Your perennials will likely need watering at some point. Because of global climate change, dry spells are becoming more frequent. All too often I see new gardeners splashing their plants with water, thinking that that will satisfy their moisture needs. Such light watering only encourages shallow roots, which make plants even more prone to drought. It also encourages fungal diseases, slugs, and snails, all of which thrive on wet foliage.

The rule of thumb: 1 inch of water once a week. It is best to give the garden a thorough soaking once a week. If using a sprinkler, place a deep pie pan in the middle of the watered area until an inch of water has gathered in it. It is best to water in the morning so that the foliage will be dry by nightfall. This reduces both the incidence of fungal diseases and slug and snail activity.

Plants growing under trees require more water, as trees outcompete perennials for water, plus their canopy acts as an umbrella. Slopes are also more prone to becoming droughty, especially if south-facing. Sandy soil too dries more quickly than loamy or organically rich soil. If you have a spot that is prone to becoming dry and you do not want to be constantly watering, select drought-resistant plants. The Perennials at a Glance section (page xxxv) provides choices.

DEADHEADING

Unless you plan to collect seeds from your perennials, it is best to deadhead as soon as the flowers fade. The advantages? First, if the plants set seed, the stimulus for them to produce additional flowers is suppressed. This is especially true for annual bedding plants. Most perennials have a set season of bloom, however, so deadheading may not necessarily encourage more blooms. Leopard's-bane, muskmallow, and mountain bluets often produce some late season flowers if promptly deadheaded. Second, deadheading prevents seed set. Producing seed is a strain on a plant. By preventing seed production, the plant puts more energy into new leaves, resulting in a more robust plant. Some perennials produce copious seeds (lupines, feverfew, and rose campion) that can produce far more seedlings than desired. Third, deadheading makes plants look tidier and even reduces the incidence of disease. Rotting petals are a prime area for fungal diseases to attack a plant.

FERTILIZING

Some people never fertilize their gardens; others do so regularly. If your soil is normally healthy and you have dug plenty of compost into the soil, it may not need additional fertilizer. This is especially true if you mulch the soil each year with a mixture of leaf mould and compost. The MUN Botanical Garden never uses chemical fertilizers on perennial plantings but mulches every May-June.

If you suspect that your soil is not ideal and your perennials are not robust enough, the addition of chemical fertilizer is warranted. Water-soluble fertilizers are quicker acting but do not last as long as granular fertilizers. As a result, you may need to use a water-soluble fertilizer every few weeks throughout the growing season. Granular fertilizers, on the other hand, are slow-acting; therefore, one application in spring is often enough. Follow the manufacturer's recommended application rates for your fertilizer choice. Fertilizers are salts and, if used too heavily, can do more harm than good.

Water-soluble fertilizers are often applied by hose applicators so that, as you water, you are fertilizing at the same time. Wetting the leaves of plants with this dilute fertilizer will not harm

them. Granular fertilizers, however, are much more concentrated—never let them touch the plant's leaves or stems. Instead, apply around the base of the plant but not touching it, just as the new spring growth reaches 10 to 15 centimetres. Scratch the fertilizer into the soil to speed up the dissolving rate.

Fertilizers come in many formulations. Generally, a three-number code, such as 10-15-10, is marked on the package. Each number represents, in order, the percentage amount of nitrogen (N), phosphorous (P), and potassium (K), commonly written as N, P, and K, in the fertilizer. These three elements are the macronutrients required by plants in relatively high doses. Nitrogen allows for more leaves and faster growth. Many lawn fertilizers are high in nitrogen to encourage rapid growth and lush green grass. For perennials, avoid fertilizers high in nitrogen, as they encourage leaves rather than flowers. Phosphorous promotes flower, fruit, and better root production; fertilizers highest in the middle number are best for perennials. Potassium

improves a plant's overall health, helps combat diseases, and improves winter hardiness. Some fertilizers also have trace elements, or micronutrients, such as iron, magnesium, or copper.

"Balanced fertilizers" are simply those that contain N, P, and K, that is, has three numbers. It does not mean that the three numbers are the same; 10-52-10, 20-20-20, and 15-30-15 are all balanced fertilizers. Non-balanced fertilizers are missing one of the main macronutrients. For example, bone meal, 2-13-0, has N and P but no K. The high amount of phosphorous, good for root production, is why bone meal is often used with transplants.

MULCHING

Mulch is a layer of material laid over the ground to cover it. It helps reduce weeds or makes pulling them easier, and it can reduce the amount of watering required in the garden as the mulch helps trap soil moisture. Generally, organic material is used. The MUN Botanical Garden uses three-year-old shredded, rotted leaves. This mulch sec-

A freshly mulched garden

onds as an organic fertilizer and is applied in a 3- to 5-centimetre-deep layer every May-June.

Other popular mulches include shredded tree bark or bark nuggets. The problem with these mulches is that, in time, the bark rots. The breakdown of bark by fungi and bacteria requires nitrogen. This nitrogen, taken from the underlying soil, results in nitrogen deficiency and possible stunting of the perennial plant's growth. Under trees and shrubs, the breakdown of shredded bark and nuggets is not as detrimental as it would be on the soil around perennials, as the plants have larger root systems that often extend beyond the mulched areas.

To reduce weeds, some new gardeners plant their perennials in slits cut in landscape fabric, which is then covered by bark mulch. In this case the mulch lasts much longer since it is not in direct contact with the soil. This tactic can be effective for trees and shrubs, as they are relatively static in their location. Some perennials, like phlox, gooseneck loosestrife, and beebalm, however, often spread quite significantly at their base, and landscape fabric deters this natural spreading.

Special gardens

COASTAL GARDEN

Gardening in Atlantic Canada's coastal areas poses some challenges. The ocean is a significant part of our region, and plenty of gardeners live in areas that are kissed by the sea (if gale-force winds off the ocean with accompanying salt spray can be considered "kissed").

The first challenge of coastal gardening is the wind. Coastal areas experience stronger winds than inland areas. Winds generated by both high- and low-pressure weather systems can hit the shore at full force, while places even a few kilometres inland can have that force diminished by forests, buildings, and other objects. Rain, when combined with wind, can do even more damage. To combat wind, gardeners should plant wind-resistant plants or erect windbreaks such as walls, fencing, or vegetation shelter belts.

The second issue is salt spray, which accompanies wind. Wind can whip up salt spray from the water's surface. The stronger the wind, the more salty the water that will be generated. When this salt-laden spray hits plants, it often evaporates, further concentrating the salt on plant leaves. Gardens within 300 metres of the shore are the most affected. Salt wicks water from the plant, resulting in conditions similar to being too dry. If too much salt accumulates on the plants' leaves or in the soil, the plants dehydrate and wilt. Evergreen plants often develop brown margins or become "burnt" on the side facing the ocean. To eliminate this, select plants that are salt- and drought-tolerant. As a rule, plants with grey-green waxy leaves, densely fuzzy leaves, or fleshy leaves are the best candidates. If the word *sea* is in the plant's common name, like sea thrift or sea lavender, that plant is generally suitable for growing near the coast. On the positive side, plants grown by the sea often show less incidence of insect pests or fungal diseases than the same plant grown inland.

In summer, coastal regions are cooler than inland regions. Even on a calm day, there is little reprieve from sea breezes. Because the ocean is colder than the land, cooler ocean air is sucked inland as warmer air rises. This can significantly lower temperatures along the immediate shoreline during the summer. Atlantic Canada is the foggiest part of the country. Coastal fog lowers temperatures, particularly in the summer. On the plus side, the ocean moderates temperatures in winter, resulting in milder temperatures along the coast than inland, allowing you to possibly grow plants that are not generally considered hardy in your zone.

Another potential coastal issue is sandy soil. Some inland areas have excessively sandy soil, but coastal areas seem to have more than their share. Soil that is too sandy, while very well drained, can be prone to drought. Sandy soil, which are often infertile, can result in stunted growth. The problems with sandy soil are easily overcome by adding organic matter in the form of compost and/or peat.

Refer to Perennials at a Glance (page xxxv) for a list of the best perennials to use in Atlantic Canadian coastal gardens.

Heritage Garden

Many of the more popular garden ornamentals grown in Atlantic Canada are considered heritage plants. Such plants were introduced several generations ago and were of such merit that they have been saved, maintained, and handed down. Gardeners of yesteryear, like gardeners today, often passed along slips of a favourite plant to a neighbour or a family relative. Over time, the plants spread from community to community until they became standards in many gardens.

Most of our heritage plants can be traced back 100 years to the British Isles or France, the ancestral homes of most Atlantic Canadians. Their plants followed the early settlers as they moved from the old to the new world. Why did they bring these plants with them? Bringing clothing and household goods would seem to be more important than plants that, for the most part, were not edible or even medicinal; many heritage plants are simply ornamental. Most

Maltese-cross and great bellflowers are classic heritage plants

likely, these plants were a reminder to the new-world settlers of the home they had left behind. It proves the strong bond that plants hold in our lives. No doubt, many of these early plants did not survive the rigours of a transatlantic trip or our local climate. Only the toughest, hardiest, and most care-free varieties could survive Atlantic Canada's relatively harsh climate. These plants have become our heritage plants.

By its nature, a heritage plant is not an unstable hybrid, unlike many of today's "new and improved" cultivars. Modern-day plants are often bred for their large, colourful blooms that create impact in the garden. However, this genetic engineering results in plants that are more susceptible to pests and diseases, that no longer provide pollen for pollinators, or that have lost their hardy and care-free nature. These older heritage plants may become important for breeding more vigour back into modern-day plants.

Heritage varieties also add to the biodiversity of garden plants. Once these varieties are lost, they are gone forever. Perennials at a Glance (page xxxv) lists the most common heritage status perennials in Atlantic Canada.

ROCK GARDEN

The old saying is that if life gives you lemons, make lemonade. In Atlantic Canada, if life gives you rocks, make a rock garden! A rock garden should be a garden on rocks—not rocks on a garden. Many of the edger or front-of-the-border plants we grow hail from high mountainous areas, that is, they are alpine plants. Although plants like sea thrift, rockcress, and pasqueflower can work perfectly well in a more classic perennial border, they thrive when you grow them in a re-creation of their original environment. Rock gardening is really an attempt to create an alpine habitat, and any gardener who has visited the alpine regions of the Rockies, Alps, or

Alpine border featuring *Campanula, Sedum, Dianthus,* and dwarf *Scabiosa*

Himalayas knows that such areas are dominated by rocks with the alpine plants tucked here and there among the rocks. Taking a slope, planting low stature plants, and throwing in a few rocks helter-skelter is not a true rock garden.

A rock garden created on a natural slope is a perfect way to use a slope rather than planting grass, which has to be mowed. However, a rock garden can be built on level ground or, alternatively, by converting a ridge of soil into a rockery. Keep in mind that most rock gardens are situated in a sunny location—after all, as there are few trees in alpine areas to shade the plants, they are well adapted to blazing sun. However, even in a shaded location, you can create a rockery for smaller ferns, primroses, and gentians. The soil should be gritty and well drained. As alpine regions are generally sloped, water is quick to drain; plus, the soil is naturally rocky. As a rule, alpine plants are not heavy feeders; they do not need rich soil. In fact, soil that is too rich may lead to soft growth which may not survive the winter.

A rock garden is composed mainly of rocks. Choose granite, sandstone, or limestone rather than mixing all three together. Naturally weathered rocks covered in lichens are more desirable than freshly quarried rock. Don't be afraid to use lots of rocks. The idea is to have planting pockets among a tumble of rocks.

Given that Atlantic Canada typically has several months of frost heaving, the rocks should be buried enough to keep them stable. If they have been just pressed into the soil, they shift over time. Instead, treat them like icebergs, with 80 to 90 per cent of the rock buried. Use an assortment of sizes, avoiding too many small rocks. Remember that you are trying to recreate an alpine environment; look at photos of such areas to provide inspiration on how to position the rocks in a natural layout.

Select plants that will stay relatively small. This is especially important if the rockery is small. The larger the rock garden, the larger the plants you can use that will still look in scale. The rock gardens at the MUN Botanical Garden or the Truro Rock Garden are of such large scale that small trees do not look out of place. For the home gardener, plants which remain less than 30 centimetres are best. Those with creeping or matlike habits such as low sedums, rockcress, and moss phlox are ideal, as are those with tufted habits such as sea thrift, auricula primrose, and Carpathian harebell. Perennials at a Glance (page xxxv) lists plants that work especially well in a rock-garden setting.

POLLINATOR GARDEN

The plight of honeybees is well known to most gardeners. All over the world, populations of honeybees are diminishing, due to a combination of diseases and parasites. Gardeners in Newfoundland are among the last in the world to potentially have healthy honeybee visitors, since the many diseases affecting honeybees are still absent from Newfoundland.

Honeybees are just one of a multitude of pollinators in our gardens. Native bees, wasps, butterflies, moths, beetles, hoverflies, and hummingbirds were our original pollinators before the introduction of honeybees. Without these pollinators, we would have no vegetables or fruit and many of our flowering plants would die, as they could not produce seed. The creation of a pollinator-friendly garden is not only beneficial to the pollinators but also to our own well-being. In addition, the flitting movement of the pollinators, especially bumblebees and butterflies, add a sense of movement in the garden and allow us to experience a sense of wild nature in our own backyards.

Pollinators need a home and food source. The easiest to provide is the food—the flowers' nectar and pollen. Each pollinator has its own flower preference. As a rule, bees prefer blue, purple, or pink flowers, especially those that are tubular. Bees can access tubular flowers, butterflies cannot. Lupines, foxgloves, and bellflowers are classic bee flowers. Butterflies prefer yellow, orange, and red flowers, especially those that are flat, making landing on them easy. Daisies as a group are among the best butterfly flowers. Even those that are purple or blue, such as fleabanes and asters, have yellow centres that act as a bull's eye for passing butterflies. Bees, however, also visit many of the more classic butterfly flowers.

Hummingbird feeders are usually red because hummingbirds prefer red flowers, especially those that are narrow and tubular, as they have

Butterflies and bumblebees love *Hylotelephium* 'Autumn Joy'

long bills and tongues that can access the nectar in such flowers. Beebalm, columbine, crocosmia, red hot poker, and cardinal flower are among the best plants for attracting hummingbirds.

As a rule, pollinator flowers should resemble their wild ancestors in appearance. Native plants are perhaps the best to use in a pollinator garden, but not all wildflowers are garden-worthy. Plant breeders are constantly trying to create larger and fuller flowers. The average gardener prefers double over single flowers. The classic peony has a fully double flower. Newer purple coneflower cultivars are now also double and in unusual shades of yellow, orange, and red. Double-flowered lilies are now available. Although they are visually attractive, these highly bred plants often have little or no nectar or pollen and are useless to pollinators. The wild versions of such plants are far better food plants for pollinators.

As for pollinator homes, you can either provide physical homes for bees or host plants for butterflies. Honeybees, of course, are kept in beehives. Bumblebees make their homes in the ground, often in abandoned mole or vole holes. Solitary bees either have very small hives in sandy ground or use holes in wood or stone. Make your own bee hotel by building a 15- to 30-centimetre-deep frame and filling it with hollow bamboo stems or blocks of wood in which you have drilled holes of varying depths and diameters, ideally 4 to 10 centimetres deep and 2 to 10 millimetres wide. Place the hotel in a sheltered site. Make it as fancy as you like, essentially creating garden art if you so desire.

Planting host plants for butterflies is a little more challenging. Many native butterflies lay eggs on native trees or wildflowers, not necessarily those that are garden-worthy. Of course, these plants will be eaten by the larvae and look rather tatty—again, not the best scenario for a formal garden. The MUN Botanical Garden plants stinging nettle, *Urtica dioica*, at the back of various borders to act as host plants for red admiral, painted lady, and green comma butterflies. In the Maritimes, plant various species of milkweed, *Asclepias*, as host plants for monarch butterflies.

Applying insecticides is unacceptable in the pollinator-friendly garden (in general, most insecticides should be avoided in all gardens). Spraying to kill troublesome aphids or sawfly larvae may also inadvertently kill the pollinators. Where possible, hand-pick and kill any troublesome insects or apply an organic insecticide to the infected plant in the late evening when pollinator activity wanes.

Gardens of note in Atlantic Canada

- Memorial University of Newfoundland Botanical Garden, 306 Mount Scio Road, St. John's, Newfoundland. Key display: perennials, rhododendrons, heritage plants, rock gardens.

- Bowring Park, 305 Waterford Bridge Road, St. John's, Newfoundland. Key display: annuals, trees and shrubs.

- Halifax Public Gardens, 5664 Spring Garden Road, Halifax, Nova Scotia. Key display: perennials, annuals, trees and shrubs.

- Annapolis Royal Historic Gardens, 441 St. George Street, Annapolis Royal, Nova Scotia. Key display: perennials, roses, heritage plants.

- Harriet Irving Botanical Gardens, 32 University Avenue, Wolfville, Nova Scotia. Key display: native plants.

- Tangled Garden, 11827 Highway 1, Grand Pré, Nova Scotia. Key display: labyrinth, arbours, perennials.

- Bible Hill Rock Garden, Dalhousie Agricultural Campus, College Road, Bible Hill, Nova Scotia. Key display: rock gardens, trees and shrubs.

- New Brunswick Botanical Garden, 15 Rue Principale, Saint-Jacques, New Brunswick. Key display: perennials, annuals, trees and shrubs, rock garden, roses.

Memorial University Botanical Garden

- Irving Arboretum, 52 Couvent Way, Bouctouche, New Brunswick. Key display: trees.

- Kingsbrae Garden, 220 King Street, Saint Andrews, New Brunswick. Key display: perennials, annuals, rhododendrons, roses.

- A.A. MacDonald Memorial Gardens, Glenelg Street East, Georgetown, Prince Edward Island. Key display: perennials, annuals, trees and shrubs.

Perennial of the Year™

In the plant descriptions in this book are references to a particular plant selection being named Perennial Plant of the Year™. In 1990, the Perennial Plant Association (PPA) (www.perennialplant.org) initiated the Perennial Plant of the Year™ program, a way to highlight certain outstanding perennials. The selection criteria is based on a perennial's suitability for a wide range of growing climates, low maintenance, multiple-season interest, and pest/disease resistance. Each year, PPA members vote for that year's winner based on a ballot of three or four choices. At vote time, members may nominate up to two plants for future consideration. The Perennial Plant of the Year™ committee reviews the nominated perennials and selects three or four to be placed on the ballot for the following year.

The winners:
1991: *Heuchera micrantha* 'Palace Purple'
1992: *Coreopsis verticillata* 'Moonbeam'
1993: *Veronica* 'Sunny Border Blue'

1994: *Astilbe* 'Sprite'
1995: *Perovskia atriplicifolia*
1996: *Penstemon digitalis* 'Husker Red'
1997: *Salvia nemorosa* 'May Night'
1998: *Echinacea purpurea* 'Magnus'
1999: *Rudbeckia fulgida* 'Goldstrum'
2000: *Scabiosa columbaria* 'Butterfly Blue'
2001: *Calamagrostis* X *acutiflora* 'Karl Foerster'
2002: *Phlox paniculata* 'David'
2003: *Leucanthemum superbum* 'Becky'
2004: *Athyrium niponicum* 'Pictum'
2005: *Helleborus* X *hybridus*
2006: *Dianthus* 'Firewitch'
2007: *Nepeta* 'Walker's Low'
2008: *Geranium* 'Rozanne'
2009: *Hakonechloa macra* 'Aureola'
2010: *Baptisia australis*
2011: *Amsonia hubrichtii*
2012: *Brunnera macrophylla* 'Jack Frost'
2013: *Polygonatum odoratum* 'Variegatum'
2014: *Panicum virgatum* 'Northwind'
2015: *Geranium* X *cantabrigiense* 'Biokova'
2016: *Anemone* 'Honorine Jobert'
2017: *Asclepias tuberosus*
2018: *Allium* 'Millenium'

Geranium X *cantabrigiense* 'Biokova'

Perennials at a glance

PERENNIALS FOR COLD, EXPOSED SITES

Aconitum napellus—Monkshood
Alchemilla mollis—Lady's mantle
Arabis caucasica—Rockcress
Armeria maritima—Thrift
Artemisia abrotanum—Wormwood
Centaurea montana—Cornflower
Dianthus deltoides—Maiden pinks
Geranium species—Crane's-bill
Hemerocallis species and hybrids—Daylily
Pulsatilla vulgaris—Pasqueflower
Saxifraga paniculata—Encrusted saxifrage
Sedum species and hybrids—Stonecrop
Symphyotrichum (Aster) novi-belgii—New York aster

PERENNIALS FOR SEASIDE GARDENS

Achillea species—Yarrow
Aconitum napellus—Monkshood
Alchemilla mollis—Lady's mantle
Armeria maritima—Thrift
Artemisia species—Wormwood, dusty miller
Dianthus species and hybrids—Pinks
Erigeron speciosus—Fleabane

New York Aster is an excellent plant for seaside gardens

Eryngium species—Sea holly
Hemerocallis species and hybrids—Daylily
Festuca glauca—Blue fescue
Helictotrichon sempervirens—Blue oat grass
Iris species and hybrids—Iris
Limonium latifolium—Sea lavender
Molinia caerulea—Purple moor grass
Sedum/Hylotelephium species and hybrids—Stonecrop
Sempervivum species and hybrids—Hen-and-chicks
Stachys byzantinum—Lamb's-ears
Symphyotrichum (Aster) novi-belgii—New York aster
Thymus species—Creeping thyme

PERENNIALS FOR ROCK GARDENS

Achillea clavennae/tomentosa—Dwarf yarrow
Anemone blanda—Windflower
Aquilegia canadensis/flabellata—Dwarf columbine
Arabis caucasica—Rockcress
Armeria maritima—Thrift
Aster alpinus—Alpine aster
Aubrieta deltoidea—Wall cress
Aurinia saxatilis—Perennial alyssum
Campanula carpatica—Carpathian harebell
Dianthus species and hybrids—Pinks
Festuca glauca—Blue fescue grass
Gentiana acaulis/septemfida—Dwarf gentian
Geranium dalmaticum/sanguineum—Dwarf cranes-bill
Gypsophila repens—Creeping baby's breath
Iberis sempervirens—Evergreen candytuft
Iris pumila—Dwarf bearded iris
Lamium maculatum—Dead-nettle
Nepeta species and hybrids—Catmint
Origanum 'Kent Beauty'—Kent Beauty oregano
Papaver alpinum/nudicaule—Alpine/Iceland poppy
Penstemon species—Beardtongue
Phlox douglasii/subulata—Moss phlox
Potentilla neumanniana—Dwarf cinquefoil

Primula species and hybrids—Primrose
Prunella grandiflora—Self-heal
Pulsatilla vulgaris—Pasqueflower
Saponaria ocymoides—Soapwort
Saxifraga paniculata—Encrusted saxifrage
Sedum species and hybrids—Stonecrop
Sempervivum species and hybrids—Hen-and-chicks
Silene flos-jovis 'Peggy'—Flower-of-Jove
Symphyotrichum (Aster) dumosum—Dwarf Michaelmas daisy
Thymus species—Thyme
Viola species—Violet

PERENNIALS FOR SHADE
Aconitum species—Monkshood
Actaea/Cimicifuga species—Snakeroot
Ajuga reptans—Bugleweed
Alchemilla mollis—Lady's mantle
Anemone species—Anemone
Aquilegia species—Columbine
Arisaema species—Jack-in-the-pulpit
Aruncus species—Goatsbeard
Astilbe species and hybrids—Astilbe
Astilboides tabularis—Shieldleaf Rodgersia
Astrantia species and hybrids—Masterwort

Hosta are classic plants for shade

Bergenia species and hybrids—Giant rockfoil
Brunnera macrophylla—Siberian bugloss
Convallaria majalis—Lily-of-the-valley
Dicentra/Lamprocapnos species and hybrids—Bleeding-heart
Epimedium species and hybrids—Barrenwort
Filipendula ulmaria—Meadowsweet
Geranium phaeum—Widow cranesbill
Glaucidium palmatum—Japanese wood poppy
Hemerocallis flava—Yellow daylily
Ligularia species—Rayflower
Hakonechloa macra—Hakone grass
Helleborus species and hybrids—Hellebore
Hosta species and hybrids—Hosta
Kirengeshoma palmata—Japanese waxbells
Lamium species—Dead-nettle
Lysimachia species—Loosestrife
Omphalodes verna—Navelwort
Pachysandra terminalis—Japanese spurge
Petasites japonicus—Japanese butterbur
Primula denticulata—Drumstick primrose
Primula X *polyanthus*—English primrose
Polygonatum species—Solomon's seal
Pulmonaria species and hybrids—Lungwort
Rodgersia species—Rodgersia
Trillium species—Wakerobin
Trollius species—Globeflower
Tricyrtis hirta—Toad lily
Vinca minor—Periwinkle
All ferns

PERENNIALS FOR WET SITES
Aruncus species—Goatsbeard
Caltha palustris—Marsh marigold
Chelone species—Turtlehead
Darmera peltata—Umbrella plant
Eutrochium species—Joe-pye weed
Filipendula ulmaria—Meadowsweet
Iris ensata—Japanese iris
Iris pseudacorus—Yellow flag iris

Iris versicolor—Blue flag iris
Ligularia species—Rayflower
Matteuccia struthiopteris—Ostrich fern
Osmunda species—Cinnamon/Royal fern
Sanguisorba species—Burnet
Primula japonica and similar species—Candela-
    bra primrose
Thalictrum species—Meadow rue
Trollius species—Globeflower

PERENNIALS FOR HOT, DRY SITES
Achillea species and hybrids—Yarrow
Artemisia species—Wormwood
Dictamnus albus—Gasplant
Echinops ritro—Globe thistle
Eryngium species—Sea holly
Euphorbia species—Spurge
Festuca glauca—Blue fescue
Gaillardia aristata—Blanketflower
Gypsophila species—Baby's breath
Helictotrichon sempervirens—Blue oat grass
Hemerocallis species and hybrids—Daylily
Liatris spicata—Blazing star
Perovskia atriplicifolia—Russian sage

Hen-and-chicks are very drought-resistant

Pulsatilla vulgaris—Pasqueflower
Rudbeckia species—Coneflower
Salvia species—Sage
Sedum/Hylotelephium species and hybrids—
    Stonecrop
Sempervivum species and hybrids—Hen-and-
    chicks
Thymus species—Thyme

PERENNIALS FOR ACIDIC SOIL
Aconitum napellus—Monkshood
Actaea/Cimicifuga species—Snakeroot
Alchemilla mollis—Lady's mantle
Anemone hupehensis—Japanese anemone
Aralia species—Spikenard
Aruncus species—Goatsbeard
Astilbe species and hybrids—Astilbe
Astrantia species and hybrids—Masterwort
Athyrium species—Lady fern
Bergenia species and hybrids—Giant rockfoil
Brunnera macrophylla—Siberian bugloss
Convallaria majalis—Lily-of-the-valley
Dryopteris species—Wood fern
Epimedium species and hybrids—Barrenwort
Filipendula ulmaria—Meadowsweet
Gentiana species—Gentians
Geum species—Avens
Hemerocallis species and hybrids—Daylily
Hosta species and hybrids—Hosta
Iris siberica—Siberian iris
Luzula species—Woodrush
Meconopsis baileyi—Himalayan blue poppy
Molinia caerulea—Purple moor grass
Osmunda species—Cinnamon/royal fern
Polygonatum species—Solomon's seal
Primula japonica and similar species—Candela-
    bra primrose
Pulmonaria species and hybrids—Lungwort
Rodgersia species—Rodgersia
Thalictrum species—Meadow-rue

Perennials for Alkaline Soil

Acanthus species—Bear's-breeches
Achillea species and hybrids—Yarrow
Arabis species—Rockcress
Armeria maritima—Sea thrift
Aubrieta deltoidea—Wall cress
Aurinia saxatilis—Perennial alyssum
Bergenia species and hybrids—Giant rockfoil
Dianthus species and hybrids—Pinks
Eryngium species—Sea holly
Gypsophila species—Baby's breath
Helleborus species and hybrids—Hellebore
Iberis sempervirens—Perennial candytuft
Pervoskia atriplicifolia—Russian sage
Potentilla species—Cinquefoil
Primula auricula— Auricula primrose
Pulsatilla species—Pasqueflower
Salvia species—Sage
Saxifraga species—Saxifrage
Saponaria species—Soapwort
Sedum/Hylotelephium species and hybrids—Stonecrop
Sempervivum species and hybrids—Hen-and-chicks
Silene species—Catchfly/campion

Heritage Perennials

Achillea ptarmica—Sneezeweed
Aconitum napellus—Monkshood
Aquilegia vulgaris—Columbine
Aruncus sylvestris—Goatsbeard
Campanula persicifolia—Peach-leaved bellflower
Campanula rapunculoides—Grandmother's blue-bells
Campanula glomerata—Clustered bellflower
Campanula latifolia—Great bellflower
Centaurea montana—Mountain bluets
Convallaria majalis—Lily-of-the-valley
Coreopsis verticillata—Threadleaf coreopsis
Delphinium elatum—Delphinium

Dianthus plumarius—Cottage pinks
Dicentra eximia—Dwarf bleeding-heart
Doronicum plantagineum—Leopard's-bane
Euphorbia cyparrisias—Cypress spurge
Filipendula ulmaria 'Flore Pleno'—Meadowsweet
Geranium macrorrhizum—Scent-leaved geranium
Geranium pratense—Meadow cranesbill
Helianthus X *laetiflorus*—Perennial sunflower
Hemerocallis flava—Yellow daylily
Hemerocallis fulva—Orange daylily
Hylotelephium (Sedum) telephium—Live-forever
Iris variegata—Bearded iris
Lamprocapnos (Dicentra) spectabilis—Bleed-ing-heart
Lilium lancifolium—Tiger lily
Lilium martagon—Martagon lily
Lilium X *hollandicum*—Orange lily
Lysimachia punctata—Yellow loosestrife
Paeonia officinalis 'Rubra Plena'—Peony
Phlox paniculata—Garden phlox
Physalis alkekengii—Chinese lantern
Polygonatum X *hybridum*—Solomon's seal
Primula veris—Cowslip primrose
Ranunculus aconitifolius 'Flore Pleno'—Fair maids of France
Rudbeckia laciniata 'Golden Glow'—Golden glow rudbeckia
Saponaria officinalis 'Flore Pleno'—Bouncing-bet
Saxifraga X *arendsii*—Mossy saxifrage
Sedum spurium—Dragon's blood sedum

Hummingbird Perennials

Alcea rosea—Hollyhock
Aquilegia species and hybrids—Columbine
Crocosmia X *crocosmiiflora*—Crocosmia
Delphinium hybrids—Delphinium
Digitalis species—Foxglove
Heuchera sanguinea—Coral bells
Kniphofia hybrids—Red hot poker
Lobelia species and hybrids—Cardinal flower

Beebalm are hummingbird magnets

Lunaria species—Silver dollar
Lupinus species—Lupine
Lychnis species—Maltese-cross, campion
Monarda species—Beebalm
Physostegia virginiana—Obedience plant
Salvia species—Sage
Scabiosa columbaria—Pincushion flower
Sidalcea hybrids—Prairie mallow

POLLINATOR PERENNIALS
All daisies
All herbs
Aconitum species—Monkshood
Arabis caucasica—Rockcress
Astilbe species and hybrids—Astilbe
Aubrieta deltoidea—Wall cress
Aurinia saxatilis—Perennial alyssum
Baptisia species and hybrids—Blue false indigo
Campanula species and hybrids—Bellflower
Chelone species—Turtlehead
Delphinium hybrids—Delphinium
Digitalis species—Foxglove
Echinops ritro—Globe thistle
Eryngium species—Sea holly
Gentiana species—Gentians
Geranium species and hybrids—Cranesbill
Hypericum species—St. John's-wort

Iberis sempervirens—Perennial candytuft
Lupinus species—Lupine
Lychnis species—Maltese-cross, campion
Monarda species—Beebalm
Paeonia hybrids—Peony (single-flowered)
Papaver species—Poppy
Penstemon species—Beardtongue
Phlox species—Phlox
Physostegia virginiana—Obedience plant
Prunella grandiflora—Self-heal
Pulmonaria species and hybrids—Lungwort
Pulsatilla species—Pasqueflower
Sedum/Hylotelephium species and hybrids—
    Stonecrop
Veronica species—Speedwell

BEST DEER-/MOOSE-RESISTANT PERENNIALS
Aconitum species—Monkshood
Ajuga reptans—Bugleweed
Artemisia species—Silver mound
Aubretia deltoidea—Rockcress
Aurinia saxatilis—Perennial alyssum
Baptisia australis—Blue false indigo
Brunnera macrophylla—Siberian bugloss
Convallaria majalis—Lily-of-the-valley
Coreopsis species—Tickseed
Dicentra (Lamprocapnos) species and hybrids—
    Bleeding-heart
Digitalis species—Foxglove
Echinops ritro—Globe thistle
Epimedium species and hybrids—Barrenwort
Euphorbia species—Spurge
Festuca glauca—Blue fescue
Galium odoratum—Sweet woodruff
Helleborus species and hybrids—Hellebores
Lamium maculatum—Spotted dead-nettle
Limonium latifolium—Sea lavender
Ligularia species—Rayflower
Nepeta species and hybrids—Catmint

Pachysandra species—Spurge
Paeonia species—Peony
Perovskia atriplicifolia—Russian sage
Rodgersia species—Rodgersia
Stachys byzantina—Lamb's-ear
Thalictrum species—Meadow-rue
Thymus species—Thyme
All ferns
All ornamental grasses

FAIR DEER-/MOOSE-RESISTANT PERENNIALS

Achillea species and hybrids—Yarrow
Actaea species—Bugbane
Alchemilla mollis—Lady's mantle
Armeria maritima—Sea thrift
Asclepias species—Milkweed
Astilbe species and hybrids—Astilbe
Crocosmia X *crocosmiiflora*—Crocosmia
Delphinium elatum—Delphinium
Dianthus species and hybrids—Pinks
Dictamnus albus—Gasplant
Echinacea purpurea—Purple coneflower
Gypsophila species—Baby's breath
Helenium autumnale—Helen's flower
Iberis sempervirens—Candytuft
Liatris species—Blazing star

Hellebores are deer and moose resistant

Lobelia species and hybrids—Cardinal flower
Monarda didyma—Beebalm
Papaver species—Poppy
Polemonium caeruleum—Jacob's-ladder
Primula species—Primrose
Rudbeckia species and hybrids—Coneflower
Salvia species—Sage
Saponaria species—Soapwort
Silene species—Campion
Tradescantia X *andersoniana*—Spiderwort
Verbascum species—Mullein
Veronica species—Speedwell
Vinca minor—Periwinkle

MOST ATTRACTIVE TO DEER/ MOOSE PERENNIALS

Aruncus species—Goatsbeard
Campanula species and hybrids—Bellflower
Chelone species—Turtlehead
Erigeron species—Fleabane
Filipendula species—Meadowsweet
Geranium species and hybrids—Cranesbill
Geum species—Avens
Helianthus species and hybrids—Sunflower
Hemerocallis species and hybrids—Daylily
Hosta species and hybrids—Hosta
Lilium species and hybrids—Lily
Lysimachia species—Loosestrife
Phlox paniculata—Phlox
Platycodon grandiflorus—Balloon flower
Sedum/Hylotelephium species and hybrids— Stonecrop
Trollius species—Globeflower

HARE-RESISTANT PERENNIALS

Achillea species and hybrids—Yarrow
Calamagrostis species—Feathergrass
Euphorbia species—Spurge
Festuca glauca—Blue fescue

Geranium species and hybrids—Cranesbill

Helictotrichon sempervirens—Blue oat grass

Iris species and hybrids—Iris

Kniphofia hybrids—Red hot poker

Lupinus species—Lupine

Monarda didyma—Beebalm

Nepeta species and hybrids—Catmint

Pachysandra species—Spurge

Papaver orientale—Oriental poppy

Pulmonaria species and hybrids—Lungwort

Rudbeckia species and hybrids—Coneflower

Thymus species—Thyme

Vinca minor—Periwinkle

Most ferns, with the exception of *Athyrium*,
Lady fern

Hares ignore iris plants

PERENNIALS

LEFT AND ABOVE: *Acanthus hungaricus*
PREVIOUS SPREAD: *Thymus serpyllum*

Acanthus
BEAR'S-BREECHES

The genus *Acanthus* contains about 30 species, many native to the Mediterranean region. Very few are hardy enough to grow in Atlantic Canada—*Acanthus spinosus*, the common bear's-breeches, is an exception. Native from Italy to western Turkey, it produces a large mound of deep green, shiny, thistlelike, basal leaves which are 60 to 80 centimetres long with deeply cut, spine-tipped lobes.

The flowers arise 90 to 120 centimetres, well above the leaves, on upright spikes. Individual flowers, which are relished by bumblebees, resemble those of snapdragon, with a white, three-lobed lip and a maroon-purple hood. A spiny bract is located beneath each flower.

This bold plant blooms from June to August and is best situated in the middle of a border.

The similar Hungarian bear's-breeches, *A. hungaricus*, native from the Balkans to Greece, has spineless foliage and pink-tinted flowers.

Grow bear's-breeches in sun to part shade in any well-drained soil. Although they tolerate variable soil pH, they prefer alkaline soil. They can be drought-tolerant but perform best if regularly watered; however, they dislike excessive wetness in winter. Plants are often slow to establish but difficult to eradicate—they can regenerate from pieces of roots left behind. Propagation is by seed or division.

To protect the crown do not remove the old leaves in autumn; mulching also helps. Both common bear's-breeches and Hungarian bear's-breeches are hardy to zone 5 and only suitable for the mildest areas. Few diseases affect *Acanthus*; they are not usually eaten by moose or deer, but slugs and snails can be bothersome.

Achillea
YARROW

The genus *Achillea* encompasses over 150 species, all native to the northern hemisphere. Named after Achilles, a Greek hero of the Trojan War, many species are weedy and not particularly

Achillea millefolium 'Summer Pastels'

Achillea millefolium 'Red Velvet'

garden-worthy. The few ornamental species are all natives of Europe.

The common yarrow, *Achillea millefolium*, is well known as a roadside weed in Atlantic Canada, but hybridizers have turned this white-flowered ugly duckling into a beautiful swan resplendent in tones of yellow, orange, pink, red, and purple. All are long-lasting cut flowers and attract bees and butterflies. Plants have mostly basal leaves that are aromatic, narrow, dissected, covered in soft hairs, and fernlike. The flowers are held on upright stems which are up to 100 centimetres long. Individual flowers are tiny but massed into dense, flat-topped clusters, blooming from June until September. Suggested cultivars for this region include 'Paprika' (dusty red), 'Terracotta' (light orange-red), 'Red Velvet' (deep red), 'Cerise Queen' (bright pink), and 'Summer Pastels' (mixed pale colours).

Bright yellow-flowered yarrow bred from *A. filipendulina* and *A. clypeolata* resemble common yarrow but the foliage is silvery and the flower stems are stiffer and grow to 120 centimetres in height.

The cultivars 'Moonshine', 'Cloth of Gold', and 'Coronation Gold' are ideal for a mid- to back border and combine beautifully with sea holly, Russian sage, wormwood, and lamb's-ears.

Sneezewort, *Achillea ptarmica* 'The Pearl', a heritage plant in Atlantic Canada, has narrow, dark green foliage and loose clusters of large, white, buttonlike flowers. It grows to 60 centimetres in height. For the front of a border or a rock garden, try a dwarf yarrow: silvery yarrow, *A. clavennae*, has silvery, hairy foliage and 20- to 30-centimetre-long stems topped with classic, white yarrow flowers; the similar woolly yarrow, *A. tomentosa*, has yellow flowers.

All yarrow are easily grown in any sunny, well-drained site; they tolerate poor, droughty soil. If, after flowering, you cut the plants back to their basal leaves, you may be rewarded with a second crop of blooms later in the season. Plants are vigorous and benefit from being divided every three to four years. They are also easily grown

Achillea ptarmica 'The Pearl'

from seed. Yarrow, hardy to zone 3, are ideal for Atlantic Canada. Pests are few and it is resistant to large herbivores. Powdery mildew may be problematic in some areas.

Aconitum
MONKSHOOD

Over 100 species of *Aconitum* are found throughout the northern hemisphere, but mostly in the Himalayan region. Only a few are common in cultivation, those primarily of European descent. The common monkshood, *A. napellus*, is a heritage plant in Atlantic Canada, where it has been grown for over 100 years—even though it is among the most toxic of our garden ornamentals.

Aconitum napellus 'Carneum'

Aconitum napellus

Common monkshood produces a tuberous root from which stems grow 100 to 120 centimetres in height. The palmate leaves are shiny, dark green, and deeply dissected. The helmet-shaped flowers grow in a narrow raceme during July and August. The flowers are typically deep blue, but other colours include white 'Album' and dull pink 'Carneum'. Virtually identical in appearance is the hybrid *A.* X *cammarum*, available in three primary cultivars: 'Bicolor' (blue and white), 'Stainless Steel' (light blue), and 'Pink Sensation' (light pink). Another monkshood hybrid, 'Spark's Variety', is deep purple-blue, blooms later in September, and may reach nearly 2 metres in height.

Wolfsbane, *A. lycoctonum*, native from northern Europe through to Mongolia, has larger leaves than common monkshood and is more compact, reaching only 85 centimetres in height. Its individual flowers are narrow. The most common cultivar on the market is 'Ivorine', with creamy white flowers. The southern European yellow wolfsbane, *A. lamarkii*, is taller than 'Ivorine', with pale yellow-green flowers.

The showy petals of monkshood are modified sepals; its true petals are small and insignificant. Monkshood grows in sun to part shade but dislikes dry sites. Staking is not generally needed if grown in full sun but may be needed if located in part shade. These tall plants are best used in the back of a border or in a wildflower garden. Combine them with other tall perennials: garden phlox, masterwort, and great bellflower. Species may be grown from seed but cultivars are propagated by division. All attract bees. The cultivars listed above are all hardy to zone 3. Monkshood is generally pest- and disease-free and resistant to large herbivores.

Actaea
BANEBERRY

The five species of *Actaea* found throughout the northern hemisphere are grown more for their decorative fruit than their small clusters of white starlike flowers produced in May and June. Flowers become red, white, or black poisonous berries in August and September. Plants form a bushy clump reaching 60 to 80 centimetres in height and have divided foliage reminiscent of that of a coarse-leaved astilbe. Two species of baneberry are native in Atlantic Canada: the red baneberry, *A. rubra*, has glossy red berries, or white on *neglecta*, and is found throughout Atlantic Canada; the other, doll's-eyes, *A. pachypoda*, whose white berries have a black "pupil" and are attached to the plant by thick red stems, is native throughout the Maritimes but not Newfoundland. From Europe comes *A. spicata*, which produces black berries, and *A. erythrocarpa*, with red. From China, Korea, and eastern Russia comes *A. asiatica*, which has black berries at the ends of thick red stems and is sure to draw comments from visitors to your garden. Baneberries make wonderful compan-

Actaea pachypoda

Actaea rubra

ion plants for hosta, astilbe, and ferns.

Woodland plants, baneberry prefer soil that is organically rich and evenly moist. In cooler coastal regions they can be grown in full sun, but in warmer inland regions they prefer part shade. Baneberry may be used in a mid-border but are also ideal for woodland and wildflower gardens. Propagation is by seed or division. They are not bothered by pests or diseases. All are rated hardy to zone 3.

Ajuga
BUGLEWEED

The genus *Ajuga* encompasses over 50 species, primarily native to Europe and Asia, but *A. reptans*, the common or carpet bugleweed, is the one most often seen in Atlantic Canada. This European species is a popular ground cover for growing in shade, on steep slopes, or in other problem areas. Plants produce low rosettes of shiny, evergreen, spoon-shaped leaves. In May and June a spike of blue two-lipped flowers emerges on stems that grow to 15 centimetres in height. These flowers are regularly visited by

TODD BOLAND

bees. After flowering, the plants produce runners from which new plants arise.

The many cultivars are primarily grown for their decorative foliage. 'Bronze Beauty', one of the older varieties, has purple-tinted foliage. 'Metallica Crispa' is similar but has wrinkled leaves. The best and largest dark-foliaged type is 'Black Scallop', which has dark purple leaves. The young leaves of 'Burgundy Glow' are purple with pink edges; they mature to grey-green with white margins. 'Golden Glow' is splashed with creamy yellow and mint green patterns. The leaves of 'Rainbow' are a combination of green, purple, and yellow.

The Chip™ series have smaller foliage and a more compact habit than most other varieties: 'Chocolate Chip', purple-tinted foliage; 'Dixie Chip', variously splashed with green, pink, and cream; 'Toffee Chip', grey-green leaves edged in creamy yellow; and 'Mint Chip', bright green foliage. All of the Chip™ series tolerate light foot traffic.

The above cultivars all have blue flowers typical of the species, but some bugleweed have pink flowers, notably 'Rosea', with green leaves; 'Pink Lightning', with white-edged leaves; the compact 'Pink Elf', with green foliage; and *A. genevensis* 'Pink Beauty', with large flowers on

Ajuga reptans 'Black Scallop'

Ajuga reptans 'Burgundy Glow'

Alcea rosea

plants that grow to 30 centimetres in height.

Bugleweed is vigorous and generally care-free, but use with caution—it can become invasive. Plants tolerate dry, poor soils but perform best if the soil is moist and fertile. If grown as a ground cover, space plants about 30 centimetres apart. It is hardy to zone 3 and may be grown throughout Atlantic Canada.

Alcea
HOLLYHOCK

Of the approximately 60 species of *Alcea*, all native from southern Europe to central Asia, the common hollyhock, *Alcea rosea*, is the most popular in Atlantic Canada. This long-time garden favourite has been cultivated in Europe since at least the 15th century. Plants produce round lobed leaves and stiff stems up to 1.5 to 3 metres

tall. From June to August, the stems are topped with a spike of 10- to 15-centimetre-diameter single or double saucer-shaped flowers. Flowers come in a variety of colours: white, pink, red, yellow, and nearly black. The thin, satiny petals are almost tissuelike.

Recommended cultivars include 'Summer Carnival' (mixed colour flowers, singles), 'Spotlight' Series (mixed singles), 'Chater's Double' (mixed doubles), 'Nigra' (black, single), 'Queeny Purple' (ruffled purple, double), and 'Fiesta Time' (ruffled deep pink, double). If hollyhock rust is a problem, try *A. filicifolia*, which is more resistant to the disease. It has deeply lobed, hand-shaped leaves. 'Happy Lights' and 'Antwerp', the most popular strains, have single flowers in an assortment of colours.

Hollyhock require full sun and well-drained soil. This is especially important in winter as these plants dislike excessive winter wetness. They are short-lived at the best of times but often self-seed. Hollyhock are susceptible to fungal spotting, as evidenced by brown or black spots, and a rust disease, which causes fine orange spots and yellowing leaves. Spider mites and Japanese beetles are common pests. As any of these can cause the leaves to be rather tatty, it is best to plant hollyhock in the back of a border behind other perennials to hide the foliage. It is hardy to zone 3 and attracts hummingbirds.

Alchemilla
LADY'S MANTLE

Among perennials grown primarily for their foliage rather than their flowers is lady's mantle. Although the genus contains over 300 species native throughout the northern hemisphere, only the eastern European garden lady's mantle,

A. mollis, is popular as a garden ornamental in Atlantic Canada. It grows in large clumps up to 45 centimetres tall and is sometimes used as a ground cover. Its cloaklike leaves are softly fuzzy and lime green, with scalloped edges. After rain, beads of water gathered on the leaves resemble drops of quicksilver. With such attractive foliage, it is best to plant lady's mantle along the front of a border where the leaves can be appreciated. Tiny chartreuse flowers are produced in airy clusters in June and July. As it freely self-seeds, the flowers should be promptly removed once they have faded.

Less common in cultivation, the dwarf lady's mantle, *A. erythropoda*, which grows to 15 centimetres in height, is ideal for a rock garden. Perhaps the prettiest is the alpine lady's mantle, *A. alpina*. It forms a clump up to 20 centimetres tall with palmately divided leaves which are matte dark green with silvery margins on the upper side and silky haired and silver-white on the underside. This rock-garden species prefers alkaline soil.

Alchemilla mollis

Cultivating any of these lady's mantle is easy in any reasonably moist soil in sun to shade. They require little care and have few pests or diseases. Propagation is by seed or division. The listed species, all hardy to zone 3, may be grown throughout Atlantic Canada.

Allium
ORNAMENTAL ONION

This genus, which encompasses over 500 species, is found throughout the northern hemisphere. The variation among them is substantial, with diminutive species reaching a few centimetres in height, to those that reach 1.5 metres. All have onionlike, aromatic, narrow foliage that arises from a bulb. The flower stems are naked and topped with a cluster of bell- to star-shaped flowers that vary from white to yellow, pink, purple, or blue, depending on the species or hybrid. The flowering season varies from May to October.

Most *Allium* prefer full sun and need well-drained soil. Smaller species are ideal for a rock garden, while the taller, ball-flowered types are wonderful additions to a perennial border. All are excellent flowers for pollinators. Pests and diseases are uncommon. Although the list of ornamental onions that can be grown in Atlantic Canada is vast, surprisingly, they are not commonly grown.

Allium collection

Allium christophii

Many ornamental onions are fall-planted, spring-blooming types that are summer-dormant. These are sold at the same time as tulips and daffodils and planted in a similar fashion. The earliest blooming, *A. oreophilum*, sometimes sold as *A. ostrowskianum*, grows to 25 centimetres tall and has a hemispherical cluster of pink flowers from late May through June. Golden garlic, *A. moly*, blooms a little later, with clusters of yellow flowers on stems up to 30 centimetres tall. Both are hardy to zone 3, multiply readily, and are excellent in a rock garden. For blooms in July, try the blue-flowered *A. caeruleum*, which has spherical clusters of flowers on 60-centimetre-tall stems. A little taller and blooming in July and August is the drumstick onion, *A. sphaerocephalum*, which has stems up to 90 centimetres tall and a small, dense, oval-shaped cluster of rose-purple flowers. These last two are ideal for the perennial border and make long-lasting cut flowers.

Perhaps the most popular and showy of the fall-planted *Allium* are the giant ball or drumstick onions, which produce white to pink spherical heads of flowers that vary from 7 to 30 centimetres in diameter, depending on the species and cultivar. These generally flower in June or July and make attractive cut flowers; even the faded flower heads are decorative if left in the garden. The shortest of these is *A. karataviense*, with two broad grey-green leaves and a baseball-sized head of silvery pink flowers atop a 20- to 30-centimetre-tall stem. The 60-centimetre-tall star of Persia, *A. christophii*, is among the most spectacular, with 30-centimetre-diameter amethyst flower heads. *A. schubertii* looks like floral fireworks with a loose but similar-sized head of rose-purple flowers. The other drumsticks are taller, reaching 90 or more centimetres, with dense, spherical heads of baseball-sized flowers in pink or white. These include *A. giganteum*, *A. aflatuense*, *A. nigrum*, and the hybrids 'Purple Sensation', 'Globemaster', 'Mount Everest', 'Globus', 'His Excellency', and 'Gladiator'. These are all rated hardy to zone 4.

Allium that keep their leaves in summer are most often used in rock-garden settings. The most common is chives, *A. schoenoprassum*, with purple-pink heads of flowers on 30- to 50-centimetre-tall stems during June. Of course, this species is grown mostly for its edible leaves. *Allium senescens* has grey-green foliage and pink flowers on 30- to 45-centimetre-tall stems during July and August. The similar hybrid 'Millenium' was chosen as the 2018 Perennial Plant of the Year™. *Allium cernuum* has unusual, nodding, July-blooming, pink flowers on 30- to 45-centimetre-tall stems. Also blooming in July and August are *A. flavum*, with pendant yellow flowers, and *A. carinatum* ssp. *pulchellum*, with pendant pink flowers. The last to bloom is *A. thunbergii*, with red-purple flowers on 30-centimetre-tall stems in September, October, and even into November. Chives is rated hardy to zone 2; the other summer-leaved types, zone 4.

Amsonia tabernaemontana

Amsonia
BLUESTAR

The genus *Amsonia*, which has 15 species, native exclusively to North America, honours 18th-century Virginian physician Dr. Charles Amson. Three species are hardy in Atlantic Canada.

The most likely to be found is eastern bluestar, *A. tabernaemontana*, which reaches a height of 90 centimetres if the soil is evenly moist, but only 60 centimetres if dry. Plants produce many upright stems clothed in narrow willowlike foliage and topped with a cluster of sky blue, star-shaped flowers in June and July. In the autumn, the foliage turns all yellow, adding an additional worthwhile element to this underrated plant. The cultivar 'Montana' has deeper blue flowers and a more compact habit than eastern bluestar, reaching just 45 centimetres tall. Fringed bluestar, *A. ciliata*, has broader leaves and slightly larger flowers than eastern bluestar on 60-centimetre-tall stems. Arkansas bluestar, *A. hubrichtii*, reaches 90 centimetres in height, has willowy stems and very narrow leaves, and tolerates heat and humidity better than *A. ciliata*. It was awarded Perennial Plant of the Year™ for 2011. A hybrid bluestar, 'Blue Ice', has lavender-blue flowers on compact 40-centimetre-tall plants.

Amsonia hubrichtii

In the garden, *Amsonia* prefer even moisture but, once established, tolerate some drought. Full sun results in more upright plants but they tolerate part shade, with the possible need of staking. *Amsonia* are useful in a middle border or a wildflower garden and make long-lasting cut flowers. Propagation is by seed or division. They are relatively care-free. Eastern and fringed bluestar are rated hardy to zone 4; Arkansas bluestar, zone 5.

Anemone
WINDFLOWER

The genus *Anemone*'s over 120 species are found in temperate regions worldwide. With such a large group, it is not surprising that there is diversity in size and flowering season, in this case, primarily spring or late summer-fall. The spring bloomers are primarily European woodland plants. In the wild they bloom before or just as the trees above

them unfurl their leaves; by mid-summer, under the deep shade of the forest, they go dormant. In the garden they follow a similar pattern and are known as spring ephemerals. They require careful situating as they can leave gaps in the garden later in the season. Ideally, anemone are placed with ferns and hosta, whose larger leaves hide the anemones' dying foliage and cover the gaps.

Anemone blanda, or Grecian windflower, is a popular fall-planted bulb; botanically, it is a tuber. It is difficult to tell the top from the bottom of the tuber, but an overnight soaking makes it more apparent. Plant tubers 5 to 8 centimetres deep, with the smoothest side on the bottom. It produces a low clump of divided fernlike foliage and solitary daisylike flowers that arise on 10- to 20-centimetre-tall stems in April and May. Popular cultivars include 'White Splendor', 'Radar' (pink), 'Pink Star', and 'Atrocaerulea' (blue).

Anemone blanda 'White Splendor' with *Pulmonaria longifolia*

Anemone X *hybrida* 'Pamina'

Anemone nemorosa, or wood anemone, produces narrow rhizomes and can form large colonies over time. Each sprout produces a pair of divided leaves and a single saucer-shaped flower with six to eight "petals" (modified sepals) on stems 20 to 30 centimetres in height. The wild form bears white flowers, but cultivars include 'Robinsoniana' (wisteria blue); 'Allenii' (lavender-blue); 'Wisley Pink', 'Royal Blue', 'Blue Eyes' (white with blue centre, double); and 'Vestal' (white, double). Similar in appearance is *A. raunculoides*, whose flowers are smaller and buttercup yellow. Both are wonderful plants to naturalize under trees and shrubs and bloom from late April through May and even into early June.

Anemone sylvestris, the snowdrop windflower, is a clumping plant with flower stems that reach 30 to 45 centimetres in height. Its flowers are also solitary and saucer-shaped with five white "petals". It blooms in late May and June. It prefers part shade and does not go summer-dormant, making it appropriate for rock gardens and border edges.

Two fall-flowering anemone species are *A. hu-pehensis*, the Japanese anemone, and the closely related *A. tomentosa*, the grapeleaf anemone. Both are native to central and northern China, and the former has also been naturalized in Japan. Both form spreading clumps of long-stemmed, trifoliate, basal leaves; the latter is distinguished by leaves with densely pubescent, whitened undersides. Both produce pink flowers, 5 to 8 centimetres in diameter, on branching stems 90 to 120 centimetres tall, from August through to October, helping to extend the flowering season. The Japanese anemone is available in several cultivars: 'September Charm' (pale pink), 'Hadspen Abundance' (medium pink with pale edges), and 'Prinz Heinrich' (semi-double pink). The grapeleaf anemone is primarily known by the cultivar 'Robustissima'. Hybrids between the two species also exist. Popular cultivars include 'Queen Charlotte' (semi-double pale pink), 'Serenade' (semi-double pink), 'Honorine Jobert' (white), 'Party Dress' (double pink), 'Pamina' (semi-double deep pink), and 'Whirlwind' (semi-double white). 'Honorine Jobert' was distinct enough to be awarded Perennial Plant of the Year™ in 2016. Several semi-dwarf compact cultivars have been released, called the Pretty Lady™ se-

Anemone 'Pamina'

ries, which reach only 30 to 50 centimetres in height: 'Pretty Lady Susan' (raspberry pink), 'Pretty Lady Emily' (semi-double medium pink), and 'Pretty Lady Diana' (deep pink).

One last anemone of note is 'Wild Swan'. This hybrid is a cross between the spring-flowering snowdrop windflower and a Japanese anemone. The result is the best of both worlds: its white petals are tinted blue on their reverse sides, on stems up to 50 centimetres tall. However, this plant starts blooming in June and continues all summer into early fall. It is not surprising that it won an award at the British Chelsea Flower Show.

Anemone prefer humus-rich, well-drained soil in full sun or part shade. Those that go summer-dormant tolerate a site that becomes dry in summer; otherwise, they need even moisture. Most need full sun in spring but can withstand shade in summer. They are ideal for planting under trees and shrubs, but they are also useful in rock gardens and, in some cases, the front of a border. Propagation is primarily by division. Pests and diseases are uncommon, but the fall-flowering anemone may suffer from mildew diseases. All are hardy through zone 4.

Anthemis
GOLDEN MARGUERITE

Despite over 180 species of *Anthemis*, most of which are native to the Mediterranean region, surprisingly few are grown in Atlantic Canada. Essentially only *A. tinctoria*, the golden marguerite, is seen—and that may not even count, as plant taxonomists now consider it as *Cota tinctoria*. Whatever the formal name, this upright plant is 60 to 90 centimetres tall, with finely divided, fernlike, pungent foliage. The flowers are single yellow daisies, produced over a long period all summer, especially if promptly deadheaded.

Several cultivars exist. 'Kelwayi' is the most

Anthemis tinctoria

common, with typical golden yellow flowers on 90-centimetre-tall plants. 'E.C. Buxton' is of similar size but has lemon yellow blossoms. 'Grallagh Gold' is deep yellow but more compact at 60 centimetres tall. 'Wargrave Variety' is pale yellow, while 'Sauce Hollandaise' and 'Susanna Mitchell' are creamy white; all reach about 60 centimetres. 'Moonlight' is a bushy cultivar reaching just 30 centimetres in height with pale yellow flowers; 'Lemon Ice' flowers have a hint of yellow.

Golden marguerite requires full sun and tolerates dry, poor soil, although it performs better if given fertile soil and regular moisture. It is apt to die out in the centre if not divided every two to three years; otherwise, it is care-free and attracts butterflies and bees. Propagation is by seed or division. Hardy to zone 3, it is suitable throughout much of Atlantic Canada.

Ideal for a rock garden in milder areas of Atlantic Canada is *A. biebersteiniana*. It has low silvery foliage and single yellow daisies atop 15- to 25-centimetre-tall stems. Ideal for coastal gardens, it is only hardy through zone 5.

Aquilegia
COLUMBINE

Columbine are stalwarts among garden plants. The genus is relatively large with over 60 species, all native to the northern hemisphere. By far the most popular is the common columbine, *A. vulgaris*, a native of Europe. The wild form produces long-stemmed, basal, grey-green leaves which are biternate and fernlike. The flowers, blooming in June and July, are held atop stiffly upright stems which are up to 90 centimetres in height. Individual flowers are nodding with five spurred petals and five petaloid sepals.

Blue is the colour of the wild flowers but modern-day cultivars come in white, yellow, pink, wine, and purple, often with contrasting white-tipped petals. Cultivars with spurless flowers are referred to as clematis-flowered or, formally, *A. vulgaris* var. *stellata*. Double-flowered clematis-flowered columbine are referred to as the Barlow series. 'Nora Barlow' is the most popular, with deep pink flowers with white tips; 'Black Barlow', a dark wine-purple. For decorative foliage, try 'Leprechaun Gold' or 'Woodside Strain', both of which have yellow-mottled foliage. Many of these modern-day columbines are more compact than the wild type, reaching 45 to 60 centimetres in height.

Columbines are promiscuous and hybridize readily with other columbine species. Long-spurred columbines, often called *A. X hybrida*, were created by hybridizing several species, most often North American natives such as *A. chrysantha* and *A. coerulea*. Among the oldest long-spurred hybrids are the 'McKana Giants', 75-centimetre-tall plants with large, often two-tone, flowers. The Music and Dragonfly series are more compact.

While the columbines listed in the previous

Aquilegia chrysantha

paragraph are best for a perennial border, many species less than 30 centimetres tall are ideal for a rock garden: *A. scopulorum* (blue flowers), *A. buergeriana* 'Calimero' (purple and yellow), *A. flabellata* 'Ministar' (blue and white), and *A. saximontana* (blue and white). For the woodland or wildflower garden, try the eastern North America native *A. canadensis* or its western counterpart *A. formosa*, both with red and yellow flowers.

Short-lived plants, columbines often self-seed around the garden. If you grow several different types, you will likely end up with interesting hybrids. They need evenly moist soil and full sun to part shade. Sawflies, a serious pest, defoliate the plants just as they bloom and often attack them again later in the season. Powdery mildew can also be a problem. If mildew is a problem for your plants, try the new mildew-resistant Winky series. All columbines attract hummingbirds. Plants are toxic if ingested; this protects them from large herbivores. Propagation is by seed, since plants are taprooted and do not divide easily. Most are hardy through zone 3.

LEFT: *Aquilegia vulgaris* double selection

Arabis
ROCKCRESS

This relatively large genus is distributed primarily in Europe. Most are weedy, with only a few suitable as garden ornamentals. The most common is *A. alpina* ssp. *caucasica*. This species, native to the Caucasus Mountains of Eastern Europe, forms a low mat of evergreen, spoon-shaped, fuzzy, grey-green leaves. From April to early June, plants send up wiry stems to 20 centimetres tall topped with a cluster of white or, less commonly, pink flowers. Individual flowers have four petals in the form of a cross. Its low stature and habit make it ideal for rock gardens or cascading over a wall. It combines well with spring bulbs. It is also reasonably wind- and salt-tolerant, lending it to use in coastal gardens. Standard white-flowered cultivars include 'Snowcap', 'Snowfix', and 'Lotti White'. In the pink shades are 'Rosea', which is light pink, and 'Lotti Deep Rose'. The most compact cultivars, less than 10 centimetres tall, are the Little Treasure series. For year-round interest, try 'Variegata', which has white-margined foliage.

Another species sometimes encountered is *A. procurrens*, a native of southeastern Europe. It has small, tight, deep green foliage and loosely clustered small white flowers on 20-centimetre-long stems. The standard cultivar is 'Glacier', but perhaps more attractive for their variegated foliage is 'Variegata' and 'Old Gold', which have white and yellow-margined leaves respectively.

These rockcress tolerate dry, poor soil but perform better if the soil is reasonably fertile and moist. They dislike too much winter wetness and high summer temperatures. Full sun is best but they tolerate part shade, where the flowers will be fewer. As the wild species are usually confined to limestone areas, the addition of lime in their growing area of the garden will be helpful. To keep plants compact and tidy, shear the old flowers by mid-June. Rockcress are not bothered by pests and diseases, although aphids and downy mildew may periodically be a problem. They attract bees and butterflies. Propagation is by seed or, in the case of variegated cultivars, cuttings. Both of the above species are rated hardy to zone 3.

Arabis caucasica 'Rosea'

Aralia cordata

Aralia

SPIKENARD

Most of the Asian and North American 68 *Aralia* species are woody plants but a few are herbaceous perennials. Three species native to Atlantic Canada—smooth sarsaparilla, *A. nudicaulis*; bristly sarsaparilla, *A. hispida*; and American spikenard, *A. racemosa*—are suitable for shady gardens. They have insignificant yellow-green flowers but produce black berries and attractive compound leaves. For the border choose Japanese spikenard, *A. cordata*, a giant, bold plant up to 2 metres in height, useful for the back of a border or a woodland or wildflower setting. With its shrublike habit, it may be planted as a stand-alone plant. Its huge leaves, up to 90 centimetres long, are compound, with heart-shaped leaflets. The minute yellow-green flowers are produced in long bottlebrush panicles in August and September and develop into black berries in autumn. The eye-catching cultivar 'Sun King' has spectacular golden yellow foliage.

Aralia prefers evenly moist, organically rich soil. It grows in sun to part shade, but 'Sun King' needs full sun to maintain its yellow foliage. The minute flowers are readily visited by bees. Insects and large herbivores are generally not a problem, but leaf spot may be. Propagation is by seed or division. These uncommon and underutilized plants are hardy to zone 3.

Aralia cordata 'Sun King'

TODD BOLAND

Arisaema triphyllum

Arisaema
JACK-IN-THE-PULPIT, COBRA LILY

Most of the approximately 180 species of *Arisaema* are native to China, with only a few hardy enough to be grown in Atlantic Canada. One species native to the Maritimes, *A. triphyllum*, grows in rich, damp, deciduous forests. As a group, *Arisaema* arise from a tuber. The divided leaves are vaguely hand-shaped. The flower is perhaps the most exotic of any hardy plant grown in Atlantic Canadian gardens, with the possible exception of orchids. *Arisaema* flowers (technically an inflorescence, as the entire "flower" is composed of many closely packed, tiny flowers) are composed of two main parts: the spathe (pulpit) and spadix (jack). The pitcher-shaped spathe often has an overlying hood.

The spadix is the clublike "stalk" inside the flower that holds the sex organs. In some species the spathe produces a long threadlike tail; in others, the spadix has the tail. Perhaps more bizarre: *Arisaema* can change sexes. Young plants are often males, while older, more mature, plants may be female or hermaphroditic. They can change sexes at any point; however, the "flowers" of either sex essentially look the same. Female flowers form closely packed red or orange berries which form a giant raspberry-like fruit in autumn.

The native Jack-in-the-pulpit, *A. triphyllum*, reaches 60 centimetres in height and produces white-striped green to dark purple-black flowers from late May through June. Each leaf has three leaflets. Similar in appearance and blooming at the same time is *A. amurense*, with greenish flowers and leaves with three to five leaflets. Green Jack-in-the-pulpit, *A. dracontium*, can reach up to 90 centimetres in height and has a horseshoe-shaped arrangement of leaflets per leaf. In this species, the spadix has a long tail-like extension that extends from the spathe like a whip. The 60-centimetre-tall *Arisaema ringens* has three leaflets. Each of its very glossy leaves may reach 60 centimetres wide, imparting a tropical effect. The flowers are dark wine with white stripes, appearing much like a cobra's head. Perhaps the most attractive of the early bloomers is *A. sikokianum*, reaching up to 60 centimetres in height and leaves with three to five leaflets which may have silvery patches in the middle of each leaflet. The flowers are dark wine with an erect white-striped hood. The brilliant white spadix is knob-shaped.

Among the late bloomers, mid- to late July, are the giants *A. consanquineum* and *A. jacquemontii*, both of which may reach 120 centimetres in height. The former species has many narrow leaflets arranged like an umbrella, and its purple white-striped flowers are produced below the leaves. The cultivar 'Poseidon' has silver-striped leaflets. *A. jacquemonti* has an umbrella-like leaf, but the leaflets are fewer and broader. Its green white-striped flowers are held above the leaves. Perhaps the most delicate of the late bloomers is the 45-centimetre-tall *A. candidissimum*, which has light pink flowers with white stripes and trifoliate leaves.

Arisaema prefer organically rich, evenly moist but well-drained soil. In the wild, they often grow in part shade, but if the soil contains enough moisture, they perform well in full sun. They are most commonly used in woodland gardens but may be dotted here and there in a border setting. As some species, like *A. jacquemontii* and *A. consangineum*, are slow to appear, often not sprouting until well into June or even early July, carefully mark the area where they are planted. Pests and diseases are not a problem. Propagation is by seed or tuber offsets. Hardiness varies from zone 3 for *A. triphyllum*, zone 4 for *A. dracontium*, zone 6 for *A. candidissimum*, and zone 5 for the remainder.

Armeria
THRIFT

Of the 100 species of thrift, all but one are restricted to Eurasia, particularly near the Mediterranean. Only *A. maritima* is naturally found in North America. As it happens, it is the most popular species grown as an ornamental. All thrift have narrow, evergreen grasslike leaves that form tight hummocks or buns. Upright, naked flower stems arise 15 to 20 centimetres above the foliage. In June each flower stem is topped with a spherical head of small reddish pink to white flowers. Although the flowers of the wild species are light to medium pink, the cultivar 'Dusseldorf Pride' is deep pink, while 'Splendens' is deep pink, with the largest flowers. 'Alba' has white flowers; 'Rubrifolia', red-tinted foliage; 'Vesuvius', dark red foliage; and the leaves of 'Nifty Thrifty' are narrowly edged in white.

Great thrift, *A. pseudarmeria*, has flower stems reaching 30 to 50 centimetres in height. Popular cultivars include the Joystick and Ballerina series

Armeria maritima

Armeria caespitosa

in red, lilac, and white. On the other hand, juniper-leaved thrift, *A. caespitosa*, is very tight and compact with flower stems reaching 5 to 10 centimetres in height. The most popular cultivars are 'Bevans' (pink) and 'Alba' (white). All thrift are ideal for a rock garden; sea and great thrift are also suitable for the front of a border.

As a group, thrift require full sun and well-drained soil. They perform better under poor soil conditions and, once established, are drought-tolerant. They prefer alkaline soil. Prompt deadheading encourages them to produce additional flowers later in the season. Pests and diseases are almost unknown. Their high salt tolerance makes them ideal for coastal gardens. Sea thrift is the hardiest, to zone 2; juniper-leaved thrift, hardy through zone 4; and great thrift, only hardy to zone 6, suitable only for the mildest areas of Atlantic Canada.

Arnica
ARNICA

The 30 species of *Arnica* are found across the northern hemisphere, but most commonly in western North America. The name is from the Greek *arni*, lamb, a reference to the softly hairy leaves of some species. From a distance, plants may be confused with leopard's-bane, *Doronicum*, but arnica blooms in June and July. The most common species grown is mountain arnica, *A. montana*, native to mountains throughout Europe. Its stems reach 60 centimetres in length and it has paired, mostly basal, leaves. The 10-centimetre-diameter yellow daisies are produced in loose clusters from late June through July. Although arnica is a medicinal plant, it is toxic if eaten raw.

Because of its clumping habit, arnica may be used in the front of a border or rock garden. The other species sometimes encountered in Atlantic Canadian gardens is meadow arnica, *A. chamissonis*, native to western North America. It too can reach 60 centimetres in length but has clustered, smaller flowers from July to early August. A runner, this species can quickly swamp more timid neighbours. It is best used in a wildflower setting.

Arnica perform best in full sun but tolerate part shade. Mountain arnica prefer acidic soil; meadow arnica, alkaline soil. Both need even soil moisture and do not tolerate drought. Arnica are wonderful plants for both bees and butterflies. Neither is bothered by pests or diseases. Propagation is by seed or division. Mountain arnica is hardy to zone 4; meadow arnica, through zone 3.

Arnica chamissonis

Artemisia
SAGEBRUSH, WORMWOOD

This large group of plants has over 200 species, distributed throughout the northern hemisphere. The genus is named after the Greek goddess Artemis, twin sister of Apollo. Many are low woody shrubs but a few are herbaceous or sub-shrubs, woody but behaving more like herbaceous plants. They are grown primarily for their ornamental foliage, which is grey-green to silver-white, fuzzy, and often pungent. Their flowers are nondescript. Several European species grow as weeds in disturbed areas throughout Atlantic Canada. Four species are commonly grown as ornamentals: *A. schmidtiana*, from Japan; *A. stelleriana*, from Japan north to Russia and east into Alaska; *A. ludoviciana*, from west-central North America; and *A. lactiflora*, from western China.

Artemisia schmidtiana, commonly known as 'Silver Mound' artemisia, is a sub-shrub which forms rounded mounds of soft, feathery, silvery white foliage, reaching a height of 25 centimetres. It makes a wonderful accent plant at the front of a border or in a rock garden. The cultivar 'Nana' is similar but smaller, reaching only 15 centimetres. 'Ever Goldy' has unusual golden grey foliage. *Artemisia stelleriana* or perennial dusty miller is matlike in its habit, lending itself to use as a ground cover. Its leaves are coarser but also silvery white, hence its use as an accent plant. The plant stems are held close to the ground, but the flower stems may reach 30 centimetres in height. To keep plants looking their best, deadhead the flowers after they fade. Popular cultivars include 'Silver Brocade' and 'Broughton Silver'. This species, which sometimes self-seeds, is cropping up as a naturalized plant along coastal regions of Atlantic Canada.

White sagebrush, *A. ludoviciana*, also has silvery

RIGHT: *Artemisia lactiflora* 'Ghizou'

TODD BOLAND

Artemisia schmitiana

white foliage but its leaves are lance-shaped and the stems upright to 100 centimetres. It is grown as an accent but better suited to the middle of a border. 'Silver King', 'Silver Queen', and 'Valerie Finnis' are the most popular cultivars. White mugwort, *A. lactiflora*, is a tall, back-of-the-border plant that reaches 150 centimetres in height. Unlike many artemisia, it has green leaves and is grown for its late-summer, terminal panicles of fluffy white flowers reminiscent of astilbe. 'Guizhou' is a cultivar with nearly black stems and very dark green leaves. Also tall is *A. vulgaris* 'Oriental Limelight', which has green leaves mottled with lemon yellow.

The silver-white-foliaged artemisia are sun-lovers and prefer dry sites. Tolerant to poor soil, wind, and salt, they are ideal for coastal gardens. They prefer alkaline soil and do poorly under acidic conditions. For an awesome display, combine them with lamb's-ears, blue sea holly, catmint, *Sedum rupestre* 'Angelina', yellow coneflower, and blue fescue or blue oat grass. The stems of white sagebrush may be cut and dried for use in flower arrangements. White mugwort, however, prefers moist soil and tolerates more shade. Artemisia are mostly pest- and disease-free. Propagation is by division or cuttings. All of the above are hardy through zone 3.

Aruncus
GOATSBEARD

Aruncus encompasses three species—or just one, according to some botanists. From a gardening point of view, there are two types: the tall goatsbeard, *A. dioicus*, and the dwarf goatsbeard, *A. aethusifolius*. The tall goatsbeard, native across much of the northern hemisphere, is a tall bold plant with large, coarse, fernlike leaves. The flowers, produced on stems up to 2 metres tall, are produced in large creamy plumes in June and July. Plants are dioecious, which means each plant is either male or female. Male plants have more attractive fluffy flowers than the females. Tall goatsbeard is a plant for the back of a border and, with its shrublike habit, may be grown as a stand-alone plant. The cultivar 'Kneiffii' has fine, divided foliage and reaches only 100 to 120 centimetres in height.

In the wild, dwarf goatsbeard is native to Korea. From a distance it may be mistaken for an astilbe. It has more filigree foliage than the tall goatsbeard and smaller, narrower plumes of

flowers. The male plants produce the showier flowers. Plants reach about 30 centimetres in height. It is better suited to the front of a border or may even be used in a large rock-garden setting. Both types are appropriate for woodland gardens or along the edges of water features. The two types hybridize readily, so if you grow both and you happen to have a female plant, you will probably end up with many offspring which are intermediate between the two parents.

Water-lovers, goatsbeard quickly suffer if the soil is too dry or of poor quality. Instead, they need organically rich, moist soil. Full sun is ideal in cooler coastal regions but, inland, part shade is advised. These plants have attractive fall colour; leaves turn warm gold on the tall goatsbeard and a blend of yellow, orange, and red on the dwarf. Pests are uncommon, but fungal spotting, present in some regions, causes leaf discoloration. Propagation is by division. Both are rated hardy to zone 3.

Aruncus dioicus

Asclepias incarnata 'Soulmate'

Asclepias
MILKWEED

About 140 species of milkweed grow in the wild, all native to the Americas. The genus name honours Asklepios, the Greek god of medicine. The common name is a reference to the milky sap of most species. Many are weedy in nature, but a few are showy. Gardeners recognize the milkweeds as being host plants for monarch butterflies. As many species of milkweed grow in agricultural areas, the plants have been removed to make room for crops. The reduction in the wild population of milkweeds has impacted the monarch population, with a dramatic decrease in their numbers. If you have a wildflower garden, you can help the monarchs by planting common milkweed, *A. syriaca*, a coarse 2-metre-tall species native to the Maritimes. The monarchs lay eggs on the plants and their caterpillars then feed on the plants. In a more formal garden setting, common milkweed is too invasive, as it spreads rapidly by underground rhizomes. There is no advantage to planting common milkweed in Newfoundland, where monarchs are not native. At any rate, common milkweed is not as showy as the more popular milkweed, the butterfly weed *A. tuberosa*.

Asclepias tuberosus

Butterfly weed is native to eastern and central North America, although it is not native to Atlantic Canada. It won Perennial Plant of the Year™ in 2017. This plant will form a clump with unbranched stems reaching 75 centimetres in height. The leaves are narrow; the brilliant orange star-shaped flowers are held in terminal flat-topped clusters during July and August. 'Gay Butterflies' has a mix of yellow, orange, or scarlet flowers; 'Hello Yellow', brilliant yellow. The flowers develop large spindle-shaped seed pods that split to reveal silky seeds. Butterfly weed is slow to establish and, because it has a taproot, dislikes being transplanted, so start with young plants. As it is late to sprout in spring, carefully mark the area where it is planted. It is a suitable species for a mid-border, a cottage garden, and especially a wildflower setting.

Native to the Maritimes is swamp milkweed, *A. incarnata*, with small vanilla-scented flowers in terminal clusters atop 100- to 150-centimetre-tall stems. It may be used in the back of a border or a wildflower garden. 'Cinderella' has rosy pink flowers; 'Soulmate', two-tone pink and white blossoms; and 'Ice Ballet', pure white.

Butterfly weed needs full sun and well-drained soil, especially in winter, as it is prone to rot if the soil is too wet. It is drought-tolerant once established and will tolerant poor, rocky soil. Swamp milkweed, as the name suggests, prefers moist to wet soil. Pests and diseases are rare on both. Propagation of butterfly weed is by seed, while swamp milkweed may be grown from seed or division. As expected, they are magnets for butterflies. Both species are rated hardy through zone 3.

Aster

ASTER, MICHAELMAS DAISY

At one time, the genus *Aster* had over 600 species. The Latin name means *star*, in reference to their starlike flowers. Recently, however, genetic information has led botanists to place many of the *Aster* into new genera. As a result, the true *Aster* now only encompass about 180 species, most confined to Eurasia.

In Atlantic Canada, the most popular true aster is the alpine aster, *A. alpinus*. It forms a low clump of spoon-shaped basal leaves. In June to July, plants produce unbranched stems that arise 20 to 30 centimetres, topped with a solitary 5-centimetre-diameter daisy. The colour of wild aster flowers is lavender-blue but cultivars offer a variety of colours: 'Albus' (white), 'Happy End' (light pink), 'Pinkie' (dark pink), 'Goliath' (lilac-blue), and 'Dark Beauty' (deep purple-blue).

Less commonly encountered is *A. tongolensis* 'Wartburg Star'. This Chinese species resembles alpine aster but its flower stems may reach 45 centimetres in height. They have purple-blue flowers up to 8 centimetres in diameter and bloom in late July. More closely resembling the standard Michaelmas daisy, Italian aster, *A. amellus*, produces 30- to 60-centimetre-tall stems and dense clusters of 2.5-centimetre-wide flowers in September. Cultivars include 'King George' (lav-

Aster alpinus

ender-blue), 'Violet Queen' (deep purple-blue), and 'Pink Zenith'.

The fall-blooming Michaelmas daisies are now known as *Symphyotrichum*. This genus has about 90 species, mostly native to North America. The tallest is the New England aster, *S. novae-angliae*. The wild version, native in Nova Scotia and New Brunswick, forms a clump of stems 1 to 2 metres tall, topped with clusters of pink-purple daisies in September and October. 'September Ruby' (reddish pink), 'Alma Potschke' (pink), and 'Hella Lacy' (lavender-blue) reach 120 centimetres. Dwarf cultivars, such as 'Purple Dome' and 'Vibrant Dome', reach about 50 centimetres and are appropriate for smaller gardens.

New York aster, *S. novi-belgii*, wild throughout Atlantic Canada, often grows by the sea. It ranges from 30 to 60 centimetres in height, is domed and bushy, and typically has lavender-blue flowers in August and September. Garden forms range in colour from white through pink to deep red and lavender-blue to dark purple-blue. Those cultivars reaching 60 centimetres high include 'Blue Lagoon', 'Diana' (pink), 'Porcelain' (pale blue), 'Crimson Brocade' (reddish violet), and 'Winston Churchill' (light purple-pink). Around 45 centimetres in height are 'White Swan', 'White Opal', and 'Royal Ruby'. The lowest, at 30 centimetres, are sometime called *S. dumosum* in the trade but chances are they are simply dwarf forms of *S. novi-belgii*. They include 'Violet Carpet', 'Pink Beauty', 'Lady in Blue', 'Hein Richard' (magenta), 'Jenny' (magenta), 'Alert' (reddish purple), 'Professor Anton Kippenberg' (deep violet-blue), and the Woods series (variable colours).

Hybrid Michaelmas daisics, including the Kickin® series, are available in a variety of stan-

NEXT PAGE: *Symphyotrichum novi-belgii*

Symphyotrichum dumosum 'Woods Pink'

dard aster colours. They form dense mounding plants up to 60 centimetres in height and smother themselves in blossoms. Another Michaelmas daisy worth trying is heath aster, *S. ericoides*. Although it may reach 100 centimetres tall, this species forms a dense mound, smothered in tiny daisies. Cultivars include 'Earl King' (pale lavender), 'Pink Cloud' (pale pink), and 'Lovely' (violet-purple).

All these Michaelmas daisies prefer full sun and well-drained, evenly moist soil. Depending on their mature height, they may be used in the back, middle, or front of a border. They are also appropriate in a cottage or wildflower garden. New York aster is particularly good for seaside gardens. All make wonderful cut flowers and are magnets for bees and butterflies. The main disease is powdery mildew, if it is grown in too sheltered a site. Spittlebugs can cause curled foliage, but otherwise these species are not bothered by pests. Propagation is by division. All are hardy to zone 4, with New York aster hardy to zone 3.

All the true aster noted above prefer full sun and require well-drained soil. Once established, they tolerate considerable drought. Excessive winter wetness is their greatest enemy. They may be used in a rock garden or in the front of a border. Their blossoms attract bees and butterflies

and are long-lasting cut flowers. Diseases are rare, except possibly powdery mildew if the location is too sheltered. The main pests are slugs, snails, and spittlebugs. Hares may nibble them, but deer and moose are not generally a problem. Propagation is by seed or division. Alpine aster and 'Wartburg Star' are hardy through zone 3, while Italian aster is rated for zone 5.

Astilbe
ASTILBE

Astilbe are among the most popular garden plants grown in Atlantic Canada. There are 18 species of *Astilbe*, most native to Asia. Gardeners usually grow hybrids from several of the Asian species. As a group, astilbe form clumps of basal, divided leaves that appear fernlike. Leaf colour is variable from light to dark green, chartreuse to red-tinted; some have dark red spring

Astilbe 'Fanal'

leaves. Plant height varies from 30 to over 120 centimetres. All produce feathery plumes of minute flowers from July to October, depending on the cultivar. Flower colour ranges from white through shades of pink and red to lilac and lavender. Wonderful for a border, they are also suitable for woodland gardens and the edges of water features, and the most dwarf forms are appropriate for rock gardens. To highlight their fine foliage, combine them with hosta, iris, and daylily.

Only a few of the more than 100 astilbe hybrids are described here. The smallest, at only 10 centimetres in height, is *A. glaberrima*, which has small pale pink plumes. *A. simplicifolia* is about 30 centimetres tall; popular cultivars include 'Sprite' (pale pink), 'Hennie Graafland' (rosy pink), 'Key West' (deep pink), 'Pink Lightning' (light pink), and 'Moulin Rouge' (red). 'Sprite' was awarded Perennial Plant of the Year™ in 1994. *Astilbe* X *crispa* 'Perkeo' has plasticlike, stiff, dark green, glossy foliage, reaches 25 centimetres in height, and has pink flowers. The Younique™ (fragrant), Partiezz™, Vision, and Music series, all new hybrids out of Holland, reach 45 to 50 centimetres. With the bonus of attractive foliage are Partiezz™ 'Karaoke Party', with chartreuse foliage, and Partiezz™ 'Surprise Party', with yellow and green foliage.

Most of the remaining hybrids are between 60 and 100 centimetres in height. Of note are 'Erika' and 'Fanal', which have dark red spring

Astilbe 'Rhythm and Blues'

Astilbe hybrids

All astilbe prefer organically rich, moist soil and do not tolerate poor, droughty sites. In coastal regions, they take full sun but in warmer inland sites, part shade is best. They attract butterflies and bees and are essentially care-free. Propagation is by division. All are rated hardy to zone 3.

Astilboides
SHIELDLEAF RODGERSIA
This plant was once included with the *Rodgersia* but is now classified as *Astilboides tabularis*. This uncommon and underrated perennial originates from China, where it grows along streams and in open damp woodlands. It forms a large clump of basal leaves. Each bright green leaf is shield-shaped and can measure up to 90 centimetres in diameter. Although it is grown primarily for its bold leaves, in July the plant produces dense plumes of tiny white flowers on arching stems up to 120 centimetres tall. It is an ideal plant for use near water features and in open woodland gardens.

Astilboides tabularis

foliage and red-tinted summer foliage. 'Color Flash Lime' has chartreuse foliage and pink flowers, while 'Color Flash' itself is chartreuse in spring but becomes flushed with purple later in the season. 'Ostrich Plume' (pink) and 'Prof. van der Wielen' (white) are *A. thunbergii* cultivars with unique drooping plumes. Both reach 90 centimetres in height. The tallest and latest-blooming astilbes, *A. chinensis*, reach 90 to 120 centimetres with narrow, stiffly upright plumes in late summer to mid-fall. 'Purple Lance', 'Purple Candles', and var. *taquetii* 'Superba' are popular. There are also dwarf, 25-centimetre-tall *A. chinensis* cultivars, which include 'Pumila' (deep pink) and 'Finale' (light pink).

This plant requires a sheltered site, as the leaves may get tattered if exposed to too much wind. Part shade is ideal but it tolerates full sun as long as the soil stays evenly moist. The leaves quickly brown if the soil is too dry. Diseases are rare but slugs may be a problem, and it may be browsed by herbivores. Propagation is by seed or, more commonly, division. It is hardy to zone 5.

Astrantia

MASTERWORT

The few *Astrantia* species are all natives of Europe. Most popular in the home garden are *A. major*, *A. maxima*, and *A. carniolica*, along with hybrids among them. All are stars in the summer border.

Masterwort plants are clumpers with long-stemmed, palmately lobed, semi-glossy leaves. The flower stems, which reach 70 to 90 centimetres in height, are held stiffly upright, topped with a loose cluster of starlike flowers in shades

Astrantia 'Star of Billion'

of silvery white, pink, or wine red. Blooms are produced from June through August. Individual flowers are unique: what appears to be a single bloom is in fact a hemispherical umbel of tiny flowers surrounded by many pointed bracts, which form a collar below the true flowers. It makes a long-lasting cut flower and may be dried for flower arrangements.

The best white cultivars are 'Star of Heaven', 'Star of Billion', 'Buckland', and 'Shaggy'. The pink shades include 'Lola', 'Roma', 'Pink Pride', and 'Primadonna'. The deepest wine red are 'Hadspen Blood', 'Ruby Wedding', and 'Lars'. With a wine and white two-tone effect are 'Star of Beauty' and 'Star of Fire'. For all-season interest, try the variegated-leaf cultivar 'Sunningdale Variegated', whose flowers are the palest pink, or 'Vanilla Gorilla', with deeper pink flowers.

Astrantia prefer organically rich, moist, heavy soil and quickly flag if soil conditions are too dry. If the soil is moist, full sun is perfect; otherwise, grow plants in part shade. Deadhead after flowering for a late-season secondary flush. As *Astrantia* is a prolific producer of seeds and seedlings, deadheading helps to prevent uncontrolled spreading. Insect and disease problems are rare, and these plants are generally ignored by large herbivores. Propagation is by seed but more often by division. The various species and cultivars listed are rated hardy to zone 4.

Astrantia 'Star of Beauty'

Aubrieta deltoidea 'Purple Gem'

Aubrieta
WALL CRESS

Although 12 species of *Aubrieta* are primarily native to the Mediterranean region, essentially only a single species, *A. deltoidea*, is commonly grown in Atlantic Canada. Sometimes called false rockcress, *Aubrieta* is a popular mat-forming plant chosen for its spring-blooming, purple-blue to red-pink flowers. The genus was named in honour of French botanical artist Claude Aubriet (1665–1742).

The plant has semi-evergreen, spoon-shaped, fuzzy, grey-green leaves. Flowers are produced in clusters atop 15- to 20-centimetre-long stems from April to June. Individual flowers have four petals in the shape of a cross. Of the many cultivars, the most popular is the Cascade, Royal, and Carpet series in blue, purple, and red. 'Purple Gem' is another worthwhile cultivar. For year-round interest, choose a variegated cultivar with white-margined leaves, notably 'Argenteo Variegata', with violet-blue flowers; 'Doctor Mules Variegated', deep violet flowers; and 'Variegated Red', violet-red flowers. 'Golden Variegata' has yellow-margined leaves and lavender-blue flowers. Unique is the dark violet-flowered 'Lime Variegated', whose chartreuse leaves are edged in darker green.

Wall cress needs full sun and well-drained soil. It prefers alkaline soil; if the soil is acidic, apply lime annually. To keep plants compact, shear faded flowers shortly after they finish blooming. Wall cress is ideal for rock gardens or cascading over a wall and attracts early-emerging butterflies and bees. Propagation is by seed or cuttings. Overall, it is a care-free plant, rated hardy to zone 4.

Aurinia
BASKET OF GOLD ALYSSUM

This plant, once classified as *Alyssum saxatile*, has now been changed to *Aurinia saxatilis*. It is native from central Europe to Turkey, especially near the Mediterranean region. Plants form low, spreading mounds 15 to 30 centimetres tall with narrow, grey-green, spoon-shaped leaves. In May and June, it produces masses of small yellow flowers. As the plants age, they may become woody at

Aurinia saxatile

the base and almost shrublike. Cutting off faded flower stems ensures that the plants stay compact and bushy. Popular cultivars include 'Basket of Gold', 'Gold Dust', and 'Golden Queen'. 'Compactum', a more compact cultivar, grows 15 to 20 centimetres tall.

In the wild, this plant grows in poor, dry, rocky sites. In the garden, it requires full sun, a well-drained site, and soil that is not too rich. Excessive winter wetness or high summer humidity will rot the leaves. Although it can tolerate various soil pH levels, this plant prefers the addition of lime. It is relatively short-lived but often self-seeds, though not aggressively. It is ideal for a rock-garden setting or cascading over a wall. All species attract early-emerging butterflies and bees and are reasonably deer- and moose-resistant. Pests and diseases are uncommon. It is hardy to zone 3.

Baptisia
BLUE FALSE INDIGO

All 25 species of *Baptisia* are native to North America. The genus name comes from the Greek word *bapto*, to dye, referring to blue clothes dye developed from the root. The species most commonly grown as a garden ornamental in Atlantic Canada is *B. australis*, native from Texas to the Great Lakes, east to the Atlantic coast. This tall, almost shrublike plant reaches 90 to 120 centimetres in height. It has large trifoliate leaves similar to those of clover. In June and July, plants produce 15 to 30 long, lupinelike spikes of blue flowers, which later develop into black swollen pods. Harvested stems with ripe pods may be used in dried-flower arrangements. It is a useful plant for the back of a border or a wildflower garden. This species was awarded Perennial Plant of the Year™ in 2010.

Baptisia Carolina 'Moonlight'

Baptisia australis

Bellis perennis 'Monstrosa'

New *Baptisia* have been bred for their 90-centimetre height, branching habit, and wide range of colours. These hybrids result from crossing with southern US species such as *B. alba* and *B. tinctoria*. These hybrids, part of the Decadence™ series, include 'Blueberry Sundae' (lavender-blue), 'Cherries Jubilee' (maroon and yellow bicolour), 'Dutch Chocolate' (maroon-purple), 'Lemon Meringue', 'Vanilla Cream', 'Pink Truffles', and 'Sparkling Sapphires' (indigo blue). 'Carolina Moonlight' is a yellow-flowered hybrid developed from crossing *B. alba* with *B. sphaerocarpa*.

False indigo, best grown in full sun, can tolerate poor, dry soil. It can form an extensive root system, making it nearly impossible to transplant once established. It is not bothered by pests or diseases, and it attracts bees. Propagation is by seed. Blue false indigo is hardy to zone 3, while the hybrids are rated for zone 4.

Bellis
ENGLISH DAISY

The approximately 10 species of *Bellis* are primarily of European descent. The Latin name *bellis* literally means daisy. Only one is commonly grown in Atlantic Canada, the English daisy, *B. perennis*. This plant has jumped the fence and is now naturalized in lawns and roadsides throughout the region. It is a low tufted plant with spoon-shaped basal leaves and 10- to 20-centimetre-long flower stems topped with a single 2- to 3-centimetre-wide, white to pink daisy. Its main blooming season is May and June. Although the wild form has single flowers, modern-day garden cultivars are usually double and have significantly larger flowers. 'Galaxy' has semi-double flowers, while 'Super Enorma' has double flowers up to 6 centimetres wide. The double-flowered 'Pomponette', 'Tasso', and 'Bellisima' have tubular petals that result in buttonlike flowers; 'Monstrosa' has double flowers with quill-like petals. The Speedstar® series have buttonlike flowers, but the plants are grown as annual or biennial bedding plants. All the preceding cultivars have a mix of flower colours that include white, pink, red, and bicolours.

English daisy prefers full sun and evenly moist soil; it can tolerate part shade but not droughty conditions. Generally a short-lived plant, it can self-seed if given a chance. The single and semi-double cultivars attract bees and butterflies. Although May–June is the main blooming season, if promptly deadheaded the flowers may bloom all summer, especially in cooler coastal regions. Overall, it is care-free. Propagation is primarily by seed. It is rated hardy to zone 3.

Bergenia
GIANT ROCKFOIL, PIGSQUEAK
All 10 species of *Bergenia*, a genus named in honour of German botanist and physician Karl August von Bergen (1853–1933), are native to Asia. Five species are grown in Atlantic Canada, along with many hybrids. Most are evergreen with rosettes of leathery round- to heart-shaped leaves that often turn purple in winter, making them valuable plants for fall and winter display. The exception is *B. ciliata*, which is deciduous. All bloom in spring, within a few weeks of the snow's melting, generally April to May. The flowers are produced in a loose cluster on leafless 30- to 60-centimetre-tall stems. Typically, flowers are in shades of pink but may be white, dark reddish pink, or purple.

The largest-leaved and tallest-flowered is *B. crassifolia*, which forms large cabbagelike clumps with magenta-pink flowers atop 60-centimetre-tall stems. *Bergenia purpurascens*, which has the best purple-red winter colour, has purple flowers on 30- to 45-centimetre-tall stems. *Bergenia cordifolia* is similar but has pink flowers. The smallest, *B. stracheyi*, reaches about 15 centime-

Bergenia ciliata

Bergenia 'Bressingham Salmon'

full shade, but the flowering will be reduced.

Bergenia are generally grown near the front of a border, in woodland gardens, or along the edges of water features. Smaller cultivars may be used in rock gardens. To complement their rather bold foliage, combine them with ferns, grasses, and iris. They have no serious insect pests or diseases. Even though these plants are generally deer-resistant, moose sometimes develop a liking for them. Propagation may be by seed or, more commonly, division. The evergreen types are hardy to zone 3, some to 2, but *B. ciliata*, rated for zone 5, is only viable in milder regions.

Brunnera
SIBERIAN BUGLOSS

The genus *Brunnera* contains just three species, all native to northwestern Asia. Only one, *B. macrophylla*, is grown as an ornamental in Atlantic Canada. The genus was named in honour of Swiss botanist Samuel Brunner (1790–1844), who discovered the plant. *Brunnera* is a clumping plant with relatively large, heart-shaped basal leaves. In May and into June, it produces loose sprays of forget-me-not-like flowers, typically blue or occasionally white, atop stems 30 to 40

Brunnera 'Looking Glass'

tres tall; its flowers open white and age to light pink. Although it is deciduous, *B. ciliata* has the unique feature of slightly pubescent leaves with wavy-edged margins. Its pale pink flowers open before leaves are produced, and its flower stems are short. Stems continue to elongate as more flowers open, eventually reaching 30 centimetres in height. *Bergenia* hybrids include 'Silver Light' (white), 'Bressingham White' (white aging to light pink), 'Baby Doll' (light pink), 'Appleblossom' (light pink), 'Winter Glow' (reddish pink), and 'Bressingham Ruby' (reddish pink). The Dragonfly™ series has small, compact foliage and abundant flowers: 'Pink Dragonfly', Dragonfly™ 'Angel Kiss', and Dragonfly™ 'Sakura'.

Bergenia are best grown in moist but well-drained, organically rich soil. They can tolerate short periods of drought but the foliage suffers if the drought is prolonged. In cooler coastal regions they may be grown in full sun but generally are best in part shade. They can even tolerate

Brunnera macrophylla 'Diane'

centimetres tall. This plant is grown primarily for its foliage; most cultivars have leaves variously marked with white or silver. It works well as an accent at the front of a border or a woodland garden but it also functions as a ground cover in part to full shade. Good companion plants are baneberry, astilbe, and ferns.

Many cultivars are available: 'Variegata' has leaves with wide white margins; 'Hadspen Cream' is similar, but its margins are cream rather than white; 'Langtrees' has silver spots along the leaf edges; and 'Emerald Mist' has more extensive silver spotting. 'Jackfrost', the first of the extensively silver-foliaged cultivars, was so striking it was awarded Perennial Plant of the Year™ in 2012. Other silver-leaved types include 'Sea Heart', which has silvery foliage with distinct green veins; 'Looking Glass', with all-silver foliage; and the striking 'King's Ransom', silvery green with creamy yellow margins. 'Mr. Morse' resembles 'Jack Frost' but has white flowers. 'Diane's Gold' has yellow to chartreuse foliage, while 'Gold Strike' leaves are irregularly mottled in yellow.

Brunnera prefer organically rich, evenly moist soil. Its leaves quickly burn along the edges if grown in soil that is too dry. It is generally care-free but slugs can be bothersome. Propagation is by division. Rated hardy to zone 3, it can be grown throughout much of Atlantic Canada.

Caltha
MARSH MARIGOLD

The 10 species of *Caltha* are all confined to the northern hemisphere. The generic name *Caltha* is derived from the Greek word *kalathos*, goblet, referring to the shape of the flower. Although it is generally a wetland plant, if provided with evenly moist soil it can tolerate a domestic flower garden. The most common species is marsh marigold, *C. palustris*, a species found throughout Atlantic Canada as well as across North America, Europe, and Asia. Marsh marigold forms a mound with mostly basal, smooth, slightly shiny, rounded leaves. The flowers, produced in late spring, are in loose clusters on stems up to 45 centimetres tall. Individual flowers are about 5 centimetres in diameter with five to nine waxy, deep yellow, petal-like sepals. Two cultivars are available: 'Alba', with white flowers and dark green foliage; and 'Flore Pleno', with fully dou-

Caltha palustris 'Flore Pleno'

ble yellow flowers that look like golden pom-poms.

Marsh marigold may be grown in full sun or part shade, in organically rich soil that is moist at all times. It is a choice plant for water-garden features but it is also suitable for wet depressions in a wildflower setting. Propagation is by seed or division. Diseases are rare and, as the plant is mildly toxic, it is not bothered by pests. Hardy to zone 2, it can be grown throughout most of Atlantic Canada.

Campanula
BELLFLOWER

The genus *Campanula* has over 500 species, ex-cluding the many hybrids. Books have been de-voted to this primarily Eurasian genus. Nearly all *Campanula* have merit as garden plants, with bell-shaped flowers in white or shades of blue. The bellflowers commonly grown in Atlantic Canada fall into three main groups: back-of-the-border types that reach 120 centimetres; mid-border types, 50 to 100 centimetres; and front-of-the-border or rock garden species, gen-erally less than 30 centimetres.

The most popular tall bellflowers are the milky bellflower, *C. lactiflora*, and the great bellflower, *C. latifolia*. The former has tall stems and a vase-like habit, with terminal panicles of outward- to upward-facing bells in July and August. This is the only common species which is fragrant. 'Prichard's Variety' (lavender-blue) and 'Lod-don Anna' (pale pink) reach 120 centimetres in height, sometimes more under rich, moist soil conditions. 'Pouffe' (pale blue) and 'Pouffe Alba' (white) are dwarf cultivars reaching just 45 centimetres. The giant bellflower may reach 120 or more centimetres with stiff upright stems and spikes of 6-centimetre-long blue or white outward- to downward-pointing, narrow bells

Campanula lactiflora

in August. This plant is a heritage perennial in Atlantic Canada.

The most popular of the mid-size group is the peach-leaved bellflower, *C. persicifolia*. It has narrow foliage and stiff stems topped with loose clusters of wide bells. If promptly deadheaded, it can bloom from July to frost. This one self-seeds readily, so be cautious. Flowers are white or shades of blue, and double-flowered culti-vars exist. 'Chettle Charm' is bicoloured; 'Kelly Gold' has pale blue flowers and bright yellow foliage. Peach-leaved bellflower also has her-itage status. Clustered bellflower, *C. glomerata*, has upright stems topped by a globular head of flowers in July. 'Superba' reaches 75 centimetres in height, with violet-blue flowers; 'Crown of Snow', 60 centimetres, with white flowers; and 'Acaulis', about 30 centimetres, with violet-blue flowers. Nettle-leaved bellflower, *C. trachelium*, reaches up to 90 centimetres with spikes of outward-facing purple-blue flowers from July to September. 'Bernice' is a double-flowered cultivar. *Campanula takesimana* and *C. punctata* reach 45 to 60 centimetres with hanging, oversized, white or pink-flushed bells from July to September. These species run: use with care. They are ideal for a wildflower garden or woodland bed. 'Elizabeth', 'Bowl of Cherries', and 'Cherry Bells' are recommended. Some lovely blue-flowered hybrids that look similar but are not as invasive are 'Viking', 'Sarastro', and 'Kent Belle'.

Of the alpine, rock-garden types, of which there are too many to thoroughly describe, Carpathian harebell, *C. carpatica*, is perhaps the most common. It forms a low mound with masses of relatively large blue or white bells in June and July. The Gem and Clips series are the most common. Dalmatian bellflower, *C. portenschlagiana*, is a low, spreading, blue-flowered species less than 15 centimetres high, while Serbian bellflower, *C. poscharskyana*, is almost a ground cover, with starry bells. Popular cultivars include 'Glandor' (blue), 'Lilacina' (pale pink), and 'E.H. Frost' (white). Thimble bellflower, *C. cochlearifolia*, a runner, spreads into the tiniest of cracks; its solitary nodding flowers arise on 5-centimetre-long stems. 'Elizabeth Oliver' (blue) and 'White Wonder' are double-flowered cultivars.

Cultivation is variable among the bellflowers. The border types may be grown in sun to part shade but the alpine types need full sun. All require well-drained soil but are not drought-tolerant. The most problematic pests are slugs, particularly on the alpine types, and spittlebugs. Diseases are generally not a problem and large herbivores usually ignore them. They all attract bees. Propagation may be by seed for species or division for cultivars. Most of the species and hybrids noted above are hardy to zone 3.

Campanula persicifolia

Centaurea
KNAPWEED, MOUNTAIN BLUETS

The genus *Centaurea* is one of the largest genera of plant families, with about 450 species, all native to Eurasia, especially around the Mediterranean. Only a few are commonly grown as garden ornamentals; way too many are weedy and considered invasive species, such as black knapweed, *C. nigra*, and brown knapweed, *C. jacea*. Perhaps the most common ornamental species is the mountain bluet or perennial cornflower, *C. montana*. This heritage plant has been grown in Atlantic Canadian gardens for over 100 years. It can survive almost anything except water-logged soil. Lance-shaped leaves are covered in white hairs. Flower stems arise to 60 centimetres and tend to flop after heavy rain or wind. The solitary flowers, which bloom in June, are up to 5 centimetres in diameter, with raggedly fringed blue petals and reddish blue centres. A hard cutting back after flowering keeps plants more compact and provides a secondary flowering later in summer. In addition to blue, *C. montana* also comes in white, and the cultivar 'Amethyst in Snow' is striking, with white petals and a reddish blue centre.

A little more refined, Persian cornflower, *C. dealbata*, can reach up to 75 centimetres tall with stiff upright stems that tolerate wind and rain. Their flowers, also produced in June, are like mountain bluet flowers but are rosy pink. Their leaves are pinnately lobed and hairy on the undersides. Giant knapweed, *C. macrocephala*, the tallest, reaches 120 centimetres, with stiff upright stems topped with solitary, thistlelike yellow flowers in July and August. While the other two are ideal for the middle of a border, *C. macrocephala* is better toward the back. All three are suitable for coastal and wildflower gardens.

LEFT: *Centaurea dealbata*

Centaurea montana

If you can find them, *C. epirota* (pink) and *C. pindicola* (white) are lovely alpine subjects for a rock garden. Both have silvery white fuzzy foliage held close to the ground and solitary 5-centimetre-diameter flowers on 5- to 10-centimetre-long stems in June.

The above *Centaurea* tolerate periods of drought but perform better under moister conditions. All are sun-lovers, although mountain bluets tolerate some shade. The flowers of all *Centaurea* are magnets for bees and butterflies and make ideal cut flowers. Giant knapweed can be attacked by a sawfly which will defoliate the plants just as they bloom. Mountain bluets may sometimes be bothered by mildew. Deer, moose, and hare generally ignore them. Giant knapweed and mountain bluets are hardy to zone 3, but Persian cornflower and the alpine types are rated for zone 4.

Chelone
TURTLEHEAD

There are only four species of *Chelone*, all native to eastern North America. In the wild they often grow in moist locations but can adapt to more typical garden growing conditions. The genus

Chelone lyonii 'Hot Lips'

name comes from the Greek word *chelone*, tortoise, referring to the turtlehead shape of the flowers. All turtleheads form clumps with stiff, unbranched, upright stems 90 to 120 centimetres long. The leaves are lance-shaped and opposite, the stems square in cross-section. From late summer to early fall, snapdragon-like, two-lipped flowers up to 3 centimetres long are produced in dense terminal spikes.

The only species native in Atlantic Canada, white turtlehead, *C. glabra*, is not commonly seen in gardens, as it requires wet conditions to do well. However, unlike the other turtleheads, it does have fragrant flowers. It is best used in a water-garden setting or in a damp depression in a wildflower garden. More commonly grown is the pink turtlehead, *C. lyonii* and *C. obliqua*. These two species are similar and, in fact, *C. obliqua* may be a hybrid derived from *C. lyonii*. Several cultivars are available, including 'Hot Lips',

whose foliage is bronzy green early in the season; 'Tiny Tortuga', a compact plant reaching just 40 centimetres; and 'Alba', with white rather than the typical pink flowers.

Turtleheads may be grown in full sun to part shade and require an organically rich, evenly moist soil. They generally do not require staking unless grown in too much shade. They attract bees and their blossoms make admirable cut flowers. This plant should be more widely grown as it is an outstanding addition to the late summer and fall border and combines well with taller ornamental grasses, obedience plant, and coneflowers. Under proper soil conditions, they are suitable for a mid- to back border and ideal for using around water gardens. Propagation is by seed, cuttings, or division. Pests and diseases are generally not a problem, although under dry conditions or if too sheltered, mildew may occur. All are rated hardy to zone 3.

Cimicifuga racemosa 'Atropurpurea'

Cimicifuga
BUGBANE

The eight species of bugbane are native to the northern hemisphere. They have all been reclassified as *Actaea*, better known as baneberries. But since they are better known in the nursery trade as *Cimicifuga*, they are described here under the older name. The most popular garden bugbane, *Actaea* (*Cimicifuga*) *simplex*, from eastern Asia, is a bold plant with large, coarse, astilbe-like foliage and flower stems that tower to 2 metres. The flowers, which bloom from September to October and even into November, are produced in narrow, arching, bottlebrush-like wands. They are white or very pale pink and highly fragrant. The cultivar 'White Pearl' is much like the wild species in appearance.

Additional cultivars are all grown for their bronze to purple foliage. 'Atropurpurea', which has purple-tinted foliage, was the first of these cultivars. 'Brunette' has darker purple leaves, while 'Hillside Black Beauty' has unusual, nearly black foliage. 'Black Negligee' has purple foliage that is more finely divided. 'Pink Spike', also known as 'Pink Spire', has purple foliage and light pink flowers. Overall, the habit of the American species, *A.* (*C.*) *racemosa*, is similar to that of *A. simplex*, but it blooms earlier in August. The cultivar 'Chocoholic' is a purple-leaved version. For a bold contrast, combine the purple-leaved bugbanes with yellow-flowered coneflower or goldenrods.

Bugbane may be grown in full sun or part shade. The soil should be well drained but evenly moist. Despite its height, bugbane is wind-tolerant and rarely needs staking. It is a beauty for the back of a border, and *A. simplex* is especially valued for its late flowers and graceful arching stems. Propagation is primarily by division. Bugbane are not bothered by pests or diseases. All are rated hardy to zone 3.

Convallaria majalis 'Albostriata'

Convallaria
LILY-OF-THE-VALLEY

There is only one species of *Convallaria*, *C. majalis*, a native of Europe. Each sprout has two or three smooth, elliptical leaves up to 20 centimetres long. From between the leaves plants produce a leafless stem up to 20 centimetres tall topped with a one-sided spike of small, bell-shaped, white flowers in May and into June. The highly fragrant flowers are suitable for dainty floral arrangements. Flowers become small scarlet berries in late summer. The variety *rosea* has pale pink flowers. 'Albostriata' is difficult to find but has exceptionally showy white-veined leaves. The standard variety is considered a heritage plant in Atlantic Canada.

Lily-of-the-valley is one of the more popular ground-cover plants for part to full shade, as they spread rapidly by underground rhizomes. It needs cooler conditions and moist soil to perform well but, once established, can tolerate some drought. Pests and diseases are uncom-

mon, and this toxic plant is not eaten by large herbivores. Propagation is by division. As it is very hardy, zone 2, it can be grown almost anywhere in Atlantic Canada.

Coreopsis
TICKSEED

The genus *Coreopsis*, with about 75 species, is confined to the Americas. Three main species are grown in Atlantic Canada as garden ornamentals. The lance-leaved coreopsis, *C. lanceolata*, is a low bushy plant with mostly basal, narrow, slightly hairy leaves and branching flower stems that reach 60 centimetres in height. Stems are topped with golden yellow daisylike flowers 3 to 5 centimetres in diameter. It blooms from June through to frost if plants are promptly deadheaded. *Coreopsis grandiflora* is similar in appearance. Hybrids and cultivars of these species

Coreopsis verticillata 'Zagreb'

Coreopsis 'Sun Up'

are often more compact, with semi-double to double flowers, including 'Early Sunrise', 'Sun Up', 'Jethro Tull', 'Sundancer', and the Leading Lady™ series.

Thread-leaf coreopsis, *C. verticillata*, has wiry stems up to 60 centimetres in height with whorls of narrow, threadlike foliage and produces yellow flowers in July and August. The cultivar 'Moonbeam' has soft primrose yellow flowers; it was awarded Perennial Plant of the Year™ in 1992. 'Zagreb' is more compact, with stiff stems up to 45 centimetres high and bright yellow flowers.

Pink thread-leaf coreopsis, *C. rosea*, is native to southwestern Nova Scotia. Its habit is much like that of the regular thread-leaf coreopsis. The flowers are also similar, but pink. A shearing in mid-late summer will keep plants tidier and encourage later re-bloom.

The red, purple-pink, and bicoloured cultivars of thread-leaf coreopsis available are mostly hybrids between *C. verticillata* and *C. rosea*. Although both parents are hardy, the hybrids are often short-lived or less hardy. Among the more reliable are 'Show Stopper' (deep pink), 'Route 66' (yellow and red), 'Sweet Marmalade' (peach), and the Big Bang™ series.

Coreopsis are excellent candidates for the front of a border or for a wildflower garden. As a group, they are sun-lovers and perform best under alkaline, drier, poorer soil conditions. Too much water, especially in winter, can lead to rot. Soil that is too rich will result in floppy plants and reduced winter hardiness. Pink thread-leaf coreopsis is an exception; it prefers even soil moisture and sandy soil. It does not tolerate heat or drought. All coreopsis attract bees and butterflies and are long-lasting cut flowers. Pests and disease are rare. Thread-leaf coreopsis is the longest-lived; the others, often short-lived, maintain themselves through self-seeding. The *C. lanceolata* and *C. grandiflora* species are rated for zone 4, while the thread-leaf species are considered hardy to zone 3. The many hybrids on the market are hardy only to zone 5.

Crocosmia
MONTBRETIA

Only a few of the garden ornamentals grown in Atlantic Canada originate in South Africa; montbretia is one such plant. While most are not

Crocosmia 'Lucifer'

TODD BOLAND

Crocosmia 'Lucifer'

hardy enough for Atlantic Canada, the hybrid 'Lucifer' is an exception. This large, bold plant can add architectural qualities to a border. Its stiff narrow leaves are swordlike, similar to those of gladiolus, but formed in clumps. In August and September branching flower stems produce spikes of bright scarlet red tubular flowers, all of which are held on the upper side of the branches. These stems may reach 90 to 120 centimetres in height; this is a plant for the back of a border, although it may also be effective as a stand-alone plant. Yellow- and orange-flowered hybrids are available but have not proven to be as hardy in Atlantic Canada as 'Lucifer'.

Crocosmia 'Lucifer' requires full sun and a well-drained site. Its bulbs (corms, to be precise) should be planted 10 centimetres deep. It is borderline hardy in zone 5 and most reliable in zone 6. It should be heavily mulched in the fall to improve its chances of winter survival. Another option is to plant the corms in a container, sunken into the

ground, then lifted and stored in a frost-free location over winter. *Crocosmia* makes a wonderful cut flower and is a magnet for hummingbirds. Pests, large or small, and diseases are not generally a problem. Propagation is by corm division. It is hardy to zone 5 if properly mulched.

Chrysanthemum
GARDEN MUM

The plants described here under *Chrysanthemum* have actually been reclassified to the genus *Dendranthema*. All gardeners are familiar with the pot mum, *C.* X *grandiflorum*. This hybrid is not hardy enough for Atlantic Canada but the similar *C.* X *morifolium*, the popular fall mum, is. The latter is often sold as an annual bedding plant in the fall but it is really a perennial which may come back each year, providing masses of double daisies in September and October. Depending on the cultivar, they may grow from 30 to 90 centimetres

Chrysanthemum X *moriifolium*

tall. Perhaps more reliable in our gardens is the hybrid *C.* X *rubellum*. Two cultivars are available: 'Mary Stoker', with pale yellow flowers that turn apricot pink, and 'Clara Curtis', with deep pink flowers. Both are bushy plants that reach 75 centimetres in height and produce clusters of single daisies from late August through to October. From Japan comes a dwarf species called *C. weyrichii*. This plant has small, glossy, divided leaves that are slightly succulent. It slowly spreads to form a colony. The flower stems reach 15 centimetres in height and are topped with solitary light pink flowers in September and October. 'White Bomb' is a white-flowered cultivar.

The above plants prefer full sun and rich, well-drained soil. Fall mums and the *C.* X *rubellum* hybrids may be used in a mid-border or the front of a border. Both are ideal cut flowers and attract bees and butterflies. The dwarf *C. weyrichii* is more suited to a rock garden. Propagation is primarily by division; to keep plants tidy, they should be divided every three years. Although large herbivores do not bother *Chrysanthemum*, they are host to many diseases and insect pests, including aphids, thrips, and spider mites. Potential disease problems include botrytis, leaf spot, powdery mildew, stem and root rot, rust, and verticillium wilt. Garden mums are rated hardy to zone 5, *C.* X *rubellum* to zone 4, and *C. weyrichii* to zone 3.

Chrysanthemum 'Clara Curtis'

Darmera peltata

Darmera
UMBRELLA PLANT

There is only one species *of Darmera*, *D. peltata*. The genus name honours Karl Darmer (1843–1918), a German horticulturist. The plant is native to western North America, where it grows along streams or in damp open woodlands. It is a clumping to running plant, with solitary leaves arising from a thick, creeping rhizome. It is unusual in that the flowers are produced before the leaves. In May and June, thick, hairy but leafless stalks arise 100 to 150 centimetres, topped with a globular cluster of pink flowers. Just as the flowers fade, leaves appear. Each umbrella-like leaf, up to 45 centimetres wide, has lobed margins. The leaves are held atop hairy stalks which are up to 150 centimetres tall. Overall, the plant resembles a small *Gunnera*, a popular huge-leaved plant grown in the Pacific Northwest, and provides a tropical effect in Atlantic gardens.

Darmera requires full sun to part shade. It loves moisture and can grow in shallow water. As a result, it is ideal for streamsides, water features, and wet depressions. It is a wonderful companion plant for rayflowers, *Rodgersia*, and Japanese iris, which have similar moisture requirements.

The blossoms make a good cut flower. Propagation is by seed or, more commonly, division. Although insects and diseases are not a problem, *Darmera* may be browsed by large herbivores. It is hardy to zone 5.

Delphinium
DELPHINIUM

Delphinium are popular back-of-the-border plants. Thanks to the cool summers, they live longer in Atlantic Canada than they would in warmer areas of central Canada and the US, where they can be short-lived. Delphinium are ideally suited to coastal areas; in Newfoundland plants over 75 years old are known. The approximately 300 species of *Delphinium* are native across the northern hemisphere but most numerous in the Himalayas. The name comes from the Greek word *delphis*, dolphin, a reference to the shape of the flower buds. The garden delphinium, *D. elatum*, is native from eastern Europe to Siberia.

Plants produce deeply divided, palmate leaves and tall stems topped by a dense elongate spike of blue-shaded flowers. Older cultivars, which often exceed 2 metres in height, require staking. Newer cultivars are more compact, but with their huge flower spikes they still benefit from support. Delphinium are available in a range of colours from white, through shades of pink, purple, and blue, along with bicolours. The Pacific Hybrid series are popular tall cultivars in mixed colours. Magic Fountain series, also in mixed colours, are more compact, at about 100 centimetres high. The New Millenium™ series, also available in a mix of colours, are the most dwarf, with plants reaching only 75 centimetres high.

Chinese larkspur, *D. grandiflorum*, is a recent introduction. The most popular cultivar, 'Blue Butterfly', reaches only 35 to 40 centimetres in

Delphinium elatum

the plus side, delphinium attract bees and hummingbirds, make admirable cut flowers, and are generally ignored by large herbivores. Propagation may be by seed but is more commonly by division. It is rated hardy to zone 3.

Dianthus
PINKS

This is one of the larger plant genera we grow in our gardens, with over 300 species, mostly native to the Mediterranean region. The name is from the Greek *dios anthos*, divine flower. With so many garden-worthy species, it is not surprising that books have been devoted to growing pinks. Quite a number of pinks are suitable for Atlantic Canada. Perhaps the longest cultivated species is the cottage pinks, *D. plumarius*. This plant has been extensively hybridized, ranging from

Dianthus deltoides

height, with branched stems and small spikes of bright blue flowers. Although a perennial, it is short-lived in Atlantic Canada and is most often annual in nature. It is worth trying in a rock-garden setting. Many other dwarf rock-garden types are worth growing but are short-lived.

Delphinium require full sun and organically rich, moist, well-drained soil. It is intolerant of poor, droughty soil. Overall, it is a high maintenance plant: even dwarf types require staking. It can be slug fodder, attacked by aphids, leaf miners, and stem borers; and it is prone to powdery mildew and fungal leaf spotting. On

TODD BOLAND

single to double flowered, in white or shades of pink or red, and combinations. These are generally mat-forming with blue-green to blue-grey, narrow evergreen foliage. In June and July, they produce stems 15 to 30 centimetres in height, topped with clove-scented flowers. It is a popular plant for the front of a border, cascading over a wall, or in a rock garden. The garden carnation, *D. caryophyllus*, is similar but has fully double flowers in a wide range of colours that includes yellow and orange. They are, however, short-lived in Atlantic Canada and mostly grown as annual bedding plants. Also popular is sweet William, *D. barbatus*, a short-lived perennial often grown as a biennial or annual. It produces dense, flat-topped clusters of white, pink, or red flowers on 30-centimetre-long stems.

Overall, maiden pinks, *D. deltoides*, are smaller than cottage pinks, with finer foliage, which is plain green or purple-tinted. What the smaller flowers lack in size, they make up for in numbers. Wiry stems reach 15 to 30 centimetres in length

Dianthus 'Starlette'

with white, pink, or red flowers in June and July. Some cultivars include 'Brilliant' (reddish pink), 'Flashing Lights' (red), 'Shrimp' (bright pink), 'Zing Rose' (rose-pink), and 'Arctic Fire' (white with red centre). Cheddar pinks, *D. gratianopolitanus*, is smaller again, with blue-grey foliage, and small pink flowers on 10-centimetre-long stems. 'Tiny Rubies' is a double-flowered cultivar.

Dianthus plumarius

Innumerable hybrids of the above species are available. These are often referred to as X *allionii* hybrids. Most have blue-grey foliage and, overall, look like compact cottage pinks. Some of the more popular hybrids are from the Witch and Star™ series. 'Firewitch' was so popular that it was awarded Perennial Plant of the Year™ in 2006. Pinks continue to be popular, and nearly every year a new cultivar is released. As a rule, the double-flowered types are not as long-lived as the singles.

All pinks are sun-lovers, need well-drained soil, and prefer alkaline soil. They are reasonably drought- and salt-tolerant and are wonderful plants for coastal gardens. All may be sheared after blooming to keep them tidy and reduce the incidence of self-seeding, especially among the maiden pinks. Shearing often results in sporadic flowering later in the season. Diseases are rare and the most common insect pests are spittlebugs, which are unsightly but do little damage.

Deer and moose ignore them but hares may nibble them. They are good butterfly flowers and those with longer stems make attractive cut flowers. Propagation is by seed or cuttings. The listed species are rated hardy to zones 3–4.

Dicentra
BLEEDING-HEART

With its unmistakable flowers, bleeding-heart is a garden mainstay in Atlantic Canada. Of the eight species of *Dicentra*, seven are native to North America and one to Japan. The standard bleeding-heart, *Dicentra spectabilis*, has now been reclassified into its own genus, *Lamprocapnos*. For many gardeners, this is one of the most elegant garden perennials; the species epithet says it all … spectacular! This eastern Asian native created quite a stir in Europe when it was first discovered, since, at the time, no other garden plants had such bizarre yet beautiful flowers. It forms

Lamprocapnos spectabilis 'Gold Heart'

Dicentra 'Burning Hearts'

a large, branching, bushy plant up to 90 centimetres tall with large, compound, matte, greygreen foliage. The flowers are held on one-sided arching racemes from the upper leaf axils. Individual bright pink flowers are distinctively heart-

Lamprocapnos spectabilis 'Valentine'

shaped with a narrow flaring petal on either side. It blooms from late April to early July. There are three cultivars: 'Alba', with white flowers; 'Valentine', red flowers; and 'Goldheart', golden yellow foliage and pink flowers.

The North American native *Dicentra* are often referred to as dwarf bleeding-hearts. Their fernlike leaves are basal and matte grey-green. Their flowers, which arise from the ground on arching, leafless stems, are also heart-shaped, although not as distinct as those of the standard bleeding-heart. The two main species, *D. eximia* and *D. formosa*, are similar, with light pink flowers produced from May to September. 'Bacchanal' is perhaps the most popular cultivar of *D. formosa*, with grey-green foliage and wine red flowers. 'Aurora' is a white-flowered cultivar. Of the several hybrid dwarf bleeding-hearts on the market, 'Luxuriant', a cross between *D. eximia* and *D. formosa*, is perhaps the most popular, with blue-green foliage and clear pink flowers. Others include 'Langtrees' (pale pink), 'Adrian Bloom' (reddish pink, blue-green foliage), 'Bountiful' (pinkish purple, green foliage), and 'Stuart Boothman' (mottled pink, green foliage).

'Candy Hearts' is a small hybrid, up to 25 centimetres high, with blue-grey foliage and flowers that are darker pink than those of 'Luxuriant'. The white-flowered version is called 'Ivory Hearts'. 'King of Hearts' is smaller again, at 15 to 20 centimetres tall, with dark pinkish red flowers. 'Burning Hearts' has the darkest red flowers of any dwarf bleeding-heart and beautiful blue foliage.

Bleeding-heart are primarily woodland plants and prefer lightly shaded, evenly moist, and moderately rich soil. They have brittle roots and rhizomes, but it seems that any piece of rhizome with an active growing point will regenerate into a new plant. If good soil moisture is maintained, they can tolerate full sun, but they thrive best in part shade. They can also tolerate deep shade, but the flowering will be less prolific if grown under shady conditions. As all have fragile stems and leaves, avoid windy sites. The standard bleeding-heart is best toward the back of a border. Be forewarned: it will go dormant by late summer and leave a gap in the garden. Dwarf bleeding-heart are suitable ground-cover plants for shady sites and ideal for woodland gardens. The Hearts hybrids are low clumpers and good for a woodland garden or shady rock garden. Overall, bleeding-heart are care-free. Propagation is by division. They are rated hardy to zone 3.

Dictamnus
GASPLANT

The genus *Dictamnus* has only a single species, *D. albus*, native to the open woodlands of southern Eurasia. The plant is bushy with glossy pinnate leaves resembling those of an ash tree. Flower stems, which arise to 90 centimetres, are topped with a spike of white to light purple-pink blos-

Dictamnus albus

soms in June and July. The flowers are elegant, as the petals often have contrasting darker veins, and stamens that project out from the flower.

The entire plant is covered in sticky glands, which exude volatile oils and a lemony fragrance. People with sensitive skin should not touch the plant, as it can cause dermatitis. On windless, hot days, it is reputed that a match lit above the plant can ignite the oils with a flash of fire, hence the common name of gasplant. After the flowers have faded, plants produce star-shaped seed pods which can be used in dried-flower arrangements. As the seed capsules mature, they split and the black, shiny seeds are forcibly ejected. Gasplant is ideal for a mid-border.

Gasplant prefers full sun and well-drained soil that stays reasonably moist. It can tolerate some drought once it matures. It is slow to establish but is a long-lived plant that improves with age. Because it produces an extensive root system, it is difficult to transplant once mature. As a result, it is propagated mostly by seed. It is a care-free plant, hardy to zone 3.

Digitalis

FOXGLOVE

Most gardeners are familiar with foxglove, a tried and true garden plant for many years; it has even naturalized itself throughout Atlantic Canada. Common foxglove, *Digitalis purpurea*, is a biennial, forming a leafy rosette of evergreen leaves the first season, then a leafy spike up to 2 metres tall in the second. The purple or white flowers are tubular and nodding, generally along one side of the stem. Plants maintain themselves in the garden by dropping copious seeds. It is a classic cottage-garden plant but also suited to wildflower gardens or the back of a border. The

Digitalis purpurea
RIGHT: *Digitalis grandiflorum*

many cultivars include 'Foxy' and 'Excelsior', along with the Dalmatian and Camelot series. The latter produces flowers all around the stem rather than just one-sided. The most striking cultivar is 'Pam's Choice', which is white with a contrasting maroon-purple throat.

About 20 other, lesser known, foxgloves exist, all native to Eurasia. Many of these are perennial. The most common, the large yellow foxglove, *D. grandiflora*, is similar to the common foxglove in habit but its July spike of flowers is pale yellow on 60- to 90-centimetre-long stems. A hybrid between the large yellow and common foxglove is *D. X mertonensis*. It is a short-lived perennial with flowers in peach to coral-pink tones. The Polkadot series is also of hybrid origin in tones of coral, peach, and apricot.

The other garden-worthy species have smaller tubular flowers in comparison to the preceding plants. Of these, perhaps the most impressive and unusual is *D. parviflora*, the small-flowered foxglove. It has narrow, shiny leaves and slender but dense candlelike spikes of rusty brown flowers on 60-centimetre-long stems in July. It is a true perennial. Similar, but biennial with larger flowers, is the rusty foxglove, *D. ferruginea*. Its flowers are the colour of Dijon mustard but the lip of the flower is white. The small yellow foxglove, *D. lutea*, is similar but with more scattered pale yellow flowers on its spikes. These last two may reach 90 centimetres in height.

Foxglove may be grown in full sun to part shade. All prefer organically rich, acidic, and evenly moist soil. They need good drainage in winter or the crowns will rot. Insect pests include aphids and slugs; possible diseases, powdery mildew and rust. Plants are toxic to mammals, including people. The spikes make an excellent cut flower and the blossoms are a magnet for bees and hummingbirds. Propagation is by seed. The above species are all hardy to zone 4.

Dodecatheon 'Aphrodite'

Dodecatheon
SHOOTINGSTAR

Most of the 17 species of shootingstar are native to North America. Botanists consider them to be a type of primrose and have reclassified them as such but, as they are best known to gardeners as *Dodecatheon*, they are described as such here. Shootingstars all have a basal rosette of narrow to spoon-shaped leaves and several naked stems that end in loose clusters of nodding flowers. The blossoms are distinct, with exerted stamens forming a point, a yellow centre, and five reflexed, curled petals—together creating a shootingstar effect and one of the most elegant flowers grown in Atlantic Canada. Shades of pink is the most common flower colour, but some species are white. The most popular and largest shootingstar, *D. meadia*, reaches 45 centimetres in height with white or pink flowers in June. *Dodecatheon pulchellum* and *D. jeffreyi* are similar but a little smaller. 'Red Wings' is a reddish

pink cultivar of *D. pulchellum*, while 'Aphrodite' is a hybrid with white flowers.

Shootingstars tolerate wet soil but thrive in humus-rich, evenly moist soil. Part shade is ideal but they tolerate full sun if the soil stays moist. They do not survive under droughty conditions. Be forewarned: plants may go summer-dormant, leaving a space in the garden. This feature makes them less desirable as a border plant, but they are lovely subjects for planting around water features, in wildflower or woodland settings, or even in a shady rock garden. Diseases are rare, but pests include slugs, snails, and root weevils. The flowers are specifically adapted for bee pollination. Propagation is by seed or division. As the above are rated hardy to zone 3, they are viable throughout much of Atlantic Canada.

Doronicum
LEOPARD'S-BANE

The nearly 40 species of *Doronicum* are native to Eurasia. All are clumping plants with serrated, heart-shaped leaves and upright stems topped with yellow daisylike flowers early in the season.

Of the two main species grown in Atlantic Canada, the most popular is *D. orientale*, aka *D. caucasicum*, the common leopard's-bane, which blooms from early May into June. There are several cultivars: 'Magnificum' grows to 60 centimetres, 'Leonardo' to 40 centimetres. Smaller still are 'Leonardo Compact' and the semi-double 'Little Leo', both of which reach about 30 centimetres. The popular 45-centimetre-tall cultivar 'Miss Mason' is considered by most botanists to be a cultivar of *D. columnae*, but some books consider it *D. orientale* or possibly a hybrid. The plantain-leaved leopard's-bane, *D. plantagineum*, is a heritage species which has been grown in Atlantic Canada for over 100 years. It is taller than *D. orientale*, growing to 80 centimetres, and

Doronicum orientale 'Miss Mason'

blooms two to three weeks later. Less commonly encountered, the great leopard's-bane, *D. pardalianches*, reaches nearly 100 centimetres and blooms from June into early July.

The common and plantain-leaved leopard's-bane are ideal for combining with spring bulbs such as daffodils and tulips. Both may be planted near the front of a border. The great leopard's-bane is better toward the back of a border and combines well with the tall ball alliums. All leopard's-bane prefer full sun and well-drained, evenly moist soil. They tolerate part shade, with the great leopard's-bane the most shade-tolerant. None are good choices for poor, droughty soil. Shear the plants severely after blooming to keep them tidy. This practice will often reward you with a few late-season blooms. All attract butterflies and bees and make excellent cut flowers. These care-free plants are propagated by seed or division. As they are very hardy, rated to zone 2, they may be grown throughout most of Atlantic Canada.

TODD BOLAND

Echinacea
PURPLE CONEFLOWER

In the wild, the genus *Echinacea* is restricted to North America and contains just nine species. In Atlantic Canada purple coneflower, *E. purpurea*, along with many of its hybrids, is most often seen. The wild species is native to the eastern US but it crosses the border into southern Ontario. It produces flower stems up to 120 centimetres tall topped by loose clusters of large purple daisies from July to October. It is an excellent plant to help extend the flower season into fall and combines wonderfully with yellow coneflowers and taller ornamental grasses like *Miscanthus* and *Calamagrostis*. Purple coneflower cultivars on the market include 'Magnus' (100 centimetres), 'Prairie Splendor' (50 centimetres), 'Elton Knight' (45 centimetres), 'Pica Bella' (60 centimetres, very narrow petals), and 'Merlot' (65 centimetres, wine-coloured stems). 'Magnus' was distinct

Echinacea purpurea

enough to be awarded Perennial Plant of the Year™ in 1998. White cultivars include 'White Swan' (90 centimetres), 'Virgin' (45 centimetres), 'Lucky Star' (100 centimetres), and 'Jade' (75 centimetres; green centre and tips). It seems that every few years another white or purple cultivar is released, each with subtle differences.

Many new *Echinacea* hybrids have been released, most with fluffy centres and often a double set of petals, in a rainbow of colours, including pink, red, orange, and yellow: 'Tomato Soup', 'Raspberry Truffle', 'Raspberry Tart', 'Secret Desire', 'Marmalade', and 'Double Scoop Bubble Gum'. These all grow from 60 to 80 centimetres tall. Unfortunately, they are often short-lived in Atlantic Canada, if not simply annual in nature. 'Cheyenne Spirit' is a single-flowered hybrid with purple, salmon, orange, or yellow flowers that bloom the first year from seed. Although it is a very attractive bedding plant, it is apt to be short-lived in Atlantic Canada; however, it does live longer than many other hybrids.

Purple coneflower, a sun-lover, requires well-drained soil. Once established, it will tolerate drought but still prefers good-quality soil. It is not fond of excess winter wetness. Prompt removal of faded flowers helps maintain flower production into early autumn. It is a mid-border plant. The flowers make attractive cut flowers and the seed heads may be used in dried-flower arrangements. This plant, a butterfly and bee magnet, is even attractive to hummingbirds. Overall, it is a care-free plant. Propagation is by seed or, in the case of the fancy hybrid, division. It is rated hardy to zone 3.

Echinops
GLOBE THISTLE

Of about 120 species of *Echinops*, natives of central and eastern Europe, western Asia, and north Africa, we grow only one in our Atlantic Canadian gardens, *E. ritro*, commonly known as small globe thistle. The name *Echinops* comes from Greek and means like a hedgehog, referring to the flowers. This is a tall, clumping plant

Echinacea 'Raspberry Truffle'

Echinops ritro 'Alba'

commonly reaching from 120 to over 200 centimetres. As such, it is best situated in the back of a border. Plants have dissected, thistlelike, but not so spiny, foliage with white hairy undersides. Stiff stems are topped with golfball-sized, spiny, globular heads which are steel blue or off-white in the cultivar 'Alba'. Flowering begins in August and continues into October, making globe thistle invaluable for the late-season garden. Combine it with Russian sage, various coneflowers, and miscanthus grass for a stunning late-summer display. Blooms make admirable cut flowers and may be dried for flower arrangements. 'Veitch's Blue' has particularly dark blue flowers on more compact 90-centimetre-high plants. The subspecies *ruthenicus* is also more compact, similarly reaching about 90 centimetres high.

As globe thistle has a deep taproot and does not tolerate transplanting, plant young plants and leave them; it is slow to establish but will improve with age. It tolerates poor, dry soil; too fertile soil results in tall plants with weak stems. Salt-tolerant, it may be used in coastal gardens. Full sun and excellent drainage are a must. The flowers are magnets for butterflies and bees. The blossoms are excellent as a fresh or dried cut flower. This care-free plant is propagated by seed or division. It is rated hardy through zone 3.

Epimedium
BARRENWORT

Of the about 65 species of *Epimedium*, found from the Mediterranean region to Japan, with the majority in China, most are garden-worthy, and many hybrids and cultivars have been made among the species. As a group they are tufted, mounding, or spreading in habit; the latter are useful as ground covers. This group of plants is as valuable for its foliage as its flowers. Generally, their leaves are trifoliate with heart- or arrow-

Epimedium grandiflorum 'Saxton's Purple'

head-shaped leaflets. Some are deciduous with attractive spring foliage and fall colour; others are evergreen with spiny-edged leaves reminiscent of holly. Only a few of the evergreen types are hardy in Atlantic Canada. Depending on the species or hybrid, it may range in height from 10 to 75 centimetres. The flowers are produced in loose panicles in May and June. Individual flowers have four petals, four petaloid sepals, and an overall starlike shape. Several have nectar spurs that extend beyond the flowers, lending an exotic appearance. Flowers are white, pink, purple, red, orange, and yellow and often bicoloured.

Several barrenworts are common in Atlantic Canada. Very popular is *E.* X *rubrum*, with bronzy spring foliage 30 to 40 centimetres tall and red flowers. Equally popular is *E.* X *versicolor* 'Suphureum', with yellow flowers and bronzy spring leaves on plants reaching up to 50 centimetres tall. The species *E. grandiflorum*, which reaches 20 to 40 centimetres in height, has many cultivars with flowers in shades of reddish to

Epimedium versicolor 'Sulphureum'

pinkish purple. Their spring foliage is often purple-tinted. *Epimedium youngianum* also has several cultivars which reach 10 to 30 centimetres, with flowers ranging from white to rosy pink or lavender. The largest is *E. pubigerum* 'Orangekonigin', which reaches up to 75 centimetres high and has orange flowers. Among the best truly evergreen types for Atlantic Canada is *E. wushanense*, with bronzy spring leaves that turn shiny green with spiny hollylike foliage. The flowers are soft yellow on stems up to 40 centimetres high. Many new barrenworts are available; all the hardy ones are well worth trying.

Barrenworts are essentially forest-floor plants and, as such, prefer dappled shade and moist, organically rich soil. It is ideal for growing under trees, along the north side of buildings, or in a shady rock garden. Only a few of the more robust species, such as *E.* X *rubrum* and *E.* X *versicolor* 'Sulphureum', can tolerate shade if the soil is dry. Combine them with hosta and ferns and position them near the front of a border, where their decorative foliage can be best appreciated. As spring growth arises quite early, avoid planting

in low-lying areas where late frosts are possible. It is mostly care-free, with the only major disease being Tobacco Rattle virus, which causes irregular yellow mottling on the leaves; infected plants should be destroyed, as the virus can spread to other ornamental plants. Propagation is by division. Most of the above are hardy to zone 5, or 4 if mulched well in fall; the evergreen types are hardy to zone 6 and, as such, are only suitable for the mildest regions of Atlantic Canada.

Erigeron
FLEABANE

Although over 200 species of *Erigeron* are found worldwide, they have their greatest diversity in western North America. Many low-growing species are ideal subjects for the rock garden, but these are mostly of interest to alpine enthusiasts. For the average Atlantic Canadian gardener, the showy fleabane, *E. speciosus*, a clumping plant with stems that reach 60 centimetres in height, is the most popular. During July and into August, it produces dense clusters of pink, purple, or lav-

Erigeron speciosus

Eryngium
SEA HOLLY

The genus *Eryngium*, with some 250 species, is cosmopolitan, with most found in South America. Despite this, the sea hollies grown in Atlantic Canadian gardens are all European natives. The most common species, *E. planum*, the common sea holly, has dark green, heart-shaped basal leaves and purple-blue stems that stiffly arise 60 to 90 centimetres, topped with clusters of steel blue flowers. Individual flowers are minute but are packed into 2- to 3-centimetre-diameter spherical umbels. Each umbel is surrounded by a collar of spiny bracts. 'Blue Glitter' and 'Blue Cap' are common cultivars with standard heights. 'Jade Frost' has white-edged leaves that contrast wonderfully with its blue flowers. 'Tiny Jackpot' reaches 35 centimetres, while 'Blue Hobbit' is the shortest, at less than 30 centimetres. 'Sapphire Blue' is a hybrid with slightly larger flowers on plants up to 75 centimetres tall. 'Big Blue' flower heads have iridescent blue, spiky bracts

Eryngium planum

ender-blue asterlike flowers. Overall, it looks like a summer-flowering Michaelmas daisy. It works well in the mid- to front border, yet it is also suitable for a cottage garden or wildflower setting. The flowers are ideal for cut flowers and both bees and butterflies are attracted to the blossoms. Among the cultivars are 'Pink Jewel' (medium pink), 'Darkest of All' (dark purple-pink), 'Prosperity' (light lavender-blue), 'Azure Fairy' (azure blue), and 'Blue Beauty' (dark lavender-blue).

Less common, the beach fleabane, *E. glaucus*, produces low, spreading clumps up to 25 centimetres tall with mauve-pink to pale lavender-blue flowers in June and July. It is ideal for the front of a border, a coastal garden, or even in a large rock garden.

Fleabane require full sun and well-drained soil but, once established, can tolerate some drought. Pests are rare, and the main concern is powdery mildew. Deer and moose generally do not bother with fleabane, but hares may be a nuisance. Propagation is by seed or division. Showy fleabane is very hardy, surviving to zone 2; beach fleabane, hardy to zone 4.

TODD BOLAND

Eryngium alpinum

up to 10 centimetres wide on 75-centimetre-tall plants. Perhaps the most outstanding sea holly is the alpine sea holly, *E. alpinum*, whose cylindrical flower heads reach 5 centimetres in length with collars of finely dissected bracts up to 10 centimetres wide. Also spectacular is *E. giganteum* 'Miss Wilmott's Ghost', whose flowers have broad, spiny, silver-grey bracts. A biennial, this species will maintain itself by self-seeding. Most sea holly bloom from July through to September.

Although they are difficult to find, other recommended sea holly are *E. amethystinum* and *E. bourgatii*. Both reach up to 50 centimetres tall with typical steel blue flowers and spiny dissected leaves. For something different, try *E. yuccifolium*: its spiny-edged, lance-shaped leaves are much like those of *Yucca*, with loose clusters of white thistlelike flowers on stems up to 100 centimetres tall.

Sea holly are all sun-lovers and require well-drained soil. They are drought-tolerant and rot if the soil is too wet in winter. This is especially true for *E. amethystinum*, *E. bourgatii*, and *E. yuccifolium*. Most are best positioned in the middle-back of a border but the dwarf cultivars are suitable for the front of a border or even in a rock-garden setting. They perform better in poorer soils, where they will be more compact and stiff-stemmed. Their salt tolerance makes them ideal candidates for a coastal garden. They are excellent companion plants for other drought-tolerant perennials like wormwood, lamb's-ears, yarrow, blue-foliaged grasses, and sedums. All make admirable cut flowers and are useful for dried-flower arrangements. They are wonderful plants for bees and butterflies, with few insect or disease problems. Their spines protect them from large herbivores. Propagation is by seed or division. As most are hardy to zone 3, they can be used throughout Atlantic Canada.

Euphorbia
SPURGE

It may be surprising that many Atlantic Canadian gardens contain perennials that are related to such plants as poinsettia and crown-of-thorns. Both of these popular houseplants are members of the genus *Euphorbia*, commonly called spurges. This worldwide genus is huge, with over 2,000 species. All have insignificant flowers—and that is where the similarity ends. Some *Euphorbia* are trees or shrubs, others are succulents with thorns and look like cactus, and many others are noxious weeds. Few are garden ornamentals, and most of them need to be used with a little caution.

The best-behaved is cushion spurge, *E. epithymoides*, also known as *E. polychroma*. This European species forms a cushionlike mound that grows up to 45 centimetres high. The leaves are oblong and softly downy, often turning lovely shades of yellow, orange, and red in autumn. The true flowers are greenish and insignificant but are surrounded by showy, bright sulphur yellow bracts. These bracts are the "flowers". It blooms in May and June and is a good candidate for the front of a border. The cultivar 'Bonfire' has purple-tinted foliage all summer, while 'Lacy' has white-variegated foliage. As cushion spurge can freely self-seed, a shearing is recommended in mid-summer.

Cypress spurge, *E. cyparissias*, a heritage plant that can jump the fence to grow in disturbed areas, runs aggressively but can be useful as a ground cover in dry, sunny areas. Plants grow up to 30 centimetres tall and have narrow, soft, blue-green foliage that turns yellow, orange, and

Euphorbia cyparissias

TODD BOLAND

pink in autumn. Their hemispherical clusters of "flowers" are chartreuse aging to orange-red, blooming from May through June.

From southwest China comes *Euphorbia griffithii* 'Fireglow' and 'Dixter', both spreading plants up to 90 centimetres tall with lance-shaped leaves that are bronze in spring, turning dark green in summer. In the fall, the foliage turns brilliant orange-red. The flowers are insignificant but are surrounded by orange bracts in June and July. As these run, they need space; they are best in a mid-border. Two hybrids between *E. epithymoides* and *E. griffithii* both look like *E. griffithii* in habit: 'Autumn Sunset' has bright yellow-orange "flowers"; 'Jessie', brilliant yellow with a thin orange margin. *Euphorbia dulcis* also runs and self-seeds. The wild form has grey-green foliage and chartreuse "flowers", but the cultivar 'Chameleon' has

burgundy-purple foliage on stems that arise to 45 centimetres. It should be sheared in mid-summer to keep the plants compact. In mild areas (zones 5–6), try the hybrid spurge 'Excalibur', which has elongated green leaves with a central white stripe and purple margins, or 'Blue Lagoon', which has blue-green foliage. Both have sulphur yellow "flowers". In sheltered sites it remains evergreen. In a rock garden try the donkey-tailed spurge, *E. mysinites*. It has trailing stems up to 30 centimetres long with spiralling evergreen blue-grey leaves and yellow "flowers" that bloom in June.

As a group, the spurges prefer full sun and well-drained soil. They are tolerant of poor, droughty soils. Pests and diseases are rare but they are sometimes eaten by large herbivores. Propagation is by seed or division for cultivars. Most are hardy to zone 4.

Euphorbia griffithii 'Fireglow'

Eutrochium maculatum

Eutrochium

JOE-PYE WEED

Historically, the eight species of North American joe-pye weed were included in the genus *Eupatorium*; today, its purple-flowered members have been moved to their own genus, *Eutrochium*. Only the white-flowered members, commonly called bonesets, are still considered to be in the genus *Eupatorium*. *Eutrochium* comes from the Greek *eu*, well, referring to the wet habitat, and *troche*, wheel-like, referring to the whorled leaves. The common name joe-pye honours a First Nations healer named Jopi, who used this plant as a herbal remedy. As a group, the joe-pye weed are tall, bold plants useful for the back of a border.

Spotted joe-pye weed, *E. maculatum*, is native throughout Atlantic Canada, growing along streamsides and pond margins. It reaches 2 metres in height, with whorls of three to five lance-shaped, rugose leaves. Stems are topped with flat-topped panicles of fluffy purple-pink flowers from July to September. The more compact 'Gateway' reaches 150 centimetres. Sweet joe-pye weed, *E. purpureum*, has vanilla-scented flowers with a more conical outline. 'Atropurpureum' has nearly black stems. For smaller gardens try the cultivar 'Little Joe', which reaches 120 centimetres in height, or 'Baby Joe', which reaches just 75 centimetres. The latter is recommended, as it has super-sized flower heads in relation to the plant. The sole European species of *Eutrochium*, *E. cannabinum*, commonly called hemp-agrimony, can reach 150 centimetres tall, with narrow whorled leaves and loose clusters of flowers. From China comes *E. fortunei* 'Pink Frost', which has white-variegated leaves and pink flowers on 90-centimetre-tall plants. Among the true *Eupatorium*, the most popular is *E. rugulosum* 'Chocolate', which has purple-tinted leaves and can reach 120 centimetres, with flat-topped clusters of white flowers.

Eupatorium maculatum

Joe-pye weed love moisture and quickly wilt if too dry. They prefer full sun and organically rich soil. These are bold plants for the back of a border but dwarf types may be used in a middle border. Both the dwarf and non-dwarf plants are ideal for planting near water features. Excellent companion plants include rayflower, Japanese iris, and *Darmera*. All joe-pye weed attract hummingbirds, butterflies, and bees. They make admirable cut flowers. Propagation is by seed or division. All are hardy to zone 4.

Filipendula
MEADOWSWEET

All 12 species of *Filipendula*, native to the northern hemisphere, produce pinnately compound leaves and small white to deep pink flowers in fluffy panicles. Of the four species grown in Atlantic Canada, the tallest is queen-of-the-prairie, *F. rubra*, a North American native which can exceed 2 metres. A bold plant for the back of a border, its compound leaves have many small leaflets, with a large, deeply lobed terminal leaflet. The large astilbe-like flower clusters are typically pale pink and fragrant and flower in July and August. 'Venusta' has deeper pink blossoms.

Filipendula rubra

Japanese meadowsweet, *F. purpurea*, is a smaller, dark pink version of 'Venusta', reaching 120 centimetres in height. The cultivar 'Elegans' has white flowers with red stamens and reaches 75 centimetres. Queen-of-the-meadow, *F. ulmaria*, is a European counterpart whose pinnate leaves have more equal-sized leaflets. This heritage plant has creamy white flowers on stems up to 120 centimetres in height. As it can prolifically self-seed, it is now naturalized throughout much of Atlantic Canada. 'Flore Pleno' is a sterile, double-flowered cultivar. For wonderful foliage, try 'Aurea', whose leaves are bright yellow, or 'Variegata', whose leaves are irregularly splashed creamy yellow. These latter species are ideal for a middle border.

Also from Europe is dropwort, *F. vulgaris* (aka *F. hexapetala*), another species that has jumped the fence in eastern North America. Atop 90-centimetre-long stems, pink buds open to creamy white flowers in June and July. Its dark green leaves

Fragaria 'Pink Panda'

have fernlike, finely dissected leaflets. 'Multiplex' or 'Flore Pleno' is a sterile double-flowered cultivar. The dwarf meadowsweet, 'Red Umbrellas' and 'Kahome', are probably hybrids between the Chinese species *F. multijuga* and *F. palmata*. 'Red Umbrellas' has red-veined leaves and pink flowers on 75-centimetre-long stems, while 'Kahome' is the most dwarf meadowsweet, with 30-centimetre-long stems topped with deep pink flowers.

Meadowsweet are plants of damp woodlands or meadows and prefer organically rich, evenly moist soil and sunny to partly shaded locations. They all prefer alkaline soil. Dropwort is native to open grasslands and can tolerate some drought. Meadowsweet are suitable to borders and wildflower gardens and near water features. Few pests, large or small, bother them. The only serious disease is mildew, which can sometimes affect queen-of-the-meadow. Propagation is mostly by division. All species mentioned above are rated hardy to zone 3.

Fragaria
ORNAMENTAL STRAWBERRY

Incorporating edible plants into standard garden landscapes is becoming increasingly trendy. Ornamental kale and cabbage are obvious examples; more recently, strawberries have made the transition. While standard strawberries are too aggressive for perennial borders, other species, with decorative variegated foliage and those with ornamental pink flowers, are good edgers along perennial borders or as ground covers. Both still produce fruit, even if smaller-than-regular strawberries.

'Pink Panda'™ has bright pink blossoms from May until frost, together with dark green, glossy, evergreen foliage. 'Lipstick' has dark reddish pink flowers in May and June, with sporadic flowerings throughout the rest of the season. Its foliage is light green. *Fragaria vesca* 'Rugen' (red fruit) and 'Yellow Wonder' (yellow fruit) are runnerless cultivars with traditional white blossoms in May and June. They are well-behaved and produce larger fruit than the pink-flowered types. Both *Fragaria vesca* 'Variegata' and *F. X ananassa* 'Variegata' have white-edged leaves but, as they produce runners, use with caution. *Fragaria chilo-*

ense or beach strawberry has smaller, glossy, ever-green foliage and white flowers on very compact plants. As it also produces runners, it may be a little aggressive. Both this and the variegated strawberries are ideal as a ground cover.

Ornamental strawberries prefer full sun and evenly moist, good-quality soil; however, they can tolerate part shade. The fruit will be eaten by birds if left unpicked. Pests and diseases are generally not a problem, but hares may eat the foliage. Propagation is by division or runners. The above are hardy to zone 2, except beach strawberry, which is listed for zone 4.

Gaillardia
BLANKETFLOWER

The genus *Gaillardia* is named in honour of M. Gaillard de Charentonneau, an 18th-century French magistrate who was a patron of botany. Its 20 species are native to North and South America. Only one is grown in Atlantic Canada, blanketflower, *G. aristata*, native in west-central North America, where it grows on dry prairies, grasslands, and foothill meadows. The wild species forms a clump up to 80 centimetres in height, with hairy, serrated, lance-shaped leaves and 7.5-centimetre-diameter daisylike flowers that are scarlet with yellow tips. The blooming season spans from July to hard frost, especially if regularly deadheaded.

Blanketflowers have had a revival in popularity. Almost every year a new cultivar is released, varying in height or colour. Plenty of compact (less than 30 centimetres in height) cultivars are available, with flowers ranging from yellow, orange, red, and burgundy to bicoloured. Many of these are hybrids between the regular blanketflower and the annual *G. pulchella*. With the infusion of an annual species, the hybrids are apt to be short-lived. Popular cultivars include the

Gaillardia aristata 'Goblin'

Mesa™ and Arizona™ series, 'Amber Wheels', 'Goblin', 'Burgundy', and 'Monarch'.

Blanketflowers, sun-lovers with a preference for alkaline soil, are drought-tolerant and require a well-drained site, especially in winter, as they are prone to rot if too wet when dormant. As many of the more popular cultivars are compact, they are best along the front of a border, but the wild species and taller cultivars are ideal for wildflower settings. Their flowers make attractive cut flowers. Pests and diseases are rare and they are not generally bothered by large herbivores. Bees and butterflies love them, and if you decide to leave the seed heads, their seeds will be enjoyed by goldfinch. It is propagated by seed or division and rated hardy through zone 3.

Gentiana
GENTIANS

The genus *Gentiana* is cosmopolitan with over 400 species, with most in the Himalayas of China. The genus name is a tribute to Gentius, an Illyrian king who may have been the discoverer of tonic properties in gentians. As a group, *Gentiana* are

Gentiana andrewsii

prized for their intensely blue flowers. Books have been dedicated to the growing of gentians. In Atlantic Canada, only a few are commonly grown, either as woodland or rock-garden subjects.

Perhaps the most impressive is the willow gentian, *G. asclepiadea*. This European woodlander produces a fountainlike clump of unbranched stems arising to 90 centimetres. The leaves are dark green and lance-shaped. The 3.5- to 5-centimetre-long, deep blue, trumpetlike flowers are produced in the upper leaf axils during August and September. As this plant produces a deep taproot, it should not be disturbed once it is planted. It can be slow to establish but is long-lived and improves with age. The cultivar 'Alba' has white flowers; 'Pink Cascade' and 'Pink Swallow' have spectacular pink blossoms.

Perhaps the tallest is the great yellow gentian, *G. lutea*. As the common name suggests, this plant can reach an impressive 2 metres. Like the willow gentian, this European species is slow to mature and difficult to transplant. It can take many years for the plant to bloom, but each year leading up to maturity, it produces a rosette of large, leathery, ribbed leaves. When it blooms, the flower stem is topped with several dense whorls of yellow starlike flowers in July.

Native to eastern North America are several species commonly called the bottle gentians: *G. andrewsii*, *G. clausa*, and *G. linearis*. These reach 60 centimetres, with a clump of unbranched stems topped with a cluster of blue to violet bottle-shaped flowers in August and September. The flowers never fully open. These are best planted in a wildflower meadow setting.

Of lower stature is the crested gentian, *G. septemfida*, native to the Caucasus region. This plant forms a low clump with sprawling, 15- to 30-centimetre-long stems. From July to September, the stems end in clusters of blue trumpets. This one is ideal for the front of a border, or the woodland, or rock garden. *Gentiana scabra* is similar. The cultivar 'Zuki-rindo' has stunning purple-pink flowers. 'True Blue', a hybrid gentian, reaches 45 centimetres in height with blue flowers in August. One of the most outstanding gentians is the trumpet gentian, *G. acaulis*, which has 5-centimetre-diameter navy blue flowers in May and June. This plant forms a low mat and is best used in a rock garden.

Gentians require evenly moist, organically rich soil. The low-stature gentians noted are sun-lovers, while the taller ones grow in sun or part shade. Most of the above prefer acidic soil, except *G. lutea*, which prefers alkaline soil. All attract bees and are usually pest- and disease-free. Propagation is most often by seed. All are rated hardy to zone 3.

Gentiana angustifolia 'Frei'

TODD BOLAND

Geranium
CRANESBILL (BORDER TYPES)

The over 400 species of the genus *Geranium* are found worldwide. The genus name comes from the Greek word *geranos*, crane, referring to the fruit shape, which is reminiscent of the head and beak of a crane. Although several weedy species are known, many are highly ornamental. Taking into account the innumerable hybrids, this is a large and varied group of garden perennials.

Many taller species are useful for a mid-border or wildflower garden. Traditionally, the most popular was meadow cranesbill, *G. pratense*, considered a heritage plant in Atlantic Canada. Still popular, with many cultivars, it is a clumping plant with stems up to 90 centimetres tall. Saucer-shaped flowers are produced in open clusters from late June through July. The colour of the wild version is purple-blue, but white and double-flowered types are available. 'Splish Splash' has white flowers flecked with purple. Several other species have purple-tinted foliage; perhaps the best of these is 'Okey Dokey'. Other similar species and hybrids include *G.* X *magnificum*, *G. himalayense*, and the hybrids 'Brookside' and 'Johnson's Blue'.

One of the tallest, *G. psilostemon*, can reach 120 centimetres. It is shrublike, with prolific magenta, black-eyed flowers from July to September. 'Dragon Heart' is similar but it reaches only 60 centimetres. 'Ann Folkard' is also similar but it has contrasting chartreuse foliage. Both of these bloom from July to frost.

Among the best pink-flowered geranium are *G. endresii* and *G.* X *oxonianum* cultivars. These bloom from late June to frost if kept reasonably moist and not too hot. *Geranium endresii* reach 40 centimetres, with a spreading habit. *G.* X *oxoniaum* 'Wargrave Pink' is similar but can reach 60 centimetres. The cultivar 'Claridge Druce' is also 60 centimetres tall but has pale pink flow-

Geranium phaeum 'Samabor'

ers; 'Katherine Adele' is pale pink with maroon-blotched foliage.

'Rozanne', a 50-centimetre-tall mounding hybrid named the 2008 Perennial Plant of the Year™, has blue flowers with a pale central eye and blooms from late June until frost. The mourning widow cranesbill, *G. phaeum*, has flowers of an unusual maroon-purple. This species can reach 80 centimetres in height. The flowers are smaller than most geranium flowers, its petals reflex back, and it blooms all summer. A white-flowered cultivar, 'Album', also exists, but perhaps the best is 'Samobor' for its striking purple-black blotched leaves.

RIGHT: *Geranium* X *oxonianum*

Among the lower growing ground-cover-habit cranesbills, the most popular and indeed another heritage species is the big-root cranesbill, *G. macrorrhizum*. This species reaches 30 centimetres in height but spreads 90 or more centimetres, and can be used as ground cover for sun or shade. The relatively small pink flowers are produced in June. The soft, sticky foliage is strong-smelling and takes on shades of yellow, orange, and red in autumn. The leaves of 'Variegatum' are thinly margined in white. The smallest of the ground-cover species, *G. dalmaticum*, reaches only 10 to 15 centimetres in height and will creep among rocks in a rock-garden setting. It blooms in early summer with light pink flowers and glossy foliage. The hybrid between *G. macrorrhizum* and *G. dalmaticum*, *G.* X *cantabigiense*, is a wonderful ground cover for sun to part shade, has glossy, fragrant foliage, and produces masses of flowers in June and July. 'Cambridge', 'Westray', 'Karmina', and 'Crystal Rose' have flowers in varying shades of pink; 'Biokova' has white blossoms with a hint of pink. It was awarded Perennial Plant of the Year™ in 2015.

One of the most popular cranesbills for the front of a border is bloody cranesbill, *G. sanguineum*, a mounding plant up to 20 to 30 centimetres in height with many bright pink flowers from late June until frost. 'Elke' has two-tone flowers, neon pink with white edges; 'Striatum' has soft pink flowers; and 'Album' has white flowers.

Geranium cinereum has a similar habit to that of *G. sanguinium* and has several cultivars: 'Ballerina', pale pink with darker veins and nearly black

Geranium 'Johnson's Blue'

centres; 'Splendens', deep magenta; and 'Purple Pillow', dark reddish purple. *Geranium wallichianum* 'Buxton's Blue' is a low spreader whose purple-blue flowers have white centres. The hybrid 'Rosetta' is similar but has pink flowers with white centres.

G. renardii is perhaps grown more for its foliage than its flowers. A low clumping plant that reaches a height of 20 centimetres, it blooms in June with white flowers veined with purple. Unlike most cranesbills, the petals are widely spaced but may be chosen for its fuzzy grey-green leaves. Notable for its foliage is the *G. renardii* hybrid 'Philippe Vapelle', but this 30- to 40-centimetre-tall mounding plant has showy purple flowers in June and July. Also grown for its foliage is the diminutive *G. sessiliflorum* 'Nigricans'; it forms a flat mat with tiny white flowers and unusual chocolate brown foliage.

Cranesbills are not fond of dry soil and perform best if the soil is organically rich. All grow in full sun to part shade, but *G. phaeum* is shade-tolerant. *G. pratense* types can get rather rangy by mid-summer and often benefit from being cut back. Many of the species listed will self-seed with abandon, especially *G. phaeum*. Overall, they are care-free. Propagation is by seed or division. Most of the above are hardy to zones 3–4, except 'Rozanne', *G. cinereum*, *G. wallichianum*, and *G. sessiliflorum*, which are rated for zones 5–6.

Geum

AVENS

The genus *Geum* is found worldwide, with the exception of Africa, with about 50 species. Only a limited number of species and hybrids are grown in Atlantic Canada. As a group, they are evergreen, with hairy basal leaves and thick rhizomes. Each leaf is pinnately compound with a

Geum 'Leonard's Variety'

single, large, deeply lobed, terminal leaflet. At least one cultivar, the European *Geum coccineum* 'Borisii', is a heritage plant. In May and June, loose flower clusters arise on wiry stems up to 45 centimetres tall. The 3.5-centimetre-diameter flowers are orange with a dense central clump of yellow stamens.

Two other popular avens are cultivars of *G. chiloense*, a species native to southern Chile. These include 'Mrs. J. Bradshaw', with double scarlet flowers, and 'Mrs. Strathedon', with double yellow flowers. If promptly deadheaded, they can be coaxed to bloom all season. Recently, a series of new hybrids has been developed called the Cocktails™ series, including 'Mai Tai' (apricot), 'Tequila Sunrise' (yellow and rose pink bicolour), and 'Banana Daiquiri' (primrose yellow).

Native to Atlantic Canada is water avens, *G. rivale*. It has unassuming nodding flowers that are an unusual shade of apricot to purple-pink. This species has been hybridized to create lovely hybrids which are a little shorter than the *G. chiloense* hybrids, reaching about 45 centimetres in height. These often have delicate nodding flowers like those of *G. rivale*—but with the large size and showiness of the *G. chiloense* or *G. coccineum* parent. These hybrids include 'Totally Tangarine' (orange, flushed pink), 'Lemon Drop' (pale yellow), 'Pink Frills' (soft pink), 'Flames of Passion' (scarlet), and 'Leonard's Variety' (coral pink). For a dwarf avens to grow in a rock-garden setting, try *G. montanum*, a European species from the Alps. It has relatively large yellow flowers in June on 15-centimetre-tall stems held above a tuft of evergreen leaves.

These avens prefer evenly moist, organically rich soil and grow in full sun or part shade. They are ideal plants for near the front of a border, in a woodland setting, or near water features. Plants benefit from being divided every three to four years. Propagation is by seed or division. These care-free plants are rated hardy to zone 4.

Glaucidium
JAPANESE WOOD POPPY

There is only a single species in this genus, *Glaucidium palmatum*. It is endemic to northern Japan, where it grows in open sub-alpine woodlands. Plants are clumpers and have a shrublike appearance. Several unbranched stems arise 45 to 60 centimetres in height. Each stem has a pair of bright green maple-leaf-shaped leaves and a single 15-centimetre-diameter mauve or white flower that looks like a cross between a peony and a poppy flower. Its blooming season is from late May through June. This connoisseur's plant may be pricey. Assuming you can track it down, it is well worth the investment, as it is long-lived and, like a fine wine, improves with age. The Royal Horticultural Society names it one of the top 200 plants in the world.

Glaucidium prefer part shade and a humus-rich, moist, well-drained soil. It will not tolerate dry soil or hot temperatures; gardeners in cooler

Glaucidium palmatum 'Album'

coastal regions have the best success. For a spectacular effect, combine it with the equally rare and desirable Japanese waxbells and Himalayan blue poppy. It is best grown in a woodland garden or partly shaded border. Pests and diseases are not generally a problem, and its flowers are attractive to bees. Propagation is primarily by seed. Larger plants may be divided; however, they have a large root system and do not transplant well. Considered hardy to zone 5, it has been known to survive in zone 4 if properly mulched before winter.

Gypsophila
BABY'S BREATH

The genus *Gypsophila*'s about 150 species are found throughout Eurasia, Africa, and Australia. The botanical name comes from the Greek words *gupsos*, gypsum, and *philos*, loving. In other words, they are lime-lovers. Despite the large number of species, only two perennial species are commonly grown in Atlantic Canada: the perennial baby's breath and the creeping baby's breath, both native to Europe. The former, *G. paniculata*, forms a large, billowy mound up to 100 centimetres in height, smothered in tiny white flowers throughout July to September. These are popular as fillers in cut- or dried-flower arrangements. This plant tolerates poor, dry soil and, as such, has jumped the fence to become an invasive species in some parts of North America. It is a good companion plant for Oriental poppy, *Papaver orientale*, which often goes dormant in mid-summer. The baby's breath can be effectively used to fill in the empty space. Two cultivars are widely available: 'Bristol Fairy', with double white flowers, and 'Pink Fairy', with pale pink flowers.

Creeping baby's breath, *G. repens*, is at the other extreme: a low creeping plant with narrow grey-green foliage, it can form mats that grow over walls and between rocks in a rock-garden setting. In June, it produces masses of tiny star-shaped flowers on 10-centimetre-tall stems. The flowers are typically white but on the cultivar 'Rosea' they are soft pink. Shear the faded flowers to keep the plants looking neat throughout the rest of the summer.

These two drought-tolerant species are sun-lovers and can grow in gravelly soil. As they dislike excessive winter wetness, they need a well-drained site. With their preference for alkaline soil, a liberal annual dusting of their soil with lime is beneficial. As perennial baby's breath's deep taproot makes it difficult to transplant the plant, it is best to start with young plants. These are care-free plants, but spittlebugs can be unsightly, even if they generally do little damage. Propagation is by seed or, in the case of creeping baby's breath, cuttings. They are hardy through zone 3.

Gypsophila repens 'Rosea'

Helenium autumnale 'Dancing Flames'

Helenium
HELEN'S FLOWER, SNEEZEWEED

All 40 species of *Helenium* are native to the Americas. The plant was named in honour of Helen of Troy, even though it is not native to the Mediterranean. The common name, sneezeweed, is not a reference to the plant's causing hay fever; rather, it was used by First Nations people as a form of snuff. Only one species of *Helenium*, *H. autumnale*, is grown in Atlantic Canadian gardens. From August to October the plants produce clusters of yellow, orange, or red 5-centimetre-diameter daisylike flowers. With its late-season blooms, it is indispensable for extending the gardening season. This is potentially a tall plant, with stems commonly reaching 120 centimetres or even up to 2 metres in height if the soil is rich and moist. Popular cultivars include 'Sombrero', in yellow; 'Mardi Gras', a blend of yellow and orange; 'Dancing Flame', all orange; 'Moerheim Beauty', in tones of orange and red; and 'Red Jewel', brick red. With its height, Helen's flower is a good choice for the middle or back of a border but it is also suitable for a wildflower garden.

Helen's flower, a sun-lover, prefers soil that stays reasonably moist. It is a magnet for bees and butterflies. Plants may need dividing every three to four years to keep them vigorous. Pinching some of the stems when they are 15 centimetres tall causes them to branch, resulting in a bushier plant. The flowers make attractive cut flowers. It is overall a care-free plant. Propagation is by seed or division. Hardy throughout much of Atlantic Canada, it is rated for zone 3.

Helianthus
SUNFLOWER

The 70 species of *Helianthus* are native to the Americas. The name comes from the Greek *helios*, sun, and *anthos*, flower—the common name is a literal translation of the Greek. Most sunflowers are annuals, but a few perennial species grow in Atlantic Canada. *H.* X *laetiflorus*, the cheerful sunflower, is a heritage plant. It is er-

Helianthus X *multiflorus* 'Sunshine Daydream'

Helianthus tuberosus

roneously called black-eyed Susan in Newfoundland, mistakenly thought to be the same plant as the true black-eyed Susan, *Rudbeckia hirta*, found native in the Maritimes. A sterile hybrid, this sunflower never sets seed but it can multiply quickly through rhizomes. Plants produce stems 120 to 200 centimetres tall, topped with open clusters of 12-centimetre-diameter yellow daisies in August and September. Although it is suitable for use toward the back of a border, its vigorous habit might merit some caution if used in a small garden. It is perfect for a wildflower garden.

Jerusalem artichoke, *H. tuberosus*, is one of the parents in *H.* X *laetiflorus*. Jerusalem artichoke can also spread rapidly, but it blooms in October, with the bonus of edible, swollen roots.

The many-flowered sunflower, *H.* X *multiflorus*, is much tamer. This is another sterile hybrid but has fully double flowers atop 2-metre-tall stems.

It will form a discrete clump. Popular cultivars include 'Sunshine Daydream' and 'Lodden Gold'. 'Capenoch Star' is a single-flowered cultivar; 'Happy Days' is a double-flowered, dwarf cultivar reaching 60 centimetres in height. Also forming a tall clump is the sunflower hybrid 'Lemon Queen': this plant can top 2 metres in an ideal location and has masses of 7-centimetre-diameter flowers in September and October.

Valued for their late flowers and use in the back of a border, perennial sunflowers are magnets for bees and butterflies. They are reasonably tolerant to drought and, although tall, if grown in full sun, their stems are stiff enough to withstand most wind. Over-fertilizing can result in floppy plants. All are attractive as cut flowers. Pests and diseases are uncommon, and large herbivores generally ignore them. Propagation is mostly by division. All are rated hardy through zone 4.

TODD BOLAND

Heliopsis
FALSE SUNFLOWER

The 15 species of *Heliopsis* are native to the Americas. The genus name comes from the Greek words *helios*, sun, and *opsis*, looking like. Certainly, the flowers and the plants themselves resemble sunflowers. A single species is grown in Atlantic Canadian gardens, *H. helianthoides*, which grows natively in meadows throughout central and eastern US and southern Canada. In the wild, plants may reach 150 centimetres tall and produce paired, triangular leaves and loose clusters of terminal golden yellow daisies 6 to 9 centimetres in diameter. If flowers are regularly deadheaded, the blooming season will run from late July through September.

Of the many cultivars on the market, single flowers are available on 'Midwest Dreams' (bright yellow, 90 centimetres), 'Hohlspiegel' (golden yellow, 120 centimetres), 'Summer Nights' (golden yellow with red centre, 120 centimetres), or 'Prairie Sunset' (like 'Summer Nights' but with purple stems and purple-tinted leaves). If variegated foliage is your prefer-

Helionopsis helianthoides 'Hohlspiegel'

ence, try 'Lorraine Sunshine' (100 centimetres), 'Summer Green' (90 centimetres), or 'Sunstruck' (dwarf, 40 centimetres), which have white foliage with contrasting green veins. Even more striking is 'Summer Pink' (65 centimetres), which has purple stems and pink, white, and green foliage. Double-flowered cultivars include 'Bressingham Doubloon' (150 centimetres), 'Double Sun' (120 centimetres), or 'Asahi' (75 centimetres). 'Double Sunstruck' is a gorgeous double-flowered version of the variegated 'Sunstruck'.

False sunflower is a sun-lover. The taller cultivars are ideal for the back of a border, the compact ones can be used in a mid-border; all are suitable for a wildflower garden. Regular watering and fertile soil results in tall plants which may require staking. False sunflower tolerates drought and poor soil, although these result in more compact plants. It attracts butterflies, birds, and hummingbirds. The blossoms are long-lasting cut flowers. Pests and diseases are uncommon, although it may be periodically attacked by aphids. It is generally not bothered by large herbivores. Propagation is usually by division but it can also occur by seed. This hardy plant can survive to zone 2.

Heliopsis helianthoides 'Asahi'

Helleborus

HELLEBORE

The hellebores are a group of perennials currently experiencing a surge in popularity. Although there are only 22 species, most native to the Balkan region of Europe, hundreds of cultivars and hybrids are available. All are grown primarily for their early-season flowers but a few are chosen for their foliage. As a group, they produce nodding to outward-facing clusters of flowers in April or May. Individual flowers have five petal-like sepals which surround a cluster of small cuplike nectaries, which are, in fact, the true petals of the plant. The wild species generally have green, white, or purple-tinted flowers but, through hybridization, they are now available in white, yellow, green, pink, and purple to nearly black. Some are spotted, bicoloured, or even double-flowered. The leaves are usually evergreen, leathery, and palmately divided, with three to 10 leaflets. Many are clumpers, reaching 40 to 60 centimetres tall when in bloom, but a few, such as *H. argutifolius*, produce trailing stems up to 100 centimetres long.

Perhaps the most popular group are the Lenten rose *H. orientalis* or *H.* X *hybridus*. As a group, they were awarded Perennial Plant of the Year™ in 2005. These have colourful flowers with spotted, bicoloured, and/or double-flowered versions. These bloom with nodding flowers from late April through May and even into June in colder areas of Newfoundland. The earliest hellebore to bloom is *H. niger*, the Christmas rose. It blooms as early as late March in the mildest areas of southern Nova Scotia, but more often from April to early May. It is the shortest of the hellebores, rarely exceeding 30 centimetres in height. Its outward-facing flowers are white fading to pink. The *H.* X *ericsmithii*, *H.* X *ballardiae*, and *H.* X *nigercors* hybrids may have white-veined and/or silvery green foliage; 'Winter Moonbeam' is one of the most striking. As a

Helleborus orientalis

Helleborus Winter Jewels® 'Cherry Blossom'

group, the flowers of these hybrids are generally white, green, or pink. Another hellebore grown for its foliage, *Helleborus foetidus* 'Wester Flisk', has finely divided foliage and burgundy stems; the cultivar 'Gold Bullion' has chartreuse-yellow foliage. The most silver foliage is found on *H.* X *sternii* 'Silver Dollar', while *H. argutifolius* 'Snow Fever' leaves are distinctly spotted with white. These last four hellebores have greenish flowers.

Hellebores prefer well-drained but organically rich soil. They are deeply rooted, slow to mature, and should not be disturbed once established. As they prefer neutral to alkaline soil, in many areas of Atlantic Canada they benefit from regular liming. They are ideal for part shade but can tolerate full shade in warmer inland areas or full sun in cooler coastal areas. Try combining them with ferns, hakone grass, and *Heuchera* to create a pleasing foliage effect. They are care-free and, because all parts of the plant are toxic, they are not bothered by insects or herbivores. Early-emerging bees take advantage of the spring supply of nectar. Propagation is by seed or, for cultivars, division. Professional propagators often use tissue culturing for mass propagation. Most are hardy to zone 4, but those with trailing stems, such as *H. argutifolius* and *H. corsicus*, are only hardy to zone 6.

Hemerocallis
DAYLILY

It is the rare garden that does not have at least one daylily. They are among the most popular perennials grown in Atlantic Canada. From only 19 species, all native to eastern Asia, have arisen thousands of hybrids, with more being added each year. As a group, they produce large clumps with grasslike leaves and naked flower stems that end in several relatively large, lilylike flowers that last a single day, hence the common name daylily. The short-lived flowers are, however, produced sequentially over several weeks. Depend-

Hemerocallis 'Purple D'Oro'

FAVOURITE PERENNIALS FOR ATLANTIC CANADA

Hemerocallis lilioasphodelus

ing on the species or hybrid, daylilies can bloom from June through to October.

The flower colour range of the species is restricted to yellow or orange, but modern hybrids are available in creamy white through every imaginable shade of yellow, orange, pink, red, to nearly purple. Many are bi- or even tricoloured. Petal edges may be frilled or the petals may be long and narrow. Some have double flowers or variegated leaves. Most modern hybrids have thicker petals than those of the wild species. Overall flower stem heights vary from 90 to 120 centimetres on the taller standard types to about 30 centimetres on the dwarf hybrids such as the Doro and Returns series.

Two species that have been grown in Atlantic Canada for over 100 years are considered heritage: the lemon-scented *H. lilioasphodelus*, with yellow flowers in June, and the tawny daylily, *H. fulva*, with orange flowers in August. The latter species can be invasive in certain parts of North America.

For these long-lived plants, cultivation is easy; they seem to thrive almost anywhere, except in soggy sites. They are drought-tolerant, reasonably shade-tolerant, salt-tolerant, and extremely hardy. However, they perform best with regular watering and full sun. The standard types are useful in a mid-border and the dwarf types

are better suited to the front of a border. All are excellent for coastal gardens and can be used as ground cover on slopes. Pests and diseases are uncommon, but newly emerging foliage may be enjoyed by slugs, deer, or moose. Propagation is by division. They may be grown throughout much of Atlantic Canada and are hardy to zone 2.

Heuchera
ALUMROOT

The genus *Heuchera* has about 35 species, all native to North America. The genus name honours Johann Heinrich von Heucher, an 18th-century German physician, botanist, and medicinal plant expert. All *Heuchera* produce mounding, basal rosettes of evergreen, round to maple-leaf-shaped, lobed leaves and wiry stems with loose sprays of tiny flowers. Many of the species are small plants and useful for a rock garden. The species that first gained popularity was coral bells, *H. sanguinea*, a native of Mexico, New Mexico, and Arizona. It has the showiest flowers, small, bril-

Heuchera sanguinea

Heuchera Dolce™ 'Black Currant'

liant red, and bell-shaped, in June and July atop wiry 45-centimetre-tall stems and is a favourite of hummingbirds. Shortly thereafter, some of the larger-leaved species were noticed, particularly *H. micrantha*, *H. americana*, and *H. villosa*. The cultivar 'Palace Purple', still available, was probably the earliest of the *Heuchera* grown for its foliage. It was so popular that it was awarded Perennial Plant of the Year™ in 1991. The modern gardening world is *Heuchera*-crazy, with innumerable hybrids available with spectacular foliage in shades of yellow, orange to nearly red, silver, silver-veined, pink, velvety purple to nearly black. Most of these colourful-leaved hybrids have insignificant flowers that are probably better removed so as to not detract from the spectacular foliage. These are plants for the front of a border or as annuals in container plantings. The Dolce™ series are highly recommended for their outstanding foliage.

Some species do have attractive flowers, in particular, hybrids using *H. sanguinea*. Of particular note is the Canyon Quartet™ series, whose small leaves form 12-centimetre-wide mounds topped with leafless, upright, 30-centimetre-tall stems. Depending on the cultivar, flowers range from light pink to deep red. These are also suitable for the front of a border or a rock-garden setting. Hybrids between *Heuchera* and the closely related foamflower, *Tiarella*, are called *Heucherella* and described under the *Tiarella* entry.

Heuchera need a well-drained site and reasonably moist soil, although, once established, they can tolerate short droughty periods. They can be grown in full sun to part shade, the latter preferable in hotter, inland locations. These care-free plants are shallow-rooted and prone to heaving in winter; the addition of fall mulch helps to prevent this problem. Propagation is by division, but professional propagators usually mass produce them by tissue culture. They are all rated hardy to zone 4.

Hibiscus
HARDY HIBISCUS, ROSE MALLOW

Hibiscus are well known as popular flowering shrubs in tropical countries. Most hibiscus are woody plants; rose-of-Sharon is a locally grown example. A few herbaceous species are available, the most popular being *Hibiscus moscheutos*, a species native to the south and eastern US and southernmost Ontario. Several additional similar hardy herbaceous species include *H. coccineus*, *H. laevis*, *H. militaris*, and *H. palustris*. The modern-day hardy garden hibiscus probably has genes from some, if not all, of the above species; commercially, all are sold as *H. moscheutos*.

As a garden ornamental, this plant can form a bushy clump over 2 metres tall. The huge flowers, up to 20 centimetres in diameter, are produced from August to October, making it a valuable plant for the late summer-early fall garden. Typical of all hibiscus, the flowers last a single day. Plants are slow to start in the spring but grow rapidly. 'Southern Belle' has flowers in white and shades of red and pink. Other tall cultivars include 'Cherry Brandy', 'Plum Fantasy',

Hibiscus moscheutos 'Luna Pink'

Hibiscus moscheutus 'Luna White'

'Fantasia', 'Peppermint Schnapps', and 'Lord Baltimore'. If space is limited, try the dwarf, 1-metre-tall Luna series, available in white, pink, and red.

Garden hibiscus require full sun and organically rich, evenly moist soil. The wild species usually grow in swamps and marshes and, as a result, will not tolerate drought. It is suitable for the back of a border and near water features. It is a good butterfly plant. Watch for insects and disease, as hibiscus can be bothered by rust, leaf spots, aphids, and especially Japanese beetle. Deer, moose, and hares are not a problem. Propagation is by division. It is hardy to zone 5, but hibiscus is only suitable for the warmer regions of Atlantic Canada as it needs a long growing season.

Hosta
HOSTA

Hosta are among the most popular perennials grown in Atlantic Canada. This genus is not large; there are only 23 species, two native to China and the rest to Japan and Korea. Given the humble beginnings, the number and variation of hosta available today is mind-boggling. Does the world need another hosta? Apparently so, as new ones are released every year and their popularity does not seem to be waning. With so many hundreds, if not thousands, of cultivars on the market, it is impossible to describe them, except as a group.

Hosta are grown primarily for their foliage. Their leaves may be shades of green, yellow, or blue. Leaves may be variegated in white or yellow along their margins, in their centres, or as mottles and streaks scattered throughout. Some have attractive wine-coloured petioles. Their bell- to trumpet-shaped flowers are usually nodding and produced on one-sided spikes. These are mostly lavender to violet but can be variously marked on the inside with darker purple; some are all white. The blooming season ranges from July through to October, depending on the species or hybrid. Hosta are generally scentless but the species *H. plantaginea* and the hybrid 'Fragrant Bouquet' are notable for their all-white, highly fragrant flowers.

The size variation is tremendous. The Amer-

Hosta 'Shademaster'

ican Hosta Society divides the plants into six size classes: dwarf, miniature, small, medium, large, and giant. Among the smallest is 'Collectors Choice', with 2- to 3-centimetre-long green leaves. At the other extreme is 'Empress Wu', whose leaves may be longer than 45 centimetres, with flower stems approaching 150 centimetres in height. In the garden setting, hosta may be used from the front to the back of a border. They are perhaps most popular in shady woodland gardens or other areas of shade where most perennials simply cannot thrive. In the wild, they grow along partly shaded streams; in the garden, regular watering is required. Overall, hosta tolerate full sun to relatively deep shade but light requirements vary with leaf colour. As a rule, those with yellow foliage or yellow variegation need the most sun; under too much shade the yellow will turn chartreuse. White variegated leaves prefer part shade. Blue foliage tolerates the most shade. Non-variegated green leaved types seem to be able to take full sun to full shade.

Although they are extremely popular, hosta are snail and slug magnets: those with thick blue foliage are the most resistant, while the thin-leaved types can be shredded by these pests. Hosta are also attacked by a disease called Hosta Virus X, which may be spread by aphids or infected pruning shears. The symptoms appear as light or dark green discolouration and/or spotting, brown streaking, or unusual leaf puckering. Infected plants lose vigour and are condemned to a long, lingering death. The virus can spread rapidly to other hosta; destroy suspected infected plants right away. As if these problems were not enough, hosta are hors d'oeuvres for hares, deer, and moose. Despite these problems, growing hosta can be addictive; you can't have just one. Propagation is by division. They may be grown throughout most of Atlantic Canada as they are hardy through zone 2.

Hypericum olympicum

Hypericum
St. John's-wort

This genus encompasses close to 500 species. Many are weedy, have insignificant flowers, or are not hardy enough for Atlantic Canada. One of the more popular in this region, *Hypericum androsaemum* 'Albury Purple', is technically a shrub which grows up to 90 centimetres tall, but in zone 5 often dies back to the ground each winter. It has paired, purple-tinted, rounded leaves. In mid-summer, the stem tips produce small clusters of 2-centimetre-wide golden yellow flowers with a central bushy clump of yellow stamens. During the autumn, flowers develop into red berries that later turn black, making for an at-

Hypericum androsaemum 'Albury Purple'

tractive fall display. Of similar appearance and habit is *Hypericum* Hypearls™, a series of hybrids grown for their decorative cream to pink fruit display. These too are shrubs that dieback to the ground over winter.

Another shrub, *Hypericum calycinum*, which reaches up to 45 centimetres in height, usually behaves as a herbaceous plant in Atlantic Canada. It produces 5-centimetre-wide yellow flowers from July to frost and, with its bushy habit, is used as a ground cover on slopes. The cultivar 'Brigadoon' has brilliant yellow foliage. *Hypericum frondosum* 'Sunburst' is similar in habit to *H. calycinum* but can reach up to 120 centimetres tall. It has blue-tinted foliage and 5-centimetre-wide yellow flowers in early summer. Also technically a shrub, it often dies back to the ground in winter to re-sprout from the base. All the above are best used in a mid-border.

Two low-spreading species popular for rock gardens, retaining walls, or the edge of borders are *H. olympicum* and *H. cerastoides*, both of which form low mounds up to 25 centimetres tall. The former has narrow blue-tinted foliage; the latter, rounded grey-green leaves. In July, the stem tips of both produce 5-centimetre-wide yellow flowers with the bushy yellow stamens typical of most *Hypericum*. *Hypericum olympicum* 'Citrinum' and 'Sul-

phureum' have light primrose yellow blossoms.

Hypericum are sun-lovers and need well-drained soil. Too much winter wetness is an enemy, but summer drought does not usually cause a problem. All attract bees and butterflies. The fruiting stems of *Hypericum androsaemum* 'Albury Purple' and Hypearls™ series make a wonderful cut stem for fall floral displays. Pests and diseases are generally not a problem. Propagation is by seed, cuttings, or division. In Atlantic Canada, the growing areas for *Hypericum* are restricted: although rated hardy to zone 5, they are more reliable in zone 6 and only suitable for the mildest coastal regions.

Iberis
PERENNIAL CANDYTUFT

The 50 species of *Iberis* are native to Eurasia, especially near the Mediterranean. The common name "candytuft" is not related to candy but refers to a town named Candia on the island of Crete, where several species grow. Only one species is commonly grown in Atlantic Canada, *I. sempervirens*, usually known as perennial candytuft. This plant is really an evergreen sub-shrub that grows to a height of 25 centimetres and forms a large, low cushion. Its small narrow leaves are

Iberis sempervirens

deep green and shiny. In May and June, plants produce terminal clusters of four-petalled white flowers that may completely conceal the foliage. After flowering, shear off the faded flower stems to keep the plants compact and tidy.

The many cultivars, such as 'Little Gem', 'Snowflake', and 'Whiteout', differ in height and flower size. For something a little different try 'Golden Candy', which has chartreuse foliage. *Iberis* is grown as an edger in a perennial border, as ground cover on embankments, for cascading over walls, or in a rock garden.

Iberis requires full sun and a well-drained site, but, once established, it is drought-resistant. It benefits from snow cover that will help prevent leaf browning in winter; alternatively, evergreen boughs may be placed over the plants in late fall. Snails and slugs may eat the blossoms, but it is rarely eaten by deer, moose, or hares. It is a popular plant for early-emerging butterflies and bees. Propagation is by seed or cuttings. *Iberis* may be grown throughout much of Atlantic Canada, as it is hardy to zone 3.

Incarvillea
GARDEN GLOXINIA

The genus *Incarvillea* has 16 species, all native to central and eastern Asia. The only species generally available in Atlantic Canada, *I. delavayi*, is often sold as a dormant root in local nurseries and box stores. It produces a rosette of dark green, fernlike leaves. The leafless flower stems, which arise to 60 centimetres, are topped with a cluster of large, pink, trumpetlike flowers in June or July. Despite being readily available, it is not an easy plant to grow in Atlantic Canada, as it is borderline hardy.

Although it is not easy to find, the dwarf garden gloxinia, *I. mairei*, is actually hardier than *I. delavayi*. It is essentially a scaled-down version of the

Incarvillea delavayi

common garden gloxinia, with oversized flowers atop 30- to 40-centimetre-tall stems. It is well worth trying to track down as it is a wonderful addition to a rock garden or the front of a border.

Both garden gloxinia are best in full sun but tolerate part shade. They need organically rich soil that is well drained, especially in winter. They do not tolerate heat and humidity well. They are both care-free plants and attract bumblebees. Propagation is by seed. As garden gloxinia is only reliable to zone 6, it is suitable only for the mildest areas of southern Nova Scotia. It may be grown in zone 5 with a good winter mulching; even then, its long-term survival is unlikely. The dwarf garden gloxinia is hardier, tough enough to survive in zone 3.

Inula
ELECAMPANE

The genus *Inula* contains about 90 species, native to Eurasia and Africa. Three species are grown in Atlantic Canada: two are large, one is dwarf. The most popular of the large species is *I. helenium*, sometimes found naturalized along

Inula magnifica

roadsides and damp meadows in the Maritimes. It is a very large plant with yellow, 7.5-centimetre-diameter sunflower-like blossoms in August and September. Plants form large clumps with lance-shaped basal leaves up to 60 centimetres long produced at the ends of 30-centimetre-long petioles. Flower stems can grow to 2 metres in height. The flowers, produced in loose clusters, have narrow and slightly shaggy petals. *Inula magnifica* is similar to *I. helenium*, with even larger leaves, up to 90 centimetres long on robust specimens. It has oval to heart-shaped leaves. It too can reach nearly 2 metres high. Both are bold plants for the back of a border or in damp wildflower gardens. They mix well with rayflower, bugbane, and giant fleeceflower.

At the other extreme is the slender-leaved elecampane, *Inula ensifolia* 'Compacta', which forms

a dense 20- to 40-centimetre-tall mound, with numerous narrow willowlike leaves. The 5-centimetre-wide yellow daisies, produced in July and August, are often solitary per stem. This plant may be used along the front of a border or in a rock garden.

All three species prefer full sun to part shade and soil that stays reasonably moist. The blossoms attract both bees and butterflies and are admirable cut flowers. Diseases and insect pests are rare, but plants may be eaten by large herbivores. Propagation is by seed or division. They are hardy to zone 4.

Iris
BEARDED IRIS
Nearly every garden in Atlantic Canada has at least one iris, as iris are among the most popular garden perennials. There are upwards of 300 species of iris, all native to the northern hemisphere, with the greatest diversity in the Middle East. The genus was named after *Iris*, the Greek goddess of the rainbow—an apt name, as iris

Iris pumila

Iris 'King Tut'

flowers are available in almost every conceivable colour. With such diversity, it is not surprising that books have been devoted to the genus. For simplicity, they are described here as two major groups: the bearded and the beardless.

Bearded iris, perhaps the most popular of all the iris, are primarily hybrids derived from several European species. All have relatively large flowers with six petals, three pointing upward (the standards) and three arching downward (the falls). On the bearded iris, a distinct tuft of hairs or beard is found at the base of the falls. The flowering season ranges from late May to early June for the dwarf bearded iris and into July for the taller cultivars. Plants form large clumps with fanlike arrangements of broad, overlapping swordlike leaves which arise from a thickened rhizome. Plant height varies dramatically from 15 centimetres for the dwarf to over 120 centimetres on the tall cultivars. The dwarf bearded iris are most popular in rock-garden settings, while the taller are used in borders.

Although bearded iris are grown primarily for their flowers, at least one species is grown for its foliage. *Iris pallida* 'Variegata' has grey-green leaves boldly margined in white, while 'Aureo-variegata' is edged in yellow. Their contrasting flowers are soft periwinkle blue.

Bearded iris prefer full sun and require well-drained soil. Ideally, their rhizomes should be at ground level, not buried. Plants benefit from being divided every four to five years, usually done four to six weeks after flowering. Once established, they can tolerate short periods of drought. They have reasonable salt tolerance and are popular in coastal gardens. The blossoms make attractive, long-lasting cut flowers. In humid, wetter areas of Atlantic Canada, they are prone to leaf botrytis, which can lead to brown spots and lesions and an overall tattering of leaves. Iris borer burrowing into the rhizomes can also be problematic. Large herbivores ignore them. Propagation is by division. These are hardy to zone 3.

Iris

SIBERIAN IRIS, JAPANESE IRIS, BEARDLESS IRIS

This group of iris is distinguished by the falls, which lack any hairs at their base. Broadly, they fall into two major groups: the Siberians, *I. siberica* cultivars, and the Japanese, *I. ensata* cultivars. Both have long, narrow, sword-shaped leaves and the plants form large grasslike clumps. The flowers of Siberian iris are smaller than those of the bearded iris and bloom several weeks later. Japanese iris flowers are larger than those of Siberian iris, flat in appearance, and the last iris to bloom, often into late July or even early August. The many cultivars among both groups are available in a wide range of colours. Both reach 90 to 120 centimetres tall. All iris are lovely as

NEXT PAGE: *Iris siberica* collection

Iris ensata 'Peacock Dance'

in shallow water. Ideal for a border, they are also popular near water features. These beardless iris are not affected by botrytis, which can devastate the bearded iris in Atlantic Canada. Iris borer is not as much a problem either, as these iris have smaller rhizomes. They are ignored by large herbivores. The Siberian and the native species are hardy to zone 2, while the Japanese species are rated for zone 4.

cut flowers. For a wonderful foliage effect, try *I. ensata* 'Variegata', which has white-margined leaves and rich purple flowers. The black Siberian iris called *I. chrysographes* 'Black Form' or 'Black Gold' is smaller than the above beardless types, reaching 50 to 60 centimetres in height; its flowers are nearly black.

Also among the beardless iris is the native blue flag iris, *I. versicolor*, and the introduced yellow flag, *I. pseudacorus*. Both are commonly found near or in shallow water but may be grown in regular garden soil if kept reasonably moist. The variegated version of yellow flag is particularly attractive and makes a bold statement in the garden. For a rock or coastal garden, try the native *I. hookeri*, sometimes sold as Arctic iris, *I. setosa* var. *arctica*. This species prefers acidic, peaty soil and is natively found where it can be kissed by the sea. It reaches 30 centimetres in height and has porcelain blue flowers in June.

The beardless iris prefer full sun and require organically rich soil that does not dry out. Japanese and blue flag iris may even grow submerged

Kirengeshoma
YELLOW WAXBELLS

The two species of *Kirengeshoma* are native to eastern Asia. The genus name comes from the Japanese name for the plant: *ki*, yellow, *renge*, lotus blossom, and *shoma*, hat, all referring to the plant's blossoms. The most common species is yellow waxbells, *K. palmata*. This woodland plant is valued as much for its leaves as its unusual late-blooming flowers. It is not regularly found in Atlantic Canadian nurseries, but spe-

Kirengeshoma palmata

cialty nurseries often offer it. It is a bushy plant with many unbranched stems that may reach 120 centimetres in height. Its paired leaves are coarsely toothed and maple-leaf-shaped, reaching 20 centimetres wide. In September and October, plants produce terminal clusters of nodding bell-like, 5-centimetre-long, yellow flowers that have thick, waxy petals. The flower shape is reminiscent of a badminton shuttlecock. It is an ideal plant for woodland gardens or shady borders but, despite its height, it should be placed closer to the front of a border so that its leaves and exotic flowers can be appreciated. It is an invaluable plant for extending the blooming season. Korean waxbells, *K. koreana*, is similar.

Yellow waxbells prefers part shade but can tolerate full sun if the soil is evenly moist. The soil should be organically rich, well drained, and acidic. It will not tolerate dry soil. Diseases are not a problem nor is it bothered by pests, with the possible exception of slugs and snails. Propagation is by seed or, more commonly, division. It is hardy to zone 5.

Kniphofia
RED HOT POKER

Not many garden ornamentals of African origin are grown in Atlantic Canada; the red hot poker is a notable exception. Many of the 72 known species are native to South Africa and neighbouring countries. Most are not hardy in Atlantic Canada but a few may be grown in sheltered areas in zones 5 to 6. The genus is named after Johann Kniphof, an 18th-century German physician and botanist. *Kniphofia* produce a clump of straplike, folded leaves reminiscent of an ornamental grass. In July to September, it produces leafless stems up to 120 centimetres in length, topped with a dense, pokerlike spike of yellow to orange tubular flowers which are magnets for

Kniphofia uvularia

hummingbirds. In Atlantic Canada, *K. uvularia* and its hybrids are most often seen. 'Royal Castle', deep orange and yellow, is the most common cultivar, but others worth trying include 'Bressingham Comet', 'Echo Mango', and 'Flamenco'.

Kniphofia need full sun and, despite looking succulent, perform best in moist, well-drained, humus-rich soil. Once established, it is reasonably drought-tolerant. It is also salt-tolerant and suitable for coastal gardens. As the crown should be dry in the winter, tie the leaves together in late fall to form a canopy over it. Plants may be used in a mid-border but, being too tender for many regions of Atlantic Canada, they seem to grow best adjacent to the south-facing side of a house, which provides shelter and reflected heat. Hummingbirds love their flowers. Pests, both large and small, as well as diseases, are rarely a problem. As it is most reliable in zone 6, the suitable growing areas in Atlantic Canada are restricted. If grown in a sheltered site, *Kniphofia* can survive in zone 5.

Lamium
DEAD-NETTLE

Close to 30 species of *Lamium* are found throughout Eurasia and north Africa, but the majority are weedy. In fact, several of these weedy species are found throughout disturbed areas in Atlantic Canada: henbit, *L. amplexicaule*, and purple dead-nettle, *L. purpureum*. In the garden, yellow archangel, *L. galeobdolon*, formerly known as *Lamiastrum galeobdolon*, and spotted deadnettle, *L. maculatum*, are both grown primarily for their decorative foliage. Yellow archangel has paired, heart-shaped leaves that are spotted and streaked with silver markings. In June, plants produce a spike of yellow, helmet-shaped flowers on 30-centimetre-tall stems. As this plant is aggressive, even invasive, use with caution. It works, however, as a ground cover in sun or shade. It is also popular in hanging baskets, where it is treated as an annual. The cultivar 'Hermann's Pride' has narrow, small leaves, bold silver spotting, and a clumping habit.

Spotted dead-nettle is less invasive but can still self-seed. It forms a low clump up to 20 centimetres tall, producing dense spikes of white, pink, or purple-red flowers in June, with scattered flowers through the rest of the summer. Although it may be grown as a ground cover, it is not as dense as yellow archangel. It is more commonly used along the front of a border or in a rock garden. Many cultivars of spotted dead-nettle are available; most are selected for their attractive foliage. Those with leaves that have a silver central stripe include 'Chequers' (purple flowers) and 'Shell Pink' (light pink flowers). 'White Nancy' (white flowers), 'Pink Pewter' (light pink flowers), 'Orchid Frost' (rose pink flowers), 'Beacon Silver' (deep pink flowers), 'Red Nancy' (purple-red flowers), and 'Purple Dragon' (magenta flowers) have all-silver leaves. For yellow foliage, try 'Aureum' (all-yellow) or 'Lemon Frost' (yellow with

Lamium maculatum 'Chequers'

a central silver stripe). Both have bright pink flowers. Perhaps the most striking are 'Golden Anniversary' and 'Anne Greenaway': both have tricolored leaves of yellow, green, and silver, with magenta-pink flowers.

Lamium prefer rich, moist but well-drained, acidic soil. Yellow archangel is reasonably drought-tolerant once established, but spotted dead-nettle needs regular moisture. Both are ideal for shade to part shade. In cooler coastal regions they may be grown in full sun but in hotter, inland areas leaves may scorch under sunny conditions. Spotted dead-nettle may not survive if the winters are too wet. Pests and diseases are rare. The pungent foliage makes them unpalatable to large herbivores. Propagation is by seed, cuttings, or division. They are rated hardy to zone 3.

Leucanthemum

SHASTA DAISY

At one time included under *Chrysanthemum*, many of the "white daisies" have now been moved to the genus *Leucanthemum*. Their position may well change again as plant taxonomists debate the various daisies. As of 2018, there are about 40 species in the genus, all native to Europe. Most gardeners are not too concerned about the taxonomy—they are simply Shasta daisies. The garden Shasta daisy grown in Atlantic Canada is a hybrid, with several species in the mix. The hybrid *Leucanthemum* X *superbum* was developed by Luther Burbank in the 1890s near snow-covered Mt. Shasta in northern California. Shasta daisy is a clumper with many unbranched stems terminating in a single large white daisy. The blooming season is generally July to September. Older cultivars reached 100 centimetres in height and were often floppy, but many of the newer ones are more compact. It is popular for the middle to back of a border. They may also be used in wildflower settings.

The over 40 cultivars of Shasta daisy available vary in height, petal shape, and petal number and range from single to fully double flower heads. 'Becky', 'Polaris', and 'Alaska' are among the more popular single-flowered tall types reaching 100 centimetres. 'Becky' was awarded Perennial Plant of the Year™ in 2003. 'Snow Lady', 'Silver Princess', and 'Snowcap' are the most compact, with single flowers on 30-centimetre-tall stems. 'Snowdrift' is semi-double with 70-centimetre-tall stems, while 'Paladin' is more compact with 50-centimetre-tall stems. 'Real Galaxy' has semi-double flowers with narrow petals on 50-centimetre-tall stems, while 'Freak!' has semi-double flowers with curly petals on 35-centimetre-tall stems. 'Crazy Daisy' is striking with fully double, shaggy flowers on 70-centimetre-tall plants.

Plant breeders have created yellow cultivars: 'Banana Cream', one of the first, with single

Leucanthemum X *superbum* 'Banana Cream'

Leucanthemum X *superbum* 'Gold Rush'

flowers; 'Real Dream', semi-double; 'Goldfinch' and 'Real Charmer', semi-double with shaggy flowers. All these reach about 50 centimetres in height. 'Goldrush' and 'Real Glory' have a wonderful bicoloured effect, with larger white outer petals and smaller yellow inner petals.

Shasta daisy prefer full sun and need a well-drained site, especially in winter. These daisies are wonderful plants for bees and butterflies and make excellent cut flowers. Consider a hard cutting back after blooming to keep the plants tidy. They benefit from being divided every three to four years. Shasta daisy are generally care-free, with few pests or diseases. Propagation may be by seed or, more often, division. The white Shasta daisy are considered hardy to zone 4; the yellow cultivars, to zone 5.

Liatris
BLAZING STAR, SPIKED GAYFEATHER

The genus *Liatris* is exclusive to North America, where there are about 40 species. As a group plants are have narrow straplike leaves and

Liatris spicata

terminal spikes of rosy purple bottlebrush-like flowers from late July to September. *Liatris*'s flowers open at the top of the spike, then bloom downward as time passes. Many species are tall and generally only suitable in a wildflower setting. One species, *L. spicata*, commonly called blazing star, is naturally more compact, making it ideal for a standard garden setting. It is native to eastern North America, where it typically grows in moist meadows. In the wild, plants can reach 2 metres in height but 100 centimetres is more typical. The plant has a cormlike root and is often sold as a dormant root in boxes or bags in the spring. The most popular cultivar, 'Kobold', is relatively compact, reaching about 75 centimetres in height. 'Floristan Violet' and 'Floristan White' reach 90 centimetres in height.

Blazing star, a sun-lover, prefers fertile, moist,

well-drained soil. It can tolerate poor soils and some drought but prefers more summer moisture than other *Liatris* species; however, it is intolerant of excessive winter wetness. It is suitable for a mid-border or a wildflower garden. *Liatris* is a pollinator plant, attracting bees, butterflies, and hummingbirds. It is also an ideal long-lasting cut flower. Pests and diseases are rare, and it is not generally bothered by hares, deer, or moose. It is hardy to zone 3.

Ligularia
RAYFLOWER

Most of the nearly 150 species of *Ligularia* are found in Asia. Despite the species diversity, only a few are grown as garden ornamentals. As a group, these bold plants with large leaves fall into two groups—those with narrow spires of small yellow daisylike flowers and those with larger flat-topped clusters of orange-yellow flowers. The former includes *L. przewalskii* and *L. stenocephala* and cultivars among them; the latter, cultivars of *L. dentata*. All bloom in July and August.

Among the first of the spire types to be introduced was *L. stenocephala* 'The Rocket', which has large, serrated, heart-shaped leaves with long flower spikes on stems up to 2 metres tall. 'Little Rocket' is a half-sized version, reaching 90 centimetres tall, while 'Bottle Rocket' is smaller again, reaching 80 centimetres. The species *L. przewalskii* resembles 'The Rocket' but has deeply serrated leaves, especially the cultivar 'Dragon Wings'. 'Dragon's Breath' is smaller, reaching 75 centimetres. If you can find them, the species *L. siberica*, *L. wilsoniana*, and *L. fischeri* are also desirable spire types.

Ligularia dentata has large rounded leaves held at the ends of long stems. Their golden orange flowers, on flat-topped clusters, are up to 9 cen-timetres wide and held on stems up to 100 centimetres long. The cultivar 'Desdemona' has slightly purple-tinted leaves. 'Othello' has deeper purple leaves, while 'Britt-Marie Crawford' and 'Midnight Lady' have dark purple foliage. 'Osiris Fantaisie' and 'Osiris Café Noir' both have a dwarf 65-centimetre-tall habit. The former has purple-tinted foliage, the latter is darker purple.

Rayflowers do best in moist, organically rich, acidic soil in full sun to part shade. They are one of the quickest perennials to wilt if they get too dry. Their large size makes them ideal for the back of a border. They are also attractive around water features. The flowers are long-lasting cut flowers and are excellent nectar and/or pollen sources for bees and butterflies. Although diseases are rare, slugs and snails can severely damage their foliage. Large herbivores generally ignore them. Propagation may be by seed or, more often, division. They are rated hardy to zone 3.

Ligularia dentata 'Desdemona'

Lilium

LILY

For some gardeners, lilies are the main focus of their gardens. For hundreds of years, lilies have captured the admiration of gardeners, and that is not likely to change. Thousands of hybrids have been developed from the over 100 lily species that occur throughout the northern hemisphere. As a group, they are bulbs from which arise unbranched stems topped with several six-petalled flowers. The blooming season ranges from June to October; flower colours include every colour except blue. With such diversity, it is not surprising that lilies have been divided into different groups: Asiatic hybrids, Martagon hybrids (the Turks-caps), Candidum hybrids, American hybrids, Longiflorum hybrids (Easter lily), Trumpet hybrids, Oriental hybrids, other hybrids, and the original species. Within each group, the flowers may be upward-facing, outward-facing, or reflexed.

Longiflorum hybrids are generally not hardy in Atlantic Canada. Candidum and American hybrids are not readily available but may be sought out by the avid lily collector. As the lily species are often more challenging to grow than the hybrids, few of them are grown in Atlantic Canada. Exceptions are *Lilium martagon*, which has fragrant, purple-pink reflexed flowers in June and July, and the tiger lily, *L. lancifolium*, with orange reflexed flowers in August and September. Both are heritage plants in Atlantic Canada. *Lilium pyrenaicum* is also easy to grow, producing yellow reflexed flowers in June with a delicious citrus fragrance. For the majority of local gardeners, the hybrids garner all the attention: the Asiatics, Orientals, Trumpets, and, more recently, the Orientpets (hybrids of Orientals and Trumpets).

Asiatic lilies are perhaps the easiest to grow and certainly the quickest to multiply into large clumps. They are available in a rainbow of co-

Lilium martagon

lours. Most have upward-facing flowers but a few may be outward-fcing or even reflexed from the influence of *L. lancifolium* genes. The Asiatics generally lack fragrance and are the earliest to bloom of the hybrids, starting in June and throughout July to early August. The Trumpet hybrids are the most finicky. They are slow to multiply, with less colour variation, but they do have a strong fragrance. As the flowers are large and heavy atop tall stems, the plants often benefit from being staked. They bloom in July or August. The Orientals generally have large,

Lilium 'Black Spider'

flat, platelike blooms and are extremely fragrant. Most face outward, but some may be upward or reflexed. The colour range is restricted to white, and pink shades to nearly red and yellow. These are slow to multiply and among the latest to bloom, from August into October.

The recent Orientpet hybrids deserve special attention. They have the best qualities of both the Orientals and the Trumpets. Although they are slow to increase, they are generally easier to grow than the Trumpets. As their huge, highly fragrant flowers are on stiff stems, they rarely need staking. These hybrids include the so-called tree-lily, which can reach 2 or more metres in height. The flower range is nearly as diverse as the Asiatics, including many bicoloured types. They may be pricier than other lilies but are well worth the expense.

Lilies prefer full sun but can tolerate part shade. Well-drained soil is needed or they will rot, especially in winter. However, they are not drought-tolerant. They are best placed in a mid-border but taller lilies are suitable for the back of a border; dwarf Asiatic hybrids, such as the 45-centimetre-tall or shorter Pixie series, for the front of a border. Lilies are attractive cut flowers. Unfortunately, they are prone to a few pests and diseases; botrytis can cause brown lesions on the leaves and bud-drop. Aphids can be problematic, and, more recently, lily leaf beetles have invaded Atlantic Canada, leading to the outright death of Asiatic lilies in particular. Hares, deer, and moose will eat all lilies if given the opportunity. Propagation is primarily through division. As most are hardy to zone 2, they may be grown throughout much of Atlantic Canada.

Limonium latifolium

Limonium
SEA LAVENDER, PERENNIAL STATICE

Only one of the about 120 species of *Limonium* is native to Atlantic Canada: *L. carolinianum*, which grows along muddy or sandy seashores, is not easy to grow in the garden. More amenable to cultivation, *L. latifolium* (also known as *L. platyphyllum*), commonly called German sea lavender, forms a mound of relatively large, leathery, evergreen basal leaves. In August and September, plants produce large airy sprays of tiny pale lavender-blue flowers that arise on stems to 75 centimetres. The overall effect is similar to baby's breath. A late bloomer, this plant extends the flowering season in a garden. With its stout taproot, it is nearly impossible to transplant once mature; it is best to start with a young plant. It may be used in a mid-border.

Sea lavender needs full sun and a well-drained site, and it is drought- and salt-tolerant. As the common name suggests, it is ideal for a coastal garden. Butterflies are attracted to sea lavender flowers. The floral sprays are suitable as cut flowers, either fresh or dried. Propagation is by seed, which can be slow, as the plants are slow to mature. This plant is overall care-free and hardy to zone 2.

Lobelia
LOBELIA, CARDINAL FLOWER

Over 400 species of *Lobelia* are found worldwide. The genus name honours Matthias de l'Obel (1528–1616), a French physician and botanist. Two species of perennials are grown in Atlantic Canada as garden ornamentals. Perhaps the more popular of the two is cardinal flower, *L. cardinalis*, a species native from New Brunswick west to Ontario and south through the eastern US. This plant has upright unbranched stems up to 120 centimetres in height, topped with a spike of bright red flowers. It is generally short-

Lobelia cardinalis

lived but will often self-seed. Cultivars such as 'Fried Green Tomatoes' are longer lived than the wild species. 'Black Truffle' and 'Queen Victoria' have dark purple foliage. The great blue lobelia, *L. siphilitica*, has a similar habit to that of cardinal flower but is longer lived and reaches a height of 90 centimetres, with spikes of blue flowers, or white in the cultivar 'Alba'. The hybrid between great blue lobelia and cardinal flower is called *L.* X *speciosa*; its cultivars come in shades of red, purple, and blue, often with bronze-tinted foliage. The perennial lobelia are best used in wildflower settings or along water features.

Perennial lobelia all require consistently moist soil in sun or part shade and do not tolerate drought. They attract hummingbirds and butterflies. Diseases are not generally a concern, but slugs can be troublesome and large herbivores may occasionally browse the plants, which are poisonous if ingested by humans. Propagation is most often by seed but large clumps of great blue lobelia may be divided. The species listed above are rated hardy to zone 4, but the hybrid is more suitable for zone 5 or higher.

Lunaria
SILVER DOLLAR, HONESTY

All four species of *Lunaria* are native to Europe. The Latin name means moonlike, a reference to its round silvery seed pods. Most familiar to Atlantic gardeners is the biennial silver dollar, also known as honesty, *L. annua*. In the first season, plants produce a rosette of coarsely toothed triangular leaves; in the second, they shoot up to 90 centimetres and produce spikes of purple-mauve four-petalled flowers throughout June. By late summer, the flowers become the silver dollar common in dried-flower arrangements. Less well known but also desirable is the perennial

Lunaria annua

honesty, *L. perennis*. Its leaves and flowers resemble those of its biennial cousin but the plants are dependably perennial and, in time, form large clumps, similar to those of garden phlox. Honesty also blooms in June and produces silver dollars, but its seed pods are teardrop-shaped.

Lunaria may be grown in full sun or part shade, with evenly moist, well-drained soil. As silver dollar self-seeds with abandon, it is best used in a wildflower setting. As a perennial, honesty does not have this habit; it can be used in a mid-border. Silver dollar is propagated by seed, while honesty is most commonly propagated by division. Blossoms are visited by butterflies and hummingbirds. Pests, either insect or mammal, are generally not a problem. The only disease of concern is leaf spot, possible if plants are grown in a sheltered site. *Lunaria* are hardy to zone 5.

Lupinus polyphyllus

Lupinus
LUPINE

Perhaps no plant is as well recognized in Atlantic Canada as the lupine. A common wildflower along roadsides, lupine is so ubiquitous that people think of them as native. In fact, lupine are primarily garden escapes from a species native to western North America. The genus *Lupinus*, with some 200 species, is found throughout the Americas and Eurasia, but the greatest diversity is in the Americas. All produce a spike of pea-like flowers, most commonly in blue, and have palmately compound leaves with seven or more narrow leaflets. Despite the many species, Atlantic Canadian gardeners most often grow *L. polyphyllus* and hybrids developed from it. The most common cultivars reach 100 to 120 centimetres in height. While purple-blue is the colour of wild lupine, today's hybrids come in white and

shades of pink, red, purple, blue, and even yellow. Many are bicoloured. The most common hybrids are the Russell Hybrids, which date to the early 1900s. More recent hybrids include the Tutti Frutti™ and Woodfield series at about 100 centimetres in height; Westcountry™ hybrids, 85 centimetres; and the Gallery and Popsicle series, 60 centimetres. The above lupines generally flower from mid-June to late July.

Lupine are naturally short-lived, but red and especially yellow hybrids are often even shorter lived as they have more tender species in their genetic backgrounds. Because of its taproots, lupines do not transplant easily; it is best to start with young plants. Use lupines in a middle border or in wildflower or coastal gardens. Plants self-seed prolifically; deadhead promptly to avoid unwanted seedlings. Garden hybrids, grown from their own seeds, often revert to purple-blue flowers.

Lupines are sun-lovers and tolerant of poor, rocky soils, which is why they do so well by roadsides. They do not thrive in droughty conditions. The flowers are magnets for bumblebees and hummingbirds. Aphids are the main pest and, in areas of poor air circulation, powdery mildew can be troublesome. Lupines, toxic to hares, deer, and moose, are avoided by them. Propagation is by seed. They are hardy to zone 3.

Lychnis
MALTESE-CROSS, CAMPION, CATCHFLY

Not many orange-flowered perennials are grown in Atlantic Canada, but Maltese-cross is a well-known exception. In fact, it has been grown in this region for so long that it is considered a heritage plant. This native of Eastern Europe is a medium to tall perennial producing clumps of unbranched stems which may reach 90 to 120 centimetres in height. The stems end in a dense rounded head of scarlet-orange flowers in July and August. Individual flowers have five deeply notched petals. It is best positioned near the back of a border. Cultivars include 'Alba', with white flowers; 'Rosea', pink; and 'Carnea', light peachy pink.

Less well known are the orange and red catchfly species from Asia: *L. cognata*, *L. fulgens*, and *L. sieboldii*, shorter plants than Maltese-cross, reaching just 30 to 45 centimetres, with smaller flower heads. Individual flowers are 3.5 to 5 centimetres in diameter. More likely to be found are hybrids *L. X haageana* and *L. X arkrightii*. Many popular cultivars from these hybrids have purple-tinted foliage, which contrasts dramatically with their fiery orange blossoms: 'Molten Lava', 'Lengai Red', 'Vesuvius', and 'Orange Zwerg'

Lychnis flos-jovis 'Nana'

('Orange Gnome') are recommended. If regularly deadheaded, these flowers bloom from July to September.

Many of the pink-flowered *Lychnis* species, such as rose campion, ragged robin, and German catchfly, have been reclassified as *Silene*, but as they are so well known under their previous name, they are included here. The red campion, *L. dioicus*, a heritage plant in Atlantic Canada, may occasionally be seen naturalized along roadsides or other disturbed areas. It is a short-lived plant but maintains itself by seeding around. From late June through August, plants produce loose sprays of 2.5-centimetre-diameter deep pink flowers on stems which are 30 to 80 centimetres tall. Each flower has five deeply notched petals. 'Alba' is a white-flowered version. Difficult to find but well worth having for their striking white-edged variegated leaves are cultivars 'Clifford Moor' and 'Valley High'.

Rose campion, *L. coronaria*, among the most striking campions, is a short-lived perennial, probably best grown as a biennial. It may be grown solely for its showy clump of silver-white woolly leaves, although the plants produce loose clusters of 2.5-centimetre-diameter magenta-pink flowers on 60- to 80-centimetre-tall stems in July and August. 'Alba' is a white-flowered cultivar, 'Angel's Blush' has white flowers with pink centres, and 'Gardener's World' has velvety red flowers. Cutting the stems back to ground level after the plant blooms ensures that the basal leaves remain attractive into the fall. It usually self-seeds if some seeds are left to mature.

The flower-of-Jove, *L. flos-jovis*, a dwarf version of the rose campion, also has beautiful silver woolly leaves and loose clusters of pink flowers in July. It is also short-lived and usually self-seeds. 'Peggy' reaches just 30 centimetres.

LEFT: *Lychnis chalcedonica* and *Trollius ledebourii*

Lychnis coronaria

Ragged robin, *L. flos-cuculi*, produces a rosette of shiny narrow leaves and loose sprays of pink flowers on 30- to 60-centimetre-long stems in June and July. Each flower has five petals with four deep clefts. An unusual feature of this plant, its sticky flower stems, which often trap flies, is the source of its other common name: catchfly. At home in a wildflower setting, it has naturalized in Atlantic Canada. The cultivar 'Jenny' has double flowers; 'Nana' is less than 30 centimetres high.

The German catchfly, *L. viscaria*, also has a basal rosette of smooth narrow leaves but its stiffly upright stems, 30 to 45 centimetres tall, produce a wandlike cluster of pink flowers in June and July. Its upper flower stems are also very sticky. 'Alba' has white flowers; 'Passion', also known as 'Splendens Plena', has double pink flowers.

The above campion prefer full sun and evenly moist but well-drained soil, especially in winter. Rose campion, flower-of-Jove, and the orange-flowered Asian species are particularly sensitive to excess wetness during winter. An exception is red campion, which can tolerate considerable shade and wet soil. All are ideal for a wildflower garden, while *L. flos-jovis* 'Peggy' and *L. flos-cuculi* 'Nana' are best in rock gardens. For a border, *L. coronaria* and *L. viscaria* are the best choices. All attract butterflies and hummingbirds. Pests and diseases are uncommon, although occasionally the plants may be attacked by leaf miners. Hares, deer, and moose rarely eat them. Propagation is by seed or division. The pink-flowered campions are hardy to zone 4; Maltese-cross, to zone 3; and the orange-flowered Asian species, rated for zone 5.

Lysimachia
LOOSESTRIFE

Nearly 200 species of *Lysimachia* are found across the northern hemisphere. The genus name honours King Lysimachus (661–281 B.C.), Macedonian king of Thrace. This group of plants should not be confused with the unrelated purple loose-strife, *Lythrum salicaria*, which is invasive in wetlands across North America. Most of the ornamental *Lysimachia* are garden thugs that quickly overpower more delicate neighbours; however, they make a splash of colour in a border if space allows. The garden loosestrifes vary from low ground covers to tall back-of-the-border clumpers. Yellow is the predominant flower colour but some have white flowers; a few loosestrifes are grown for their ornamental foliage.

The European garden loosestrife, *L. punctata*, is a heritage plant in Atlantic Canada. Its presence in the wild often indicates that a homestead was once in the area. It is a clumping plant with many unbranched stems reaching 100 centimetres in height. The stems are topped with a leafy spike of 2.5-centimetre-wide, cup-shaped, yellow flowers in July and August. Soft lance-shaped leaves are produced in whorls of three or four. 'Alexander' has white variegated leaves, tinted pink in spring; 'Golden Alexander' has yellow-edged leaves. Both are compact, reaching 60 centimetres in height, and less vigorous than the wild species.

Lysimachia punctata

Lysimachia clethroides

Perhaps the most elegant species of *Lysimachia* is the gooseneck loosestrife, *L. clethroides*, another vigorous spreader. Reaching 90 centimetres tall, the unbranched stems of this eastern Asia species end in a dense tapered spike of white star-shaped flowers during August and into September. These spikes, which form a distinctive arch above the foliage, are attractive to butterflies. It is a admirable cut flower.

Fringed loosestrife, *L. ciliata*, native to eastern North America, is also a thug and an abundant self-seeder, with stems reaching 90 centimetres tall. From July and into September it produces solitary or paired yellow flowers among the axils of the upper leaves. 'Firecracker' has burgundy-purple leaves in spring, which become purple-tinted in summer. The spring stems are often used in floral arrangements.

Creeping Jenny, *L. nummularia*, is a ground cover for sun or shade with trailing stems that root as they clamber over the soil surface. Throughout the summer, solitary, yellow, nearly stemless flowers are produced from the leaf axils. 'Aurea', a cultivar with yellow foliage, is popularly used in hanging baskets.

Loosestrife require full sun to part shade. The clumpers benefit from being divided every three to four years to keep them in check. They all prefer moist to wet soil and are suitable for damp depressions. With their robust habit, they are effective in wildflower gardens. Creeping Jenny, a viable lawn substitute, tolerates limited foot traffic. Pests and diseases are rare, although garden loosestrife may occasionally be attacked by moth caterpillars. Loosestrife are hardy through zone 4 or even into zone 3, if mulched in winter.

Macleaya
PLUME POPPY

The two species of plume poppy originate in China and Japan. The genus name honours Alexander Macleay (1767–1848), colonial secre-

Macleaya cordata

tary for New South Wales, Australia. The more common species is *M. cordata*, a bold clumping plant with unbranched stems reaching 2.5 metres in height. Plants have scallop-edged, grey-green leaves. In July and August the stems are topped with airy plumes of tiny petal-less flowers. *Macleaya microcarpa* 'Kelway's Coral Plume' has blue-tinted leaves and bronzy pale pink plumes. Although they are not well known, both species are well suited to the back of a border. Suggested companion plants include rayflower, bugbane, and elecampane.

Plume poppy grows in full sun to part shade and prefers sandy but consistently moist soil. If growing conditions are ideal, they quickly form large clumps. Although their tawny seed heads are attractive, prompt deadheading prevents self-seeding. Despite their height, plume poppy rarely require staking. Overall, they are a care-free plant. Propagation may be by seed or division. Both are rated hardy to zone 3.

Malva

MUSK MALLOW, MALLOW

Malva are native to the Old World. Many of the 25 *Malva* species are weedy and several are tropical; two species are often grown in Atlantic Canada. The European musk mallow, *M. moschata*, is a heritage plant and a naturalized species that grows along roadsides, in old fields, and in disturbed areas. Despite its being so common, many gardeners include this classic cottage-garden plant in their landscape designs. Although musk mallow is relatively short-lived, it self-seeds with abandon. It forms a bushy plant up to 80 centimetres tall. From July to September, plants produce satiny 3-centimetre-diameter flowers in white or pink. Each flower has five notched wedge-shaped petals. The leaves are round in outline but divided and feathery.

Malva alcea 'Fastigiata'

Less weedy is hollyhock mallow, *M. alcea* 'Fastigiata', which forms upright clumps that reach 100 centimetres tall. The flowers, produced in the upper leaf axils, are pink and up to 5 centimetres in diameter. Striped mallow, *M. sylvestris* 'Zebrinus', resembles a smaller-flowered hollyhock and reaches 120 centimetres in height. Its spikelike flowers are pale lavender with a contrasting dark purple-veined centre. This striking beauty is only hardy enough for the mildest coastal regions of Atlantic Canada. It is sometimes sold as an annual and worthwhile as such, since it has a long blooming season.

The mallows prefer full sun and well-drained soil. They can be reasonably drought-tolerant once established. Both European musk mallow and hollyhock mallow are ideal plants for cottage or wildflower gardens. Hollyhock mallow is tidy enough to be used in a mid-border. Both mallows are attractive to butterflies and unlikely to be bothered by large herbivores. The only serious insect pest is Japanese beetle. Powdery mildew may be a problem in some areas. Propagation is primarily by seed, as these taprooted plants are difficult to divide. Musk mallow is hardy to zone 3; hollyhock mallow, zone 4.

Meconopsis
HIMALAYAN BLUE POPPY, WELSH POPPY

With their unique sky-blue poppy blossoms, Himalayan blue poppies are an instant favourite whenever they are seen. Overall, they are challenging to grow, but gardeners in Atlantic Canada, particularly those along the coast, are among the lucky few in Canada to have a good chance of success. Himalayan blue poppies need cool summers and flag when temperatures rise above 25°C, especially when combined with high humidity.

About 40 species of *Meconopsis* exist, but *M. baileyi* (aka *M. betonicifolia*) is the best suited for Atlantic Canada's climate; it is also the longest-lived species. Most *Meconopsis* are biennials or monocarpic, meaning that they flower only once. Even *M. baileyi* can be monocarpic—unless you prevent its blooming the first time it tries. This may seem counter-intuitive, but if all the flowers are cut off during the first year it tries to bloom, the plant will become perennial.

Himalayan blue poppies come in shades of blue. 'Lingholm' is one of the best cultivars for its vibrant colour and longevity; other cultivars include 'Alba' (white) and 'Hensol Violet' (purple). Its flowers bloom in late June to early July

Meconopsis baileyi

on flower stems that arise 80 to 150 centimetres. Individual flowers are up to 8 centimetres in diameter.

Included within the genus is the Welsh poppy, often called *M. cambrica*. This European native is unlike the Asian forms, and many botanists now place Welsh poppy in the genus *Papaver*, the true poppies. Since they are still popularly known under their former name, they are included here. Welsh poppy looks much like Iceland poppy, forming a tuft of fernlike leaves from which flower stems arise to 50 centimetres. The flowers are

Meconopsis cambrica

5 to 7 centimetres in diameter, most commonly yellow, but orange and scarlet cultivars are available. If deadheaded, it will bloom from June to frost. Deadheading is advised as the plants can self-seed vigorously if given the chance. Welsh poppy are taprooted and difficult to transplant once established, but like dandelion, often regenerate from remaining pieces of roots.

Himalayan blue poppies need consistently moist, organically rich, acidic soil. In the coolest regions, they perform well in full sun but generally dappled shade is best. Welsh poppies tolerate poorer soil and some drought and simply go summer-dormant if conditions are too dry. It blooms best in full sun but still flowers in part shade. Pests and diseases are rare, and hares, deer, and moose ignore them. Propagation is by seed. Himalayan blue poppies are hardy to zone 3, Welsh poppies to zone 4.

Monarda
Beebalm

There are about 20 species of *Monarda*, all native to North America. The genus was named in honour of Spanish botanist Nicolás Monardes, whose 1574 book described plants of the New World. *Monarda didyma*, the scarlet beebalm or Oswego tea, native to eastern North America, is the species most often encountered in Atlantic Canadian gardens. This plant forms a clump of many unbranched stems that reach 30 to 120 centimetres in height, depending on the cultivar. The leaves are opposite, stems square, and the entire plant smells like bergamot orange, the flavour used in Earl Grey tea. Each stem is topped with a 9- to 12-centimetre-diameter head of tubular flowers in July and August. Plants found in the wild have red flowers, but hybrids come in white, pink, purple, and red shades. Cultivars

Monarda didyma 'Blue Stocking'

Monarda didyma 'Jacob Cline'

best suited for Atlantic Canada are 'Jacob Cline' (red, 120 centimetres tall), 'Violet Queen' (violet, 120 centimetres), 'Prairie Night' (dark purple, 120 centimetres), 'Blue Stocking' (violet purple, 100 centimetres), 'Cambridge Scarlet' (red, 75 centimetres), and 'Fireball' (dark red, 70 centimetres).

If your gardens are plagued by powdery mildew, try 'Gardenview Scarlet' (red, 120 centimetres), 'Marshall's Delight' (hot pink, 120 centimetres), 'Fire Marshall' (red, 85 centimetres), 'Grand Parade' (lavender purple, 60 centimetres), 'Grand Marshall' (purple, 50 centimetres), 'Grand Mum' (light pink, 45 centimetres), 'Petite Wonder' (soft pink, 30 centimetres), or 'Petite Delight' (hot pink, 30 centimetres).

A western prairie species, *M. fistulosa*, or wild bergamot, is sometimes seen but it prefers drier conditions than those experienced in Atlantic Canada. It has lavender flowers but the same distinctive fragrance as scarlet beebalm.

Scarlet beebalm prefers full sun and reasonably moist soil. It may be used toward the middle of a border or in a wildflower garden. It does not tolerate droughty soil. Wild bergamot, on the other hand, is drought-tolerant. Pests are few but it is often bothered by powdery mildew, except for the mildew-resistant cultivars noted above. Beebalms attract bees and hummingbirds and are wonderful cut flowers. Because of beebalm's fuzzy leaves and pungent smell, hares, deer, and moose do not find it particularly palatable. Propagation is by seed for wild bergamot but by division for scarlet beebalm. Scarlet beebalm is rated hardy to zone 3, wild bergamot to zone 2.

Nepeta
CATMINT

Nearly 250 species of *Nepeta* are found native in the Old World. Although some gardeners grow catnip, *N. cataria*, the most frequently grown ornamental in Atlantic Canada is *N.* X *faassenii*, a hybrid between *N. racemosa* and *N. subsessilis*. The numerous cultivars available vary in height from 20 to 75 centimetres. The leaves are small, grey-

Nepeta X *faassenii* 'Walker's Low'

green, and aromatic. Lavender-blue flowers are individually small but produced in numerous showy spikes from June to September. Shearing the plants after the first flush of blooms keeps them bushy and encourages continuous blooming. These plants are suitable for the front of a border, a rock garden, a cottage garden, a wall edge, or even in a herb garden.

'Six Hills Giant', one of the largest cultivars, reaches 75 centimetres in height. Despite its name, 'Walker's Low' also grows to 75 centimetres. It was named Perennial Plant of the Year™ in 2007. 'Joanna Reed' reaches 60 centimetres; 'Blue Wonder' and 'Dropmore', 45 centimetres; 'Select Blue', 35 centimetres; and 'Kit Cat', only 20 centimetres. Unfortunately, 'Kit Cat' is not as floriferous as many of the other cultivars. Others include 'Ice Blue', which is pale blue; 'Blue Whisper', pale lavender; 'Candy Cat', light violet; or 'Sweet Dreams', pink.

Catmint prefers full sun but will tolerate part shade, although flower production is curbed with less sun. It is drought-tolerant and survives in poor, rocky soils. The plants may rot in winter if the soil is too rich or too wet. Catmint attracts butterflies and bees and, to a lesser degree, the household cat. It is rarely bothered by any insects, diseases, or large herbivores. Propagation is by division or cuttings. All are rated hardy to zone 3.

Oenothera
SUNDROPS, EVENING PRIMROSE

The approximately 145 species of *Oenothera* are all native to the Americas. Although there is some variety in leaf shape and height, all have similar-shaped four-petalled flowers with an X-shaped stigma. Yellow is the most common flower colour, but they also come in white or pink. Most *Oenothera* species hail from dry climates, but several are native to Atlantic Canada. *O. biennis*, the common evening primrose, is biennial, forming a rosette the first year, then flowering, setting seed, and dying in the second. Similar in appearance and also native is *O. oakesiana* and *O. parviflora*. All three may be used in a wildflower garden. Small-flowered evening primrose, *O. perennis*, is a European species naturalized in Atlantic Canada. Although perennial, it has small flowers compared to most evening primrose, but it could be used in a wildflower garden.

Among the ornamental perennial species, the most common is probably sundrops, *O. fruticosa* (*O. tetragona*). Sundrops open in the day rather than in the evening. This clumping plant reaches 60 centimetres in height, with stems terminating in a cluster of 5-centimetre-diameter yellow flowers in June and July. Plants spread quickly and benefit from division every three to four years. 'Highlights' is a common cultivar; 'Summer Solstice' has bronze-tinted foliage; 'Fireworks' and 'Yellow River' are more compact, reaching only 45 centimetres. If you are a lover of variegated foliage, try 'Spring Gold' or 'Crown of Gold', both of which have white-edged leaves. Sundrops are suitable for the middle of a border, a wildflower garden, or a cottage garden.

Missouri sundrops, *O. fremontii* (aka *O. macrocarpa*), is a low-growing species with long, narrow, silvery green foliage and huge 7.5-centimetre-diameter yellow flowers from July to September. As it reaches only 30 centimetres and has trailing stems, it is best grown in a rock garden. 'Shimmer' is the most popular cultivar.

Hybrid sundrops 'Lemon Drop' and 'Cold Crick' form a compact clump with narrow

Oenothera tetragona

leaves, stems to 30 centimetres in length, and 2.5- to 3-centimetre-diameter yellow flowers in August and September. Heat-lovers, they are best grown in inland areas. Showy evening primrose, *O. speciosa*, has pink flowers throughout the summer; it is not reliably hardy and tends to be short-lived in Atlantic Canada.

Oenothera are sun-lovers but sundrops tolerate part shade. Both tolerate poor soil and prefer soil that is on the dry side. Good winter drainage is important. Overall, they are care-free plants. Propagation is by seed or division. Common sundrops are hardy to zone 3; Missouri sundrops, zone 4; and 'Lemon Drop', 'Cold Crick', and showy evening primrose, zone 5.

Omphalodes
NAVELWORT

Botanists do not agree on the number of *Omphalodes* species in existence; many have been reclassified in recent years. The two grown in Atlantic Canada are European natives. The most reliable navelwort, *O. verna*, one of the best ground cov-

ers, grows well in sun or shade and reaches 25 centimetres in height, producing heart-shaped leaves and numerous small sprays of forget-me-not-like flowers in May and June. 'Alba' is a white-flowered cultivar. Plants spread rapidly, making them one of the best for covering a large space in a short time. Do not plant navelwort close to other flowers—it can form a tidal wave. A pleasing effect, though, can be created by planting daffodils to naturalize among it.

Blue-eyed Mary, *O. cappadocica*, is similar in habit but slower to spread than navelwort. Its slightly narrower foliage has a glossy hue. Even more floriferous, it forms a sea of blue mostly in June. There are two cultivars: 'Cherry Ingram', violet blue; 'Starry Eyes', two-tone blue and white.

Both species prefer evenly moist, rich soil. The only likely pest is slugs, but these vigorous plants quickly recoup. Diseases are rare; hares, deer, and moose ignore them. Propagation is by division. *Omphalodes verna* is hardy to zone 5; because *O. cappodococa* is hardy to zone 6, it is only reliable in the mildest areas of Atlantic Canada.

Omphalodes verna

FAVOURITE PERENNIALS FOR ATLANTIC CANADA

Origanum
OREGANO

Only a handful of herbs are also considered suitable in a perennial flower garden. Oregano, *O. vulgare*, fits into this category, especially if you wish to attract pollinators. This plant forms a large clump with stiff, slightly woody stems 45 to 80 centimetres tall. The small, opposite leaves are rounded and intensely fragrant; hence, their popularity in cooking. In July and August, plants produce a terminal cluster of tiny pale mauve-pink flowers that attract bees and butterflies. Dried flower stems make wonderful additions to dried-flower arrangements. Oregano flowers should be deadheaded promptly as plants seed about if given the opportunity and may even become invasive. In addition to its use in a mid-border, oregano is suited to a wildflower garden, where its self-seeding may be more acceptable. Greek oregano is not as reliable in Atlantic Canada nor are its flowers as showy; however, it does not spread like wild oregano and its flavour makes it more desirable as a garden herb.

Origanum 'Kent Beauty'

Origanum vulgare

'Kent Beauty', perhaps the most ornamental oregano, forms a low trailing mound with blue-green foliage. From July to frost it bears drooping heads of hoplike flowers in a blend of pink, green, and cream. It may be grown in rock gardens or to cascade over a retaining wall.

Oregano, a sun-lover, requires well-drained soil. It is drought-tolerant and performs well in poor, gravelly soil. It does like alkaline soil, so lime should be applied regularly. Pests and disease are rare, and oregano's strong smell usually deters hares, deer, and moose. Propagation is by seed, cuttings, or division. Oregano is hardy to zone 4, but 'Kent Beauty' is reliable only to zone 6 (zone 5, if the site is very well drained) and only suitable for the mildest coastal areas of Atlantic Canada.

Pachysandra terminalis 'Silver Edge'

Pachysandra
SPURGE

Of the only five species of *Pachysandra*, four are native to Asia and one to southeastern North America. The name is derived from the Greek *pachys*, thick, and *andros*, male, which refers to the thick stamens. The most popular species is Japanese spurge, *P. terminalis*, grown as an evergreen ground cover in shady areas. Plants have leathery, toothed, oval leaves that are slightly glossy. Stems reach 20 centimetres in height and plants spread by underground rhizomes. Small terminal spikes of tiny white flowers are produced in May and June; although they are not very noticeable, they are wonderfully fragrant. 'Green Sheen' and 'Green Carpet' are popular cultivars. A variegated cultivar, 'Variegata' or 'Silver Edge', is less vigorous than the non-variegated green-leaved types. Fragrant pachysandra, *P. ax-*

illaris, is similar, but its tiny flowers are in clusters among the upper leaf axils.

The Allegheny spurge, *P. procumbens*, is the North American species. It is not as reliably evergreen as the other spurge and can look tattered in the spring. Its leaves are matte green but often purple-tinted with pale green veins when young. Its flowers are similar to those of Japanese spurge.

Pachysandra prefer organically rich, evenly moist soil but are surprisingly drought-tolerant once established. Dappled shade is best for all, but they also do well in shady conditions. Full sun often leads to bleached leaves. Pests and diseases are generally not a problem. Propagation is by division. Japanese spurge is the hardiest, zone 4 or even 3 if snow cover is reliable. Allegheny spurge is hardy only to zone 5; fragrant pachysandra, rated for zone 6, is suitable only for the mildest regions of southern Nova Scotia.

Paeonia lactiflora 'Sarah Bernhardt' (left) and 'Karl Rosenfield' (right)

Paeonia

PEONY

The genus *Paeonia* has 25 to 40 species, depending on which botanist you follow. The genus name comes from the Greek physician of the gods, *Paeon*, who was later turned into a flower by the Greek god Pluto. Most peony are native to Eurasia; two species are found in western North America. Peonies are a staple in many Atlantic Canadian gardens. Two species, *P. officinalis* and *P. lactiflora*, are, in fact, heritage plants in the region. The oldest cultivated peony was the European *P. officinalis*, a species once used as a medicinal plant. It forms a clump with coarse divided leaves and unbranched stems reaching about 60 centimetres in height. In June to early July, the stems terminate in a solitary, fragrant, cup-shaped, crimson flower that is up to 12 centimetres in diameter. Generally, either the double 'Rubra Plena' or the single-flowered pink 'Mollis' are seen in local gardens.

The most popular species is *P. lactiflora*, native to eastern and central Asia. This plant has been hybridized for over 100 years, with new cultivars still appearing. Generally, this species grows to 90 centimetres tall, with waxier foliage and larger flowers than other peony. It blooms about two to three weeks later than *P. officinalis*. Older hybrids were bred to have fully double pompomlike flowers; but as the stem often flops under the weight of the flowers, especially when exposed to wind and rain, staking is required. Newer cultivars have semi-double or even single flowers which do not require staking. The flower colours range from white, through pale yellow, coral, and shades of pink to deep red. The traditional cultivars, still popular, include the pink

Paeonia lactiflora 'Coral Charm'

TODD BOLAND

Paeonia officinalis 'Plena Rubra'

'Sarah Bernhardt', the white 'Festiva Maxima', the deep red 'Karl Rosenfield', and the raspberry red 'Felix Crousse'. A newer cultivar, with a brilliant coral-pink colour, is 'Pink Hawaiian Coral'. Popular free-standing cultivars have a single ring of wide petals with a central "fluff" of narrow white to yellow petals or stamens. Some recommendations: 'Bowl of Beauty' (pink with white centre), 'Gay Paree' (deep rose pink with white centre), 'Primevere' (pale pink with yellow centre), 'Red Magic' (red with yellow centre), and 'Moon of Nipon' (white with yellow centre). If space is limited, try the Patio series, which are compact with stronger stems reaching 50 to 70 centimetres tall. Cultivars are all named after famous European cities.

The Itoh peony are hybrids between tree peony (shrubs beyond the focus of this book) and herbaceous species. These have the wide colour range and matte green foliage of the tree peony, with a herbaceous habit. The stems are strong and the semi-double flowers are fragrant, over 15 centimetres in diameter, and bloom in July. Colours include white, yellow, apricot, coral, pink, red, and purple, many with two-tone effects. These are expensive to purchase but worth the investment.

Additional hardy herbaceous peony species are not easy to obtain. Look for *P. anomala*, *P. veitchii*, *P. daurica*, *P. obovata*, and *P. tenuifolia*. Peony are sun-lovers and require a deep, rich, fertile soil that stays reasonably moist. As they prefer alkaline soil, a yearly application of lime is beneficial. Use them in a mid-border or a cottage-garden setting. The blossoms make a good cut flower. Peony do not tolerate transplanting well and may take several years to resume blooming after being moved. Ideally, they should be planted with at least 5 centimetres of soil above the top of the root. Too much shade, or being planted too deep, reduces blooming. As these plants are mildly toxic, pests are rare. Although ants are attracted to their sticky buds, they do no damage. Among diseases, botrytis and blight may be problematic under high humidity and poor air circulation. Propagation of hybrids is by division; species may be grown from seed. Most are hardy to zone 3.

Papaver
POPPY

It is the rare person who does not recognize a poppy. Between 70 and 100 species are found in the northern hemisphere, many of which are annuals or not hardy enough to be grown in Atlantic Canada. Many are alpine in nature and essentially rock-garden plants. All typically have four to six satiny petals and exude a milky sap when cut. Perhaps the most well-known poppy species in Atlantic Canada is the Oriental poppy, *Papaver orientale*, which has been grown in the region long enough to be considered a heritage plant. This plant forms a large rosette of elongated, deeply lobed, almost fernlike foliage covered in stiff hairs. The naked flower stems arise to 75 centimetres and are topped by a solitary,

RIGHT: *Papaver nudicaule*

Papaver orientale

large, typically orange flower in June or July. The base of the petals typically has a large black spot. Many cultivars are available in white, shades of pink, purple, red, and orange, with single or fully double flowers. The plants have several drawbacks: the flowers flop in the rain and the plants go summer-dormant, leaving a gap in the garden. Plant a late-summer perennial such as yellow or purple coneflowers nearby to hide this gap. This poppy is taprooted and not easy to transplant once established. However, if moved, it often regenerates in the original location from remaining pieces of root.

The other poppies suitable for Atlantic Canada are mostly rock-garden plants or those used as edging. Iceland poppy, *P. nudicaule*, forms a tuft of matte light green leaves from which arise multitudes of naked flower stems 30 to 45 centimetres high, topped with flowers in white, shades of yellow, salmon, orange, or pink. If promptly deadheaded, it may bloom all season. Otherwise, the main flowering season is from late May through June. For a dwarf version of Iceland poppy, choose the alpine poppy, *P. alpinum*, which reaches only 20 centimetres. It flowers primarily from May into June. Both of these species are apt to be short-lived, lasting just two or three seasons, but if a few seed heads are left to ripen, they will self-seed.

Papaver alpinum

Less common, the Atlas or Moroccan poppy, *P. atlanticum*, produces a flat blue-green rosette of hairy leaves and stems up to 45 centimetres tall, topped with solitary single or semi-double orange flowers. It starts to bloom in June and, if deadheaded, blooms until frost. It self-seeds readily if given the chance.

Poppies are sun-lovers and require well-drained soil, especially in winter. Oriental poppy prefers organically rich soil that does not get droughty. The rock-garden types are tolerant of poor, rocky soil. The Atlas poppy is drought-resistant. All are essentially pest- and disease-free and not bothered by hares, deer, or moose. Propagation is primarily by seed. Iceland and alpine poppies are hardy to zone 2; Oriental poppies, zone 3; and Atlas poppy, zone 4.

Penstemon
BEARDTONGUE

Although there are some 250 species of *Penstemon*, primarily in North America, few are grown as ornamentals in Atlantic Canada. The genus name comes from the Greek words *penta*, five, and *stemon*, stamen, referring to each flower's having five stamens. Most *Penstemon* are found in dry regions of western North America; Atlantic Canada's winters are too wet for many of them, with the exception of those species native to eastern North America or the wet Pacific Northwest. Although some large-flowered *Penstemon* are available, many of which have been developed from *P. hartwegii*, these are essentially annual bedding plants or simply not reliably hardy. The hardy species generally have smaller flowers. One beardtongue available in Atlantic Canada is *P. digitalis*. This eastern North American species typically forms a clump of basal leaves and several stiffly upright stems 90 to 150 centimetres high topped with a loose cluster of white, two-lipped, tubular flowers in June or July. The most popular cultivar, 'Husker Red', has maroon foliage and pale pink flowers on 60- to 90-centimetre-tall stems; it won Perennial Plant of the Year™ in 1996. 'Husker Red Superior' has consistent dark foliage. 'Dark Towers' also has deep wine red foliage but shell pink flowers. Closely related to *P. digitalis*, *P. hirsutus* has dark green foliage and two-tone white and lavender flowers. 'Pygmaeus' reaches only 20 centimetres and is suitable for the front of a border or a rock garden.

Penstemon barbatus, another frequently seen beardtongue, is also clumping, with upright stems 60 to 90 centimetres tall topped, in this case, by a spike of one-sided, tubular, red flowers. The several cultivars, probably of hybrid origin, range from white, through shades of pink,

Penstemon digitalis 'Husker Red'

red, and purple-blue. This species, as well as *P. digitalis* and *P. hirsutus*, are short-lived but often reseed themselves. Choose for a mid-border and cottage or wildflower garden.

For the front of a border or in a rock garden, the Pacific Northwest evergreen sub-shrub species such as *P. fruticosus*, *P. cardwellii*, and *P. davidsonii* are long-lived perennials which bloom in June with relatively large tubular flowers in shades of pink or purple. The plants form spreading mats with flowers stems reaching 10 to 20 centimetres in height.

Beardtongue prefer full sun and need a well-drained soil. Excess winter wetness can kill the plant. The taller types are reasonably drought-tolerant, unlike the Pacific Northwest species, and are suitable for cut flowers. All beardtongue attract bees and hummingbirds. None are generally bothered by pests or diseases. Propagation is by seed or cuttings. The taller species noted above are hardy through zone 3; those from the Pacific Northwest, rated for zone 4.

Perovskia
RUSSIAN SAGE

Although Russian sage is not a true sage, it does have wonderfully fragrant foliage reminiscent of sage. The common species grown in Atlantic Canadian gardens, *Perovskia atriplicifolia*, is shrub-like but dies back to within a few inches of the ground each winter. It has a narrow habit, reaching 90 to 150 centimetres tall. The grey-green leaves are opposite, narrow, and finely dissected. The flowers are produced in numerous narrow spikes with pale lavender-blue, two-lipped flowers from August to October. This plant won Perennial Plant of the Year™ in 1995. Its airy habit makes it ideal for the back of a border or near a house foundation. It combines nicely with sea holly, sedum, and wormwood. Several cultivars

Perovskia atriplicifolia

of varying height are available: 'Filigran', 150 centimetres; 'Rocketman', 90 centimetres; 'Little Spire' and 'Peek-a-blue®', 75 centimetres; and 'Silvery Blue' and 'Lacey Blue', 50 centimetres.

Russian sage loves a sunny, hot, dry site. Excess winter wetness is an enemy. Cut plants back in the spring to within 15 centimetres of the ground as new growth will form at the base of the woody stems. The plant's pungent smell protects it from pests, and diseases are not a problem. Propagation is by cuttings. It is rated hardy to zone 4.

Persicaria

FLEECEFLOWER, BISTORT

Like several other plant genera, this group has gone through several name changes. In older literature, most of the plants listed here were included in the genus *Polygonum*, but it is now split into several new genera and many garden-worthy species have been moved to *Persicaria*. As a group, the ornamental species produce narrow spikes of tiny flowers, usually white through shades of pink. Several have attractive foliage. As most are robust plants, they are not suitable for small gardens. The height range depends on the species. Dwarf fleeceflower, *Polygonum affine*, has matted, narrow, leathery leaves that take on burgundy tones in autumn. It is an effective ground cover for either sunny or shady areas. Throughout the summer, it produces red to pink spikes on stems up to 20 centimetres tall. Similar, but with tiny leaves, is creeping fleeceflower, *Po-lygonum vaccinifolium*. At 10 centimetres in height, it is perhaps better used in a rock garden than as a ground cover. Pink bistort, *Persicaria bistorta* 'Superba', forms a spreading mound with narrow triangular leaves and many spikes of soft pink flowers on 75-centimetre-tall stems. It is also suitable as a ground cover or toward the middle of a border; because it is a rapid spreader, it can swamp timid neighbours.

Mountain fleeceflower, *Persicaria amplexicaulis*, has a bushy habit, forming spreading mounds 45 to 95 centimetres high. It has heart-shaped foliage and numerous narrow spikes from mid-summer through autumn. Popular cultivars include 'Orange Field' (salmon rose, 95 centimetres tall), 'Taurus' (crimson red, 75 centimetres), and 'Pink Elephant' (pink, 45 centimetres). For the back of a border try white or giant fleeceflower, *Persicaria polymorpha*, which is shrublike in appearance, forming a clump up to 120 centimetres tall. It

Polygonum vaccinifolium

Persicaria polymorpha

Petasites japonicus var. *giganteus*

is often used as a stand-alone plant due to its size. It has relatively large narrow leaves and numerous fluffy spikes of off-white flowers from late July to early September. Despite its size, it is well-behaved and less prone to spreading than many *Persicaria*. Grown for its foliage is tovara, *Persicaria virginiana* 'Painter's Palette', also a tidy shrublike plant reaching 120 centimetres or taller. Although it produces narrow deep pink spikes in September and October, its foliage is the selling feature: large rounded leaves irregularly splashed and spotted with white and a central pink V-shaped blotch. Because it is late to appear in spring, carefully mark the spot where it was planted.

Fleeceflower may be grown in sun or part shade. As most of the ornamental varieties prefer evenly moist soil, they are suitable for planting near water features. Wildflower gardens are another viable location, if the soil is not too dry. Fleeceflower are not generally bothered by any diseases or pests, large or small. Pink bistort, white fleeceflower, and dwarf fleeceflower are hardy through zone 3; mountain and creeping fleeceflower, to zone 4; tovara, the least hardy, to zone 5 or higher.

Petasites
BUTTERBUR

Seventeen species of *Petasites* are found across the northern hemisphere. The genus name, from the Greek *petasos*, a broad-brimmed hat, refers to the large leaves of most butterbur species. Only one species is commonly grown in Atlantic Canada, the Japanese butterbur, *P. japonicus*, primarily for its large, bold foliage, which may reach 75 centimetres in diameter, atop thick 100-centimetre-tall stems. The flowers are valued for their early bloom and unusual shape: they often emerge through late-lying snow in April and May and, at first, the flower bud looks like a pale green baseball, but it quickly elongates to 30 centimetres, producing a dense cluster of off-white flowers surrounded by leafy bracts. After the flowers start to set seed, the leaves emerge. 'Variegatus' has leaves variously streaked and blotched with white. Most impressive is *P. japonicus* var. *giganteus*. Its leaves, which may reach 120 centimetres in diameter, atop stems that are over 2 metres tall, offer a tropical effect. Japanese butterbur, however, is invasive; to keep it in check, grow the plant in a large tub that is sunken into the ground.

Japanese butterbur grows in part or full shade

but demands humus-rich and very moist, if not boggy, soil. It is best used in wet depressions or open woodlands or near a water feature. Diseases are not a problem and herbivores ignore it. However, slugs feast on the emerging leaves and what starts as a small slug hole can become a large gap as the leaves mature. Bees appreciate the early pollen and nectar supply of the flowers. Propagation is by division. This species is hardy to zone 5.

Phlox

CREEPING PHLOX, WOODLAND PHLOX, GARDEN PHLOX

Phlox, a genus exclusive to North America, with some 67 species, generally fall into one of three groups: creeping or moss phlox, woodland phlox, and border or summer phlox. Creeping phlox are mat-forming plants, with evergreen, needle-like foliage; in Atlantic Canada *P. subulata* and *P. douglasii* are the most common species. These phlox are ideal for rock gardens or for cascading over retaining walls. The flowers of *P. subulata* are on short stems; *P. douglasii*, nearly stemless. Both bloom from late May through June and are white, pink shades, red, and purple to nearly blue, most with contrasting darker "eyes". Suggested cultivars include 'Emerald Pink', 'Emerald Blue', 'Red Wings', 'Crackerjack' (bright red), 'Purple Beauty', 'Candy Stripe' (white and pink stripes), and 'Snowflake'. For showy foliage, try 'Nettleton Variation', which has white-edged leaves and bright pink flowers.

Of the two main woodland phlox, *Phlox stolonifera* produces leafy, creeping stems and rosettes. In June, loose clusters of fragrant lavender flowers emerge on 20- to 30-centimetre-tall stems. As the name suggests, 'Sherwood Purple' is a dark purple cultivar. *Phlox divaricata*, the other woodland phlox, has stems that reach 30 to 45 centimetres tall. Popular cultivars include 'Clouds of

Perfume' (powder blue), 'Blue Moon' (lavender blue), and 'May Breeze' (pale ice blue).

Not commonly available in Atlantic Canada is *Phlox* X *procumbens*, a hybrid between *P. subulata* and *P. stolonifera*, which forms an evergreen mat with small lance-shaped leaves and fragrant flowers on 15-centimetre-tall stems. 'Variegata' is a particularly attractive cultivar with white-edged leaves that take on pink tints during the winter. Becoming more readily available locally are crosses between *P. subulata* and *P. divaricata*— the Paparazzi™ series. These low growers, for woodlands or shady rockeries, have flower stems

Phlox subulata 'Oakington Blue Eyes'

TODD BOLAND

that reach 20 centimetres in height. They come in the standard *P. subulata* colours.

Summer phlox, *P. paniculata*, are among the most popular perennials in Atlantic Canada. This is not surprising: they have showy fragrant flowers. Older cultivars are now considered heritage plants. Today's border phlox have come a long way from their ancestors. The species and older cultivars often reached heights of 2 metres and had relatively small purple-pink to white flowers. Now there are 100 or more cultivars, some as short as 45 centimetres, with flowers twice as large as the wild forms and available in white, through shades of pink, purple, red, and orange. Bicolour cultivars are also available.

As a garden plant, phlox form clumps of many stiffly upright, unbranched stems that terminate in a rounded cluster of flowers from late July to early October. Many of the modern cultivars grow between 80 and 100 centimetres tall and are best used in a mid- to back border. Consider 'David' (white), 'Laura' (purple, white eye), 'Blue Boy' (medium blue), 'Franz Shubert' (pale pink), 'Starfire' (red), 'Bright Eyes' (pink, red eye), 'Nicky' (dark magenta), and 'Orange Perfection' (salmon orange). Many of these are prone to powdery mildew, except 'David', which is con-

---

Phlox paniculata 'Harlequin'

Phlox divaricata 'May Breeze'

sidered the most mildew-resistant of any *P. paniculata* cultivar. For this distinction it was awarded the 2002 Perennial Plant of the Year™.

For the smaller garden or for use near the front of a border, many dwarf cultivars that stay below 50 centimetres are available: 'Red Riding Hood' (red), 'Tequila Sunrise' (salmon pink), 'Peppermint Twist' (bicolour pink and white), 'Purple Kiss' (lavender blue, with a white eye), and 'Watermelon Punch' (deep pink, with a white eye). The Flame™ series all reach about 40 centimetres in height and are reasonably resistant to powdery mildew.

Summer phlox also have several cultivars with variegated foliage. These are attractive all season long, even more so when the flowers contrast with their foliage. Suggested cultivars include 'Harlequin' (white-edged leaves, magenta flowers), 'Goldmine' (bright yellow-edged leaves, reddish pink flowers), 'Becky Towe' (cream-yellow-edged leaves, rose pink flowers with a red eye), 'Shockwave' (cream-yellow-edged leaves, lavender-blue flowers), or 'Norah Leigh' (broad white edges and pale pink flowers with a red eye); all reach 75 to 90 centimetres tall.

Creeping or moss phlox need full sun and gritty, well-drained soil. They are drought-tolerant. Woodland phlox are better suited to part shade, with organically rich soil that stays evenly moist, but, once established, they can tolerate some drought. Summer phlox need full sun and evenly moist, organically rich soil; they do not tolerate drought conditions. They make admirable cut flowers. All phlox attract butterflies; the taller woodland types and summer phlox, hummingbirds. Woodland and summer phlox are susceptible to powdery mildew; adequate spacing and good air circulation helps alleviate this problem. The main insect pest is spittlebugs, which can cause the leaves to curl. Deer, moose, and hares generally ignore them. Propagation is by division for summer phlox or cuttings for woodland and creeping phlox. All the above phlox are hardy to zone 3, with the exception of *P. stolonifera*, *P.* X *procumbens*, and Paparazzi™, which are rated for zone 5.

Physalis
CHINESE LANTERN

Most of the 80 species of *Physalis* are tropical plants from Central and South America and are commonly referred to as ground cherries. A single species, Chinese lantern, *P. alkekengi*, native across Eurasia, is considered an ornamental as well as a heritage plant in Atlantic Canada. Plants form large colonies with many unbranched stems 40 to 90 centimetres tall. In July and August, it produces solitary, white, star-shaped flowers from the upper leaf axils. When pollinated, a green husk forms around the developing berry. In September and October, this husk turns orange and becomes the ornamental lantern. Once the husk turns orange, the stems may be used as a cut flower or dried. In the garden, the fall foliage is bright yellow. Too aggressive for use in a border, Chinese lantern should be grown in its own bed or in tubs or used in

Physalis alkekengi

Physalis alkekengi

relatively shiny. From August to October, plants produce 30- to 45-centimetre-long spikes of pink to pale lilac, narrow, snapdragon-like flowers. It is particularly valued for its late blooms, which help extend the garden into the fall. It is a favourite plant for hummingbirds and bees and makes suitable cut flowers. Cultivars worth considering include 'Bouquet Rose' (bright pink, 120 centimetres), 'Red Beauty' (lilac-pink, 90 centimetres), 'Miss Manners' (white, 90 centimetres), and 'Summer Snow' (white, 90 centimetres). Compact cultivars which reach only 50 centimetres include 'Crystal Peak White' and 'Vivid' (bright pink). For attractive foliage and flowers, try 'Variegata', which has white-edged leaves and lavender-pink flowers and reaches 90 centimetres in height.

Obedient plant prefers evenly moist soil that is acidic but not too organically rich; otherwise,

Physostegia virginiana

wildflower settings, where its invasive qualities are not a problem.

Chinese lantern prefer full sun and need evenly moist soil. Although they may tolerate some drought, husk production is reduced. Pests and diseases are rare, and its toxic foliage makes it unappealing to large herbivores. Propagation is by seed or division. It is very hardy, zone 2, and grows throughout much of Atlantic Canada.

Physostegia
OBEDIENT PLANT

This uncommon garden plant is worthwhile because it is a late bloomer. All 12 species are native to North America. A single species is grown in Atlantic Canada, *P. virginiana*, a native wildflower throughout much of the US. This narrow upright plant produces many unbranched stems that may reach 120 centimetres in height. The sharply toothed narrow leaves are paired and the plants may flop. Full sun is best, but plants perform well in part shade. It is ideal for a mid- to back border but can also be used in wildflower or cottage gardens. Overall, it is a care-free plant. Propagation is by seed or division. It is hardy through zone 3.

Platycodon
BALLOON FLOWER

The genus *Platycodon* has a single species, *P. grandiflorus*. This bellflower relative is native to eastern Asia. The genus name comes from the Greek *platys*, broad, and *codon*, bell. The plant forms a clump with several unbranched stems arising from a thick taproot. The wild form can reach 80 centimetres or taller, but many of the cultivars are shorter. The flowers are produced in loose clusters at the ends of the stems in August and September. The flower buds are large and look balloonlike immediately before they burst open to reveal the 5- to 8-centimetre-diameter, outward-facing, bell-shaped flowers. The colour of the wild forms is purple-blue, but modern cultivars may be pink, mauve, white, or white with blue veins. Recommended cultivars include the Fuji series, which are blue, pink, or white and reach 60 centimetres tall; the dwarf Astra series reach 25 centimetres in the same colour range. The smallest, 'Sentimental Blue', is only 20 centimetres tall. Double-flowered cultivars include 'Double Blue', which reaches 60 centimetres, and the dwarf version, 'Astra Double Blue', 25 centimetres. The taller forms are ideal for a

Platycodon grandiflorus and *Coreopsis verticillata*

Platycodon grandiflorus 'Roseus'

mid-border, but the dwarfs may be used both along the front of a border or in rock gardens.

Balloon flowers prefer full sun but tolerate part shade. They need even moisture and organically rich soil. As they are taprooted, they do not tolerate being transplanted; set them as young plants and leave them to improve each year. As balloon flowers are late to emerge in the spring, carefully mark the spot where it was planted. The blossoms make attractive cut flowers. Pests and diseases are rare. Propagation is by seed. Balloon flower is hardy to zone 3.

Podophyllum
MAYAPPLE

Of the nine *Podophyllum* species, one is native to North America, the rest to Asia. The name comes from the Latin *podos*, foot, and *phyllon*, leaf, referring to the footlike leaf shape of the American mayapple, *P. peltatum*. The American mayapple, native in southern Ontario, Quebec, and points farther south, is an attractive plant with parasol-like leaves. Each 30- to 45-centimetre-tall stem has either a single leaf or a pair of leaves. In May and June, plants produce a nodding white flower held under the paired leaves. This later develops into a yellow applelike fruit. This species should be used with care: it can run quickly, swamping its neighbours, and may go summer-dormant, leaving a bare patch in the garden. It is not suitable for a border, but it can be attractive in a woodland or wildflower setting.

Far more desirable are the Asian species. The most popular is the Himalayan mayapple, *P. hexandrum*. The best varieties have olive green leaves with brown mottling. A clumper, it stays tidy in the garden and it does not go summer-dormant. Its leaves are single or paired on each 50-centimetre-long stem. In May, it produces a single white to pink flower that sits atop the paired leaves. This later becomes a red, teardrop-shaped, tomato-like fruit. Very pricey but highly recommended for their unusual leaves in the shape of umbrella, starfish, or even

Podophyllum hexandrum

Dysosma pleiantha X *veitchii*

squares, are cultivars of *P. delavayi*, *P. versipelle*, and *P. pleianthum*. The leaves may be all-green or brown-spotted. 'Spotty Dotty', a clumper with either single or paired leaves on 30- to 50-centimetre-high stems, is particularly attractive. Its red flowers, in nodding clusters beneath the paired leaves, later develop into green fruit. Like Japanese wood poppy, *Glaucidium*, these plants are long-lived and improve with age. Combine them with ferns, hellebores, trillium, and astilbe for a sharp contrast in leaf shape.

Mayapple prefer part shade and evenly moist, organically rich soil. They are ideal under deciduous trees, where they can get some sun in the spring when actively growing and blooming, and find some shade in mid-summer. In a border, use the Chinese species near the front where their decorative leaves can be best appreciated. They are not bothered by diseases and the most likely pest is slugs feeding on the fresh spring growth. Propagation is by seed or, more commonly, division. American mayapple is hardy to zone 4; Himalayan, zone 5; and the remaining Chinese species, zone 6. If provided a good winter mulch, the Chinese species should survive in zone 5.

TODD BOLAND

Polemonium
JACOB'S-LADDER

The more than 30 species of *Polemonium* are native to the northern hemisphere. The most popular is *P. caeruleum*, also known as Jacob's-ladder, a European native that is a heritage plant in Atlantic Canada. This plant forms an upright clump with unbranched stems reaching 60 to 75 centimetres in height. The fernlike leaves are compound with small leaflets. The cobalt blue flowers, produced in open clusters, bloom in June or July. Prompt deadheading often results in a secondary blooming in late summer. There are two variegated cultivars: 'Brise d'Anjou' and 'Snow and Sapphires'. The Asian *P. yezoense* is similar to *P. caeruleum* but is only 45 to 60 centimetres tall. It has two cultivars with purple-tinted foliage: 'Bressingham Purple' and 'Purple Rain'. All the above are ideal for a mid-border.

Polemonium caeruleum

P. reptans, from eastern North America, reaches 30 to 40 centimetres in height. As it is more mounding in habit than the previous two species, it is more useful along the edge of a border or in a rock-garden setting. The cultivars most commonly grown, 'Stairway to Heaven' and 'Touch of Class', are both variegated.

The often short-lived *Polemonium* maintain their presence by self-seeding, making them suitable in a wildflower setting. Deadheading may extend their lifespan. If the variegated and purple-leaved cultivars are left to self-seed, keep only those seedlings that exhibit the decorative foliage; remove any that revert to all-green.

All the above *Polemonium* prefer evenly moist and organically rich soil. They perform well in full sun to part shade but tolerate considerable shade. Their moisture requirements make them useful in wet areas. Pests, both large and small, are rare and the only disease of concern is powdery mildew, if the site is too sheltered. Propagation is by seed or division. Hardiness ranges from zones 3 to 4.

Polemonium 'Brise D'Anjou'

Polygonatum multiflorum

Polygonatum
SOLOMON'S SEAL

Around 60 species of *Polygonatum* are found throughout the northern hemisphere, but most commonly in Asia. The genus name, from the Greek *poly*, many, and *gonu*, knee joint, refers to the jointed plant rhizomes. As a group, these flowers are small; plants are grown more often for their bright green foliage, which is distinctively ribbed and located on either side of arching stems, than for their flowers.

Two species, and the hybrid between them, are grown in Atlantic Canada. Solomon's seal, *P. multiflorum*, a European native, is nearly identical to, and often confused with, hybrid Solomon's seal, *P.* X *hybridum*. Usually what is grown in gardens as *P. multiflorum* is actually the hybrid. The hybrid, a heritage plant in Atlantic Canada, was a classic cottage-garden plant. Both *P. multiflorum* and *P.* X *hybridum* can reach 125 centimetres in height and produce 2-centimetre-long, bell-shaped, nodding white flowers with green tips in twos or threes from the upper leaf axils. They bloom in May and June and have a light fragrance. The common Solomon's seal produces blue-black berries, but the hybrid is sterile, never producing fruit.

This differentiates the two. Both have variegated versions, but they are difficult to obtain.

Originally from Asia, the fragrant Solomon's seal, *P. odoratum*, resembles *P. multiflorum* and *P. X hybridum* but is a smaller-stature plant, reaching about 60 centimetres. Its highly fragrant flowers are almost always in pairs. It also develops blue-black berries later in the season. The variegated cultivar, 'Variegatum', most often grown, was selected as Perennial Plant of the Year™ in 2013.

Solomon's seal prefer organically rich, evenly moist soil from full sun to dense shade. All spread by rhizomes and can form large colonies. Fragrant Solomon's seal is generally slower growing than the other two. Common and hybrid Solomon's seal are suitable for the back of a border; fragrant Solomon's seal is better in a mid-border. With their moisture requirements, all are ideal for wet areas, and their vigorous habit is suited to wildflower settings. All parts of the plant are toxic to humans. Pests and diseases are not a problem but deer and moose may be. The common and hybrid Solomon's seal are hardy to zone 2; the fragrant Solomon's seal, zone 3.

Polygonatum odoratum 'Variegatum'

Potentilla thurberi

Potentilla
CINQUEFOIL

Well over 300 species of *Potentilla* exist, some of which are native in Atlantic Canada; others have been naturalized in the region. Rock gardeners have a variety of options: there are many low, alpine types. Few are available to be used as herbaceous ornamentals for a perennial border. The main species grown is the Himalayan cinquefoil, *P. nepalensis*, a clumping plant with basal rosettes of evergreen strawberry-like leaves. Its wiry 45-centimetre-tall stems are topped in mid-summer with an open spray of 2.5-centimetre-diameter purple-red flowers. 'Miss Willmott', whose flowers are deep pink with a red eye, is the most widely available cultivar. Newer cultivars are 'Shogran', which is bright pink with a red eye, and the similar but more compact 'Ron McBeth'. With a similar habit to Himalayan cinquefoil's is scarlet cinquefoil, *P. thurberi*, listed sometimes as *P. sanquinea*. This American native is taller, reaching 70 centimetres. 'Monarch's Velvet' has particularly dark red flowers. Hybrids between the previous two are also available and form clumps up to 40 centimetres tall. These usually have semi-double blossoms. 'Volcan' is deep red; 'William Rollinson', two-tone orange and yellow;

Potentilla megalantha

and 'Arc-en-ciel', scarlet red. Overall, the above cinquefoils are similar in appearance to garden avens, *Geum*, which is not surprising, as they are related. These are all suitable toward the front of a border or in a cottage-garden setting.

As an edger or in a rock garden, there are three reasonably available cinquefoils to choose from. Spring cinquefoil, *P. neumanniana*, a low creeper that reaches only 15 centimetres tall, has numerous small yellow flowers in late spring. Woolly cinquefoil, *P. megalantha*, produces a clump of large, hairy, strawberry-like leaves and, in June, clusters of 3- to 4-centimetre-diameter, cup-shaped, yellow flowers emerge atop 25-centimetre-tall stems. *Potentilla* X *tonquei*, a hybrid with trailing stems, produces red-eyed apricot flowers throughout the summer.

The above cinquefoil thrive in full sun and well-drained soil. They can tolerate some drought, once established. The border types, which may be used as cut flowers, should be promptly deadheaded to extend their blooming season. Pests are not generally a problem, but the border types may occasionally be bothered by mildew. Propagation is by division or, in the case of spring and woolly cinquefoil, seed. All the above are hardy to zone 4, possibly zone 3, if given extra mulch in winter.

Primula
PRIMROSE

Because there are over 500 species and innumerable hybrids, the following description of primroses will not do them justice. For simplicity, they have been divided into early bloomers (April and May) versus late bloomers (June or later). Among the early bloomers, the most popular are the English primroses, *Primula* X *polyanthus*, and hybrids between *P. vulgaris* and *P. veris*. These have been highly bred over the centuries and now include every conceivable colour, with both single- and double-bloom forms. Some have solitary flowers but most produce flowers in small clusters. Closely related and blooming concurrently are the Julian primroses, *P.* X *pruhonicensis*, with masses of solitary flowers in rich magenta, red, and shades of pink. *P. veris*, cowslip, and *P. elatior*, oxlip, are also popular and readily available.

Blooming several weeks later is the Auricula primroses. Like the English primroses, they have been highly bred and are available in virtually every colour, in both single and double forms. Unlike the lettucelike leaves of the English primroses, the Auricula have spoon-shaped, matte green, smooth leaves. Although many species fall under the Auricula group, they are mostly grown by specialists. Both the English and Auricula primroses reach 15 to 20 centimetres in height when in bloom.

The other popular group of early bloomers are the drumstick primroses, *P. denticulata*, originating from the Himalayas of Kashmir. The wild form has lilac flowers, but modern cultivars come in a range of colours from white through shades of purple and pink to nearly red, all with a contrasting yellow eye. The flowers are produced in perfect spheres on stems reaching 30 centimetres tall.

In Atlantic Canada many primroses bloom in

RIGHT: *Primula* X *polyantha*

FAVOURITE PERENNIALS FOR ATLANTIC CANADA

June and July or even later. These are all native to eastern Asia. One of the largest groups of later-flowering primroses are the Candelabra or Japanese primroses. These produce a basal rosette of leaves from which rise unbranched, naked stems reaching 45 to 60 centimetres in height. The flowers are produced in several whorls, each above the other. Flower colours include white, shades of pink to nearly red, purple, yellow, and orange, all with striking yellow eyes. This group contains several species and hybrids, including *P. pulverulenta*, *P. japonica*, *P. beesiana*, *P. bulleyana*, and *P. chungensis*. Requiring similar conditions and blooming a little later is *P. florindae*, which can reach 60 to 90 centimetres in height. Its yellow, orange, or red flowers are in nodding clusters.

The other group of later-flowering primroses are low-growing clumpers with rounded, maple-leaf-shaped foliage. They reach 20 to 30 centimetres tall and have flowers in shades of pink. These include *P. heucherifolia*, *P. cortusoides*, and *P. sieboldii*. Another species which may not bloom until July or even August is *P. capitata*. Its flowers are deep purple and produced in a dense, slightly rounded cluster, similar to those of the drum-

Primula florindae

Primula 'Wanda'

stick primrose. The undersides of their spoon-shaped leaves are covered in a white powder. *P. vialii* produces an unusual and eye-catching rocketlike flower spike on stems up to 45 centimetres tall. The lavender-pink flowers emerge from a contrasting red calyx. *P. vialii* is the last primrose to bloom, often well into August.

English and drumstick primroses prefer part shade and organically rich, evenly moist soil. Auricula primroses prefer sun and require a well-drained, grittier soil. As they also prefer alkaline soil, dust them with lime annually. The later-blooming primroses prefer full sun and require acidic, organically rich soil that stays moist; they are intolerant of the slightest drought. All of the early blooming primroses are ideal for the front of a border or for use in rock gardens. English, drumstick, and candelabra primroses are also suited to woodland gardens or near water features. Drumsticks and candelabra primroses make attractive cut flowers. All primroses are visited by bees and butterflies. Diseases are generally not a problem, but pests can include slugs, snails, and root weevils. Propagation may be by seed or, more commonly, division. As all the above are hardy to zone 3, they may be used throughout much of Atlantic Canada.

Prunella
SELF-HEAL

Prunella encompasses fewer than 10 species, all native to Eurasia. The purple-blue-flowered heal-all, *P. vulgaris*, is naturalized in Atlantic Canada and a common wildflower in moist fields and roadsides. Two species, considered garden-worthy in Europe, have only recently appeared in North American gardens. Self-heal, *P. grandiflora*, forms a low mound up to 20 centimetres high with paired, oval leaves. The two-lipped flowers are produced in dense, almost rounded spikes held just above the foliage. If deadheaded, it blooms from June to September. The Freelander series comes in blue, pink, and white cultivars: 'Bella Blue' is violet-blue; 'Loveliness', pale purple. Cutleaf self-heal, *P. laciniata*, is similar overall to the above except its leaves are cut with a pair of narrow lobes; its flowers are white or pink.

Self-heal may be grown in full sun or part shade, preferably in acidic soil. As both species are moisture-lovers, they are ideal for the edges of moist borders. Their small size suits them for rock gardens as well. Self-heal is apt to be short-lived but self-seeds if given a chance. They attract bees and butterflies. Pests and diseases pose no problems. Propagation is most often by seed. Self-heal is hardy to zone 4; cutleaf self-heal, zone 5.

Prunella laciniata

Pulmonaria saccarata

Pulmonaria
LUNGWORT

The dozen or so species of *Pulmonaria* are primarily native to Europe. The Latin name is derived from *pulmo*, lung, referring to the spotted leaves, which look like a human lung. In the garden, the most common species are *P. officinalis* and *P. saccharata*, both of which have white spotted leaves and nodding clusters of flowers from April to June. Flowers change from pink to blue as they age and form spreading evergreen clumps up to 30 centimetres tall. The difference between the two species, both of which are considered heritage plants in Atlantic Canada, is subtle, and hybrids also occur. Many cultivars have emerged, some of which have permanently blue flowers, such as 'Purple Haze' (purple-blue) and 'Roy Davidson' (pale blue); others have pink flowers, such as 'Bubble Gum' and 'Dora Bielefeld'. All-white cultivars include 'Sissinghurst White' and 'Opal'. Recent breeding has emphasized developing plants with all-silver foliage. Perhaps the most popular of these are 'Majeste' and 'Excalibur', which have nearly all-silver foliage. Others with significant silver coloration include 'Moonshine', 'Silver Shimmers', 'Silver Bouquet', and

139

Pulmonaria rubra 'Redstart'

'High Contrast'. 'Raspberry Ice' has striking grey-green leaves that are spotted and edged in white; its flowers are raspberry pink.

Of similar size and habit is *P. angustifolia*, which has all-green deciduous leaves and brilliant blue flowers. 'Azurea' and 'Blue Ensign' are cultivars suited to Atlantic Canada. A little larger in size, reaching 45 centimetres in height, *P. rubra* has all-green leaves but is evergreen. Its deep coral-pink flowers bloom so early that it may literally be in flower as the snow melts around it. 'Redstart' is the most popular cultivar. For its decorative foliage, try 'David Ward', whose leaves are edged in white. Less commonly seen is *P. longifolia* ssp. *cevennensis* or *P. longifolia* 'Bertram Anderson', both with heavily spotted, narrow, deciduous leaves and bright blue flowers. These bloom a little later than the other lungwort species; they spread by underground runners but are not invasive.

Lungwort prefer organically rich, moisture-retentive but well-drained soil. They do not tolerate too-dry soil. If the soil is reasonably moist, lungwort can tolerate full sun; otherwise, part shade is best. They can even tolerate reasonably heavy shade. Lungwort are an important early pollen and nectar source for bees. Pests and diseases are not a problem. Propagation is by division. Most lungwort are hardy to zone 3, but *P. rubra* is rated for zone 4.

Pulsatilla
PASQUEFLOWER

The 33 species of *Pulsatilla* are found in grassland to alpine regions across the northern hemisphere. The genus name, from the Latin *pulsare*, to ring or to sound, refers to the flowers' bell shape. All are suited to rock gardens or for the edge of a border. As a group, they form a clump of basal feathery to fernlike leaves. From late April to June, solitary flowers arise on stems 15 to 45 centimetres high, depending on the species. The 10- to 15-centimetre-diameter flowers may be nodding or upright, bell- to saucer-shaped. They have no petals but the large sepals are petal-like. The centre of the flowers has a mass of yellow anthers. Flower colours, depending on the species, range from white and yellow, through shades of pink and purple, to nearly red and blue. The flowers are replaced by ornamental plumelike seed heads, reminiscent of dandelions.

The most popular species is the European *Pulsatilla vulgaris*, the common pasqueflower. It blooms within a few weeks of snowmelt and produces flowers first, followed later by the leaves. The May-blooming flowers start off nodding but become erect once they fully open. Flower colours includes white and shades of pink and purple. 'Red Cloak', also known as 'Rote Glocke', is

Pulsatilla vulgaris

Pulsatilla pratensis 'Nigricans'

deep crimson red. 'Papageno' comes in a mix of colours and has ragged or fringed sepals, which are often semi-double.

Small pasqueflower, *P. pratensis*, also European, has small, usually nodding, flowers. The entire plant, flowers included, are covered in soft silky hairs. The flowers are typically dark purple, but the cultivar 'Nigricans' has unique, nearly black, flowers. The giant of the genus, but not often available, is the alpine pasqueflower *P. alpina*, with stems reaching 30 to 45 centimetres in height. It is also the last of its genus to bloom in June. Flowers are typically white but the variety *apiiflora* has lemon yellow flowers. Other species to consider include *P. georgica*, *P. bungeana*, *P. ambigua*, and *P. turczaninovii*.

All pasqueflowers prefer full sun and a well-drained, humus-rich, but gritty, alkaline soil. Winter wetness is not tolerated but, once established, these plants can tolerate some drought. As pasqueflowers do not tolerate transplanting, plant them when they are young. Their toxicity, if ingested, makes them resistant to most pests, both large and small. Diseases are also rare. Bees are attracted to the copious pollen production of the blossoms. Propagation is by seeds. They are hardy throughout most the region, rated for zone 2.

TODD BOLAND

Ranunculus
FAIR MAIDS OF FRANCE

Gardeners do not generally think of buttercups as a garden ornamental; rather, they are seen as obnoxious weeds. Some 600 species are found worldwide, many of which are weedy or unattractive. Several are wonderful alpine plants for a rock garden but, of the garden-worthy perennial border species, only one is suitable for Atlantic Canada: Fair Maids of France, *Ranunculus aconitifolius* 'Flore Pleno'. Native to Europe, this species has single, white buttercup-like flowers. The double form is the most ornamental. This plant forms a bushy, 45- to 60-centimetre-tall mound. Its white pompomlike flowers are produced in open sprays throughout June and into early July. As the flowers are sterile, the plants cannot self-

Ranunculus aconitifolius 'Flore Pleno'

Ranunculus aconitifolius 'Flore Pleno'

seed and are well-behaved. The glossy leaves are relatively large, rounded in outline, but deeply cut and lobed. This plant is ideal for a front to mid-border but, as it goes summer-dormant, it can leave a gap in the garden. Plant a late-flowering tidy perennial like yellow or purple cone-flower nearby to hide this space. This rare garden plant is a heritage plant in Newfoundland, where the first instances of its being planted as a garden ornamental date to the mid-1800s.

Fair Maids of France prefer full sun to part shade, with organically rich, evenly moist soil. The only major pest, a leaf miner that can speed up the summer dormancy of the plant, does no permanent damage. Diseases are rare and its toxins make it distasteful to large herbivores. Propagation is by division. It is rated hardy to zone 5.

Rodgersia
RODGERSIA

The five species of *Rodgersia* are all native to the woodland regions of eastern Asia. The genus was named after US Admiral John Rodgers, commander of the expedition which discovered *R. podophylla* in the 1850s. Today, four of the species are grown for their bold foliage and large *Astilbe*-like plumes of white or pale pink flowers, produced in July. All produce thick rhizomes from which arise a clump of compound leaves to 100 centimetres. The flower stems can reach 150 centimetres in height. The most common species, *R. podophylla*, has palmately compound leaves with five to seven jagged leaflets. There are two cultivars: 'Braunlaub', which has bronzed foliage, and 'Rotlaub', whose newly emerging leaves are vivid red, becoming bronzed as they mature. Both can be shy bloomers and are grown primarily for their foliage. *R. podophylla* is a quickly spreading species. The leaves

Rodgersia aesculifolia

of the similar *Rodgersia aesculifolia* have serrated rather than ragged edges. This clumping plant consistently produces white or pale pink plumes. 'Irish Bronze' and 'Cherry Blush' have distinctly bronzed foliage.

Rodgersia pinnata resembles *R. aesculifolia* but its leaflets are pinnately compound rather than palmately compound and the flowers usually pink. 'Elegans' and 'Superba' both have green leaves but dark pink plumes; 'Fireworks', bronze-edged leaves; and 'Chocolate Wings', deep bronze leaves. *Rodgersia sambucifolia* has pinnate leaves but typically white flowers. *Rodgersia* are ideal subjects for waterside or woodland gardens. Position them in a mid-border so that their foliage can be appreciated.

All *Rodgersia* prefer part shade and evenly moist, humus-rich soil. Intense sun can scorch the foliage. Because their leaves are early to emerge in spring, and may be damaged by late frosts, avoid planting in low-lying areas. The flowers attract bees and butterflies. Diseases are rare but slugs and snails may damage emerging leaves. Large herbivores ignore them. Propagation may be by seed but more commonly by division, particularly the cultivars. They are reliably hardy in zone 5, but, if given a thick winter mulch, may grow in zone 4.

Rudbeckia

BLACK-EYED SUSAN, CONEFLOWER

The genus *Rudbeckia* is native exclusively to North America. The genus name honours Swedish botanist Dr. Olof Rudbeck, founder of the Uppsala Botanical Garden in Sweden. Of about 25 species, four are regularly grown in Atlantic Canada. Black-eyed Susan or gloriosa daisy, *R. hirta*, is native to the region, growing along roadsides and in old meadows. The wild form creates a large clump up to 90 centimetres tall with rough,

Rudbeckia hirta

hairy, elliptical leaves and open clusters of large, 10-centimetre-diameter, golden yellow daisies. Modern cultivars, of which there are many, are generally more compact, often less than 60 centimetres in height. The wild form is suitable for a wildflower garden, while modern cultivars are ideal bedding plants but have been bred to behave more like annuals than perennials. Even as a perennial, plants are apt to be short-lived. This species often reseeds itself; offspring from cultivars may resemble its wild ancestors. Deadheading prevents reseeding and encourages the plant to bloom from July to frost.

Tall coneflower, *R. laciniata*, is definitely a plant for the back of a border as it can easily exceed 2 metres in height. In August and September, and even into October, it produces loose sprays

NEXT PAGE: *Rudbeckia fulgida* 'Goldstrum'

Rudbeckia nitida 'Herbstonne'

tober. It is a mainstay for a late-summer border and, when massed, provides a striking display. It is best used in a mid-border but is also ideal in a cottage garden or even a wildflower garden. The most popular cultivar, 'Goldstrum', reaches 60 centimetres in height; it was awarded the 1999 Perennial Plant of the Year™. For the front of a border try 'City Garden', 'Little Goldstar', or 'Little Suzie', all of which grow to 30 centimetres in height.

All *Rudbeckia* prefer full sun and an evenly moist, organically rich soil. Black-eyed Susan is the most drought-tolerant, but all *Rudbeckia* can tolerate some drought once they become established. All attract bees and butterflies. All *Rudbeckia* make ideal long-lasting cut flowers. The only likely disease is powdery mildew, if the growing site is too sheltered. Pests are not a problem; even hares, deer, and moose ignore them. Propagation may be by seed or more commonly by division. All except 'Herbstsonne' are hardy to zone 3; 'Herbstsonne', to zone 5.

of 10-centimetre-diameter yellow flowers. Its leaves are pinnate and 15 centimetres or longer. A popular cultivar in Atlantic Canada is 'Golden Glow', also known as 'Hortensia', a heritage plant with double flowers. Tall coneflower can be robust and swamp close neighbours. This plant may require staking if grown in a windy location. Shining coneflower, *R. nitida* 'Herbstonne', a hybrid between *R. laciniata* and *R. nitida*, can exceed 2 metres and may require staking. Its yellow petals droop, exposing the green cone. It blooms in September and October and adds colour to the late-season garden.

Perhaps best suited for Atlantic Canadian conditions is *R. fulgida*, the common yellow coneflower. It forms a compact clump about 75 centimetres tall with heart-shaped leaves. Plants produce masses of 10-centimetre-diameter yellow flowers in August, September, and into Oc-

Salvia
PERENNIAL SAGE

The genus *Salvia* is a large plant group with close to 1,000 species found in Eurasia and the Americas. It includes annuals, biennials, perennials, and low shrubs. As a whole, they are primarily found in dry habitats and most release a pungent fragrance when their leaves are bruised. Essentially one hybrid is grown in Atlantic Canada, *S. X sylvestris*, often erroneously referred to as *S. nemorosa*. Called perennial sage or woodland sage, this hybrid is one of a few sages that tolerates moisture. It is a clumping plant with many upright stems reaching 60 to 75 centimetres tall. Its paired wrinkled leaves are slightly grey-green and fragrant when rubbed. The tubular, generally deep blue flowers are in narrow terminal spikes from July to early August; they attract bees, in particular, but hummingbirds and butterflies visit them as well. It makes a long-lasting cut flower.

Perhaps the most popular cultivar, 'May Night', named Perennial Plant of the Year™ in 1997, has deep purple-blue flowers on plants reaching 75 centimetres in height. Others include 'Amethyst' (light purple), 'Blue Queen' (vibrant blue), 'Caradonna' (deep blue), 'Burgundy Candles' (deep blue), 'Rose Queen' (light pink), 'Rose Wine' (medium pink), and 'Lyrical™

Salvia nemorosa

White'. More compact forms reach 40 to 50 centimetres tall include 'Merleau™ Blue' (deep blue), 'East Friesland' (purple), 'Blue Hill' (medium blue), and 'Snow Hill' (white), while the most compact, reaching just 30 centimetres, are 'Maras', 'Sensation Blue Sky', and 'Sallyrosa™ April Night', all in shades of blue, and 'New Dimension Rose' in rose pink. Less common and more difficult to find is the whorled sage, *S. verticillata* 'Purple Rain'. It has a similar habit, reaches up to 45 centimetres, and has rounded clusters of flowers scattered along the length of the spikes.

Culinary sage, *S. officinalis*, sometimes grown as a garden ornamental, especially those species with colourful foliage, is really a sub-shrub with a woody base. The species has crinkled, greygreen, pungent foliage and whorls of blue, two-lipped flowers in July. As a bonus, it can be used in cooking. Grown for its purple-flushed foliage is the cultivar 'Purpurea'. The young leaves of 'Tricolor' are edged in pink or purple and mature to being edged in white. 'Icterine' has yellow-edged leaves.

The above sages all require full sun for maximum growth. The taller cultivars are ideal for a mid-border, the more compact near the edges. While an organically rich, well-drained but evenly moist soil is preferable, they also tolerate a poorer, dry soil. Prompt deadheading often extends the blooming season into early fall. The only disease that is likely to occur is powdery mildew; better spacing and more air circulation often deters this. The pungent foliage means that few pests, including large herbivores, bother them. Propagation may be by seed or, in the case of cultivars, division or cuttings. Woodland sage is hardy through zone 4; culinary sage is only reliable in the mildest regions of Atlantic Canada, zone 6, but can be overwintered indoors in colder areas.

Sanguisorba

BURNET

There are about 20 species of *Sanguisorba*, all native to the northern hemisphere. The genus name comes from the Latin *sanguis*, blood, and *sorbere*, to soak up, from the reputed power of these plants to stop bleeding. This plant is not often seen in gardens—yet—but it has attractive architectural elements and will probably become more popular as plant breeders begin to develop cultivars. All *Sanguisorba* form large mounds with many basal, pinnate leaves that give the plant a fernlike appearance. From July to September, upright stems arise 90 to 120 centimetres, topped with many bottlebrush-like flowers ranging in colour from burgundy red to white depending on the species.

Canada burnet, *S. canadensis*, is native in Atlantic Canada, usually found growing near the sea or along larger rivers. It has grey-green leaves and stiffly upright, white bottlebrush flowers 10 to 20 centimetres long. Japanese burnet, *S. obtusa*, is similar but its leaves are all-green and its flowers arching and bright pink. Alaskan burnet, *S. menziesii*, another lookalike, has maroon flowers that contrast with its blue-tinted foliage. Great burnet, *S. officinalis*, has leaves similar to those of Alaskan burnet but with small oval-shaped bottlebrushes. Great burnet is pale pink and not as showy as some of the other burnets; but 'Tanna' and 'Red Thunder' cultivars are maroon and look like airier versions of the Alaskan burnet. For lovers of variegated foliage, try *S. minor* 'Little Angel', which forms a compact mound with

Sanguisorba canadensis

Sanguisorba obtusa

monly grown in Atlantic Canada. Bouncing-bet, *S. officinalis*, one of the taller *Saponaria*, forms a clump with paired, smooth, lance-shaped leaves and unbranched stems up to 90 centimetres tall. The flowers are in terminal clusters throughout August and September and make an attractive cut flower. Individual blossoms are light pink, fragrant, and about 2.5 centimetres in diameter. European in origin, bouncing-bet has been naturalized in many areas of North America. In the garden, the heritage double form 'Flore Pleno' is most commonly grown. As it is a fairly aggressive plant, use it with caution in a border. It is perhaps better suited to a cottage garden or a wildflower setting.

The other popular species is rock soapwort, *S. ocymoides*, a dwarf, trailing semi-evergreen species often seen in rock gardens, cascading over retaining walls, or growing as a ground cover on sunny embankments. In June, the plants are smothered in a profusion of pink blossoms held

white-edged leaves and small deep pink bottle-brushes on 60-centimetre-tall stems.

All the burnets are moisture-lovers. They are grown in organically rich soil in full sun but they can tolerate some shade. As they are robust, they should be used with caution in a border; they are better suited to a wildflower garden or near water features. The blossoms make an attractive cut flower. Overall, they are care-free plants, with few pests or diseases. Propagation is by division. Canada burnet is rated hardy to zone 3; the other burnets, zone 4.

Saponaria
SOAPWORT, BOUNCING-BET

Between 30 and 40 species of *Saponaria* are found wild in Eurasia. Many are low-growing alpines and, although attractive garden plants, are best in a rock garden. Only two species are com-

Saponaria officinalis 'Flore Pleno'

TODD BOLAND

Saponaria ocymoides

Saxifraga X *urbium* 'Aureopunctata'

atop 15-centimetre-tall stems. 'Alba' and 'White Tip' have white blossoms. This species attracts bees and butterflies.

Both soapworts require full sun with average well-drained soil but tolerates drought and gravelly soil. If the soil is too rich, bouncing-bet is apt to flop. Rock soapwort tends to rot in winter. Diseases are not generally a problem, nor are the soapworts bothered by large herbivores. The main insect pest is leaf miners, which can cause cosmetic damage to the foliage. Propagation is by seed or, in the case of the double bouncing-bet, division. Both are hardy through zone 3.

Saxifraga
SAXIFRAGE, LONDON PRIDE

The genus *Saxifraga*, with over 440 species found throughout the northern hemisphere, is best known for its multitude of alpine species, many of which are wonderful additions to rock gardens. However, only three are commonly encountered: London pride, mossy saxifrage, and encrusted saxifrage. London pride, perhaps the most common, is a heritage plant in Atlantic Canada. It is a natural hybrid, formally known as *Saxifraga* X *urbium*. Plants are matlike, produc-

ing many evergreen rosettes with spoon-shaped, dark green, leathery leaves. It is a good ground cover for semi-shady locations. In May and June, airy clusters of small white or pale pink starlike flowers are produced on 20- to 30-centimetre-tall stems. For decorative foliage, try 'Aureopunctata', which is irregularly spotted and splotched with yellow.

Mossy saxifrage, *S.* X *arendsii*, another evergreen species often grown as a cushionlike ground cover in part shade, is slower growing than London pride but has denser foliage and, from a distance, appears mosslike. In May and June, plants produce numerous 1.5-centimetre-wide cup-like flowers atop wiry 15-centimetre-tall stems. The flowers are typically white, pink, or red. Cultivars include 'White Pixie', 'Peter Pan' (pink), and 'Purple Robe' (red), and, recently, the Touran™ series in white, pink, or red. For colourful foliage, try 'Bob Hawkins', with white-edged leaves that give the plant a frosted look, or 'Cloth of Gold', with brilliant yellow leaves. Both produce white flowers.

Several species of saxifrage are referred to

as encrusted saxifrages; *S. paniculata* is the most common. All encrusted saxifrage have evergreen leaves which form tight rosettes, not unlike a miniature hen-and-chicks (*Sempervivum*). The overall plant habit is hummock- or cushionlike. In June, it produces sprays of small white or pale pink flowers on 15-centimetre-tall stems. This is an alpine plant best used in a rock garden or alpine trough.

London pride and mossy saxifrage tolerate full sun if the soil is evenly moist and the plants are grown near the cooler coastlines. Elsewhere, they perform better under semi-shaded conditions. London pride can tolerate considerable shade. Both are drought-intolerant. Encrusted saxifrage needs full sun but tolerates part shade in hot areas. It can also tolerate some drought but ideally the soil should be well drained but retain some moisture. As encrusted saxifrage prefers alkaline soil, a liberal annual dusting with lime is beneficial. All of the above saxifrages benefit from having their flower stems sheared after blooming to keep the plants neat and compact. Overall, they are all care-free. Propagation is most commonly by division, but encrusted and mossy saxifrages may be grown from seed. London pride and mossy saxifrages are hardy to zone 4, the encrusted saxifrage to zone 2.

Saxifraga X *arendsii*

Scabiosa

PINCUSHION FLOWER, SCABIOUS

As garden ornamentals, essentially two pincushion flowers are grown in Atlantic Canada. The common pincushion flower once known as *Scabiosa caucasica* is now classified as *Knautia caucasica*. It is a European species now naturalized throughout Atlantic Canada and an attractive garden plant for a cottage garden, wildflower garden, or mid-border. It forms a clump of basal leaves and wiry stems reaching 60 centimetres in height and producing loose sprays of 5- to 7-centimetre-diameter flowers from July to September. The most common flower colour is lavender-blue but cultivars are available from white, pink, shades of lavender, to deep violet.

More popular is the dwarf pincushion flower, *S. columbaria*, which is similar to the above species except the flower stems reach 45 centimetres and, if deadheaded, produce a procession of blooms from June to October. Popular culti-

Scabiosa columbaria Flutter™ 'Rose Pink'

vars include 'Mariposa Blue', 'Mariposa Violet', 'Harlequin Blue™', 'Flutter™ Deep Blue', and 'Flutter™ Rose Pink'. 'Moon Dance', a pale yellow variety with smaller flowers, is occasionally seen. *Scabiosa* hybrids on the market include 'Butterfly Blue', winner of Perennial Plant of the Year™ in 2000. Other hybrids are 'Pink Mist' and 'Vivid Violet'. *S. columbaria* and its cultivars are all ideal for a front to mid-border. The

Scabiosa 'Butterfly Blue'

smallest pincushion flower, *S. columbaria* 'Nana' or 'Blue Note', reaches just 20 centimetres. In addition to their placement in the front of a border, these may also be used in a rock garden.

At the other extreme is the giant scabious, *S. gigantea*, known today as *Cephalaria gigantea*. The plants can grow to over 2 metres in height and they have pale yellow flowers. It blooms in August and September and is best suited to the back of a border.

Pincushion flowers prefer full sun and soil that is well drained, especially in winter. Once established, they can tolerate considerable drought. All attract bees, butterflies, and hummingbirds. They are suitable as cut flowers. Pests and diseases are not usually a concern. Propagation is by seed or division. The giant scabious is hardy to zone 3; common pincushion flower, zone 4; and the dwarf pincushion flower, zone 5.

Sedum
STONECROP: CREEPING TYPES

With over 470 species of *Sedum* and so many popular as garden plants, it is difficult to do them justice. The following is not an exhaustive list. The taller, more herbaceous border-type stonecrops have been moved into their own genus, *Hylotelephium*, and are described in the next Sedum entry.

The true *Sedum* are essentially rock-garden plants, used along the edge of a border or for cascading over walls. Many are popular as ground cover for sunny embankments. They are indispensable for green (living) roofs. Perhaps the most popular, and one with heritage status, is *S. spurium*. This plant has creeping stems and spoon-shaped fleshy leaves and, in mid-summer, produces flat-topped clusters of pink star-shaped flowers atop 15-centimetre-tall stems. Cultivars

Sedum spurium 'Album'

vary in flower and leaf colour: 'Red Carpet' has red-tinted foliage which turns burgundy in fall; 'Dragon's Blood' is similar but has deeper pink-red flowers; 'Voodoo' was selected for its dark red foliage; 'Album' has green leaves and white flowers; and 'Tricolor' has green leaves edged in white and pink, and light pink flowers. *Sedum kamtschaticum* has a similar habit to that of *S. spurium* but it is a little more compact, with yellow flowers. The cultivar 'Variegatum' has white-edged foliage. *Sedum hybridum* is a *S. kamtschaticum* lookalike with green foliage and yellow flowers. *Sedum selskianum* is distinguished by its narrow, slightly hairy leaves.

Another popular group of creeping sedums,

Sedum collection

the reflexed stonecrop, *S. reflexum*, aka *S. rupestre*, are mat-forming, but evergreen, and have crowded, fleshy, conifer-like leaves. This species has blue-tinted foliage and upright flower stems that reach 20 centimetres high, topped with a flat cluster of yellow flowers. 'Blue Spruce' has the bluest foliage. Popular, and rightly so, is 'Angelina', which has bright yellow summer foliage, turning orange in winter. Fairly new on the market is *S. hakonense* 'Chocolate Ball'. It has maroon-brown needlelike foliage, is very dense and compact, looking like a dwarf conifer, and produces yellow flowers.

Sedum acre is less than 10 centimetres tall, with scaly foliage and yellow flowers. It is a little weedy, but the creamy yellow-foliaged 'Aureum' is less aggressive. *Sedum album*, also small, has rounded, jellybean-like leaves. 'Murale' has slightly red-tinted foliage and white flowers, and 'Coral Carpet' foliage is strongly red-tinted with pale pink flowers. Both species are popular for green roofs.

Sedum are easily grown in full sun and well-drained soil. Their superior drought and salt tolerance make them popular for coastal gardens. They also tolerate poor, gravelly soil. Pests and diseases are generally not a problem, although aphids may sometimes be troublesome and hares may nibble on the growths. Propagation is by division or cuttings. Most of these sedums are hardy through zone 3.

Sedum
STONECROP: BORDER TYPES
Recently botanists have separated the taller border-type stonecrops into their own genus, *Hylotelephium*. Unlike many of the true sedum, which are evergreen, *Hylotelephium* are herbaceous and, in autumn, dieback to small overwintering buds. Perhaps the most popular is *H. spectabile*,

Hylotelephium spectabile 'Autumn Joy'

or showy stonecrop, a bushy plant with many unbranched, upright stems reaching a height of 60 centimetres. The leaves are grey-green and rounded and the flowers are in flat-topped clusters with numerous pink star-shaped flowers. The species is rarely seen in gardens, but its cultivars are: 'Autumn Joy', 'Brilliant', 'Neon', and 'Stardust', the latter with white flowers. If space is limited, try 'Pure Joy' or 'Thundercloud', both of which form 20-centimetre-tall mounds with light pink flowers. Or try a variegated version of 'Autumn Joy' called 'Autumn Charm'. *Hylotelephium telephium*, a similar-looking heritage plant with smaller flower heads, has many cultivars:

'Hab Grey', pink-grey foliage and cream-yellow flowers; 'Matrona', grey-green, purple-tinted foliage, and rose-pink flowers; and 'Purple Emperor', deep purple foliage and rose-pink flowers. More recent are the Candy™ series: 'Cherry Truffle', 'Chocolate Drop', and 'Raspberry Truffle', all which have dark purple foliage. Grown for their spectacular variegated foliage are cultivars of *H. erythrostichum* such as 'Frosty Morn', with white-edged leaves, and 'Mediovariegata', whose leaves are yellow with a green edge. As all of the above grow to about 40 centimetres tall, they are suitable for the front to middle portion of a border.

TODD BOLAND

Hylotelephium cauticola 'Lidakense'

Low-growing cultivars suitable as edgers or for use in rock gardens include *H. ewersii*, with grey-green foliage; *H. sieboldii*, blue-grey, scalloped-edged foliage; and 'Vera Jameson', purple-tinted foliage. The darkest purple-foliaged low growers include *H. cauticola* 'Lidakense' and hybrids 'Bertram Anderson' and 'Plum Perfection'. The Sunsparkler® series has tight mounded habits on plants generally less than 15 centimetres high. These hybrids are selected for their colourful foliage: 'Lime Zinger', green leaves edged in red; 'Lime Twister', cream-edged green leaves; 'Firecracker', rich purple-red foliage; and 'Dazzleberry', purple-blue foliage.

Hylotelephium are easily grown in full sun and well-drained soil but adapt to poor, gravelly soil. Excessively damp soil is not well tolerated. Their superior drought and salt tolerance make them popular for coastal gardens. They combine well with blue oat and blue fescue grasses, sea holly, and lamb's-ears. All attract bees and butterflies, and the longer-stemmed cultivars are ideal for cut flowers. Overall, they are care-free plants. Propagation is by division or cuttings. Most of the above are hardy through zone 3.

Sempervivum
HEN-AND-CHICKS, HOUSELEEK

There are about 40 species of *Sempervivum*, primarily native to the Mediterranean region. The Latin name *sempervivum* literally translates to always alive, a testament to the plant's ability to survive for many years. Houseleeks, with their succulent rosettes, are reminiscent of other desert plants, yet they are extraordinarily hardy. The innumerable hybrids and cultivars all produce rosettes of leaves held close to the ground. These rosettes may vary from less than 1 centimetre to nearly 20 centimetres in diameter. The foliage may be shades of green, chartreuse, light reddish pink, to nearly black, and grey- or blue-tinted. They may also be smooth or covered in white hairs. When mature, the rosettes form a thick upright flower stem which varies from 10 to more than 30 centimetres in height, depending on the cultivar. The yellow, pink, to deep red starlike flowers are produced in flat-topped clusters in July and August. After they bloom, the rosette dies, but not before it produces numerous chicks around its base. Houseleeks are popular in rock gardens but are also ideal for growing in containers, and the larger rosette types are useful for the front of a border. They pair well with low sedums.

All houseleeks require full sun and well-drained, gritty soil. Their drought and salt tolerance make them ideal for coastal gardens. They are essentially pest- and disease-free. Blossoms are visited by both bees and butterflies. Propagation is easy through the separation of the chicks from the hen. Most are hardy throughout the region, rated for zone 3.

RIGHT: *Sempervivum* hybrid

FAVOURITE PERENNIALS FOR ATLANTIC CANADA

Sidalcea
PRAIRIE MALLOW, CHECKER MALLOW

The 20 species of *Sidalcea* are all native to west-central North America. Of the three hybrids grown in Atlantic Canada, 'Party Girl' is the most popular, with unbranched stems that reach 90 centimetres in height and spikes of deep pink, five-petalled, 5-centimetre-diameter flowers. It blooms from mid-July through September. Overall, the plant looks like a dwarf hollyhock. 'Elsie Heugh' (75 centimetres) and 'Little Princess' (60 centimetres) have bushier habits and paler pink flowers and bloom several weeks earlier than 'Party Girl'.

Prairie mallow prefers full sun and well-drained soil but does not tolerate hot, dry weather. Acidic soil is best, as plants can become chlorotic and yellow under alkaline conditions. It is frequently visited by bees, butterflies, and hummingbirds. Propagation may be by seed or division. 'Party Girl' needs a sheltered site or staking; 'Elsie Heugh' and 'Little Princess' are more wind-tolerant. In the garden, use them in a mid-border. All are suitable as cut flowers. Although diseases are rare and large herbivores ignore prairie mallow, Japanese beetle may be a problem. All are rated for zone 4.

Silene
CAMPION

The genus *Silene*'s 700 or more species are found primarily in the northern hemisphere. Many are either weedy or alpine plants grown by specialist rock gardeners. Most of the larger species, including Maltese-cross, red and rose campion, and sticky catchfly, were included in the genus *Lychnis* and are described in this book under that

Sidalcea malviflora 'Party Girl'

name. Among those plants originally considered in the genus *Silene*, only a few are grown as garden ornamentals. Fringed campion, *S. fimbriata*, is an old-fashioned cottage-garden plant. It is a clumping plant that reaches up to 90 centimetres in height with paired oval to heart-shaped leaves and loose terminal clusters of nodding white flowers in July. The flowers resemble miniature balloons before they open. Each blossom's five petals are delicately fringed along their margin. Zadwadskis catchfly, *S. zadwadskii*, occasionally offered in Atlantic Canada, has a low rosette of glossy, narrow, evergreen leaves and in July produces loose clumps of white flowers on 20- to 25-centimetre-tall stems.

The only other widely available *Silene* is rock campion, *S. uniflora*, sometimes known as *S. maritima*. It is a creeping, mat-forming plant with paired, usually matte grey or blue-tinted evergreen foliage and loose clusters of balloonlike

Silene fimbriata
LEFT: *Silene zadwadskii*

buds that open to five-petalled white flowers throughout June and July. As each petal is deeply cleft, the flowers appear to have 10 petals. 'Compacta' has a dense, mounding habit; 'Rosea' has flowers with a delicate pink flush. For outstanding foliage, try 'Druett's Variegated', whose leaves are widely margined in white. 'Swan Lake' has double flowers. More rarely seen is alpine catchfly, *S. alpestris*, a creeping plant with bright green shiny leaves. In July it has airy clusters of small white flowers reminiscent of baby's breath. Both of these *Silene* species are ideal for rock gardens or cascading over retaining walls.

Silene prefer full sun and well-drained soil. They are reasonably drought-resistant once established. Rock campion is highly recommended for seaside gardens. Fringed campion may be used as a cut flower. Propagation is by seed, cuttings, or division. Diseases are rare but plants may be eaten by slugs and snails and nibbled by hares. They are hardy to zone 4.

Solidago 'Crown of Rays'

Solidago
GOLDENROD

Most Atlantic Canadian gardeners are familiar with goldenrods, as they are often encountered along roadsides and in waste areas, open woodlands, and peatlands throughout the Atlantic Canada. Most of the approximately 100 species are North American in origin. All may be grown in wildflower settings as they are superb for attracting bees and butterflies. Most, however, spread too aggressively to use in formal garden settings. Lance-leaved goldenrod, *Solidago graminifolia*, now called *Euthamnia graminifolia*, is an exception—although this species can clump up in a short time, it is easily controlled by division and prompt deadheading once the flowers have died. It forms clumps of unbranched stems 75 to 90 centimetres tall, with flat-topped clusters of tiny yellow flowers, in August and September.

Plant breeders have begun to hybridize and select goldenrods to create more garden-worthy ornamentals. For the back of a border, try 'Fireworks', which reaches a height of 120 centimetres. 'Crown of Rays', 'Golden Baby', and 'Golden Fleece', suitable for a mid-border, reach 70 centimetres. For the front, consider 'Little Lemon', which reaches 45 centimetres and has lemon yellow flowers compared to the deep golden yellow of many of the other cultivars.

All goldenrods require full sun and well-drained soil. They do not, however, tolerate dry conditions. All attract bees and butterflies and make admirable cut flowers. Overall, goldenrod are care-free plants. Propagation of wild types may be by seed, but cultivars are propagated through division. All are hardy throughout much of Atlantic Canada, rated for zone 3.

Stachys
LAMB'S-EARS, BIG BETONY

The genus *Stachys* includes over 300 species. The majority have insignificant flowers and a weedy habit, however, and only three species are commonly used as garden plants. The most popular is lamb's-ears, *S. byzantina*, sometimes called *S. lanata*. Native to southeast Europe, this plant is grown for its silvery, densely hairy leaves. Plants form a clump up to 15 centimetres tall, with tongue-shaped leaves that are up to 10 centimetres long. These leaves are often evergreen in sheltered sites. In July and August the plants produce a spike of insignificant pink flowers on stems up to 45 centimetres tall. Most gardeners prefer to cut off the flowers, as they detract from the foliage. The cultivar 'Silver Carpet' has been selected for its non-blooming habit. 'Fuzzy Wuzzy' mounds to 20 centimetres tall, with 15-centimetre-long leaves; 'Helene von Stein', also known as 'Big Ears', has huge leaves up to 20 centimetres long. 'Primrose Heron' has chartreuse-yellow fuzzy foliage.

Big betony, *S. macrantha*, a heritage plant in Atlantic Canada, is seldom sold in garden centres but is still found in older gardens. Plants form a mounding clump with paired, triangular leaves that are crinkled and have round-toothed edges. In June and July, it produces stems that are up to 60 centimetres tall that terminate in a showy spike of 2-centimetre-diameter, purple-pink, two-lipped flowers. Prompt deadheading keeps plants tidy and may encourage a secondary flush of blooms. Its blossoms attract bees, and it makes a good cut flower.

Fairly new on the gardening scene is wood betony, *S. officinalis* 'Hummelo'. This plant also forms a low mound up to 20 centimetres in height with paired, spoon-shaped leaves that are crinkled and have scalloped edges. In July and August, it produces stiff, nearly leafless flower stems up to 60 centimetres tall, topped with a

Stachys byzantinum 'Helen von Stein'

narrow dense spike of reddish purple flowers. Plants attract bees, butterflies, and hummingbirds and are suitable as cut flowers. 'Pink Cotton Candy' is a light pink cultivar.

The betonies prefer evenly moist soil; they do not tolerate drought. Lamb's-ears, on the other hand, do tolerate drought. All prefer full sun. These plants are best used toward the front of a border or in a cottage-garden setting. The betonies are also suitable near water features. They are not bothered by pests, large or small, or diseases. Propagation is most commonly by division, although wood betony is also grown from seed. All are hardy through zone 3.

Stachys macrantha

Stokesia 'Blue Danube'

Stokesia
STOKES ASTER

The sole species of *Stokesia*, *S. laevis*, a native of the southeastern US, is closely related to the cornflowers, *Centaurea*. The genus was named in honour of English physician and botanist Jonathan Stokes (1755–1831). Plants form a mound up to 60 centimetres tall with many 7-centimetre-diameter, lavender-blue, daisylike flowers from July to September. Several cultivars are available. In periwinkle blue tones are 'Blue Danube', 'Peachie's Pick', 'Blue Star', and 'Mel's Blue'; 'Silver Moon' has white flowers; 'Honeysong Purple' and 'Purple Parasols' are purple-pink; 'Colorwheel' is light pink; and 'Omega Skyrocket' is pale lavender and much taller than most other cultivars, with stems up to 120 centimetres tall. With the exception of 'Omega Skyrocket', the others are suited to the front of a border or a cottage-garden setting. Prompt deadheading greatly extends the blooming season of *Stokesia*.

Stokesia prefers full sun and evenly moist, sandy soil yet can tolerate considerable drought once established. Excess winter wetness is the main threat to its survival. Blossoms attract both bees and butterflies, and pests and diseases are rare. This plant makes an attractive cut flower. Propagation is by seed and division. This plant is rated for zone 5, but as it is more reliable in zone 6, it is really suitable for the mildest regions of Atlantic Canada.

Tanacetum
PAINTED DAISY, FEVERFEW

About 160 species of *Tanacetum* are all natives of the northern hemisphere. Many were classified in the genus *Chrysanthemum*, while the painted daisy was specifically, and still is, in some circles, called *Pyrethrum*. Today, the proper name for painted daisy is *Tanacetum coccineum*. A 60- to 90-centimetre-tall clumping plant, it produces many upright wiry stems topped with solitary 7.5-centimetre-diameter daisylike flowers in mid-summer. The leaves are bright green, narrow but finely divided, and produce a pungent fragrance when rubbed. Available cultivars have single or double flowers, in a range of colours from white, through shades of pink, to dark red. 'Robinson's Mix' is a

Tanacetum parthenium

Tanacetum coccineum

Thalictrum rochebruneanum

popular cultivar; 'James Kelway' has the darkest red flowers; and 'Vanessa' has double deep pink flowers. Painted daisy is best used in a mid-border or can be mass-planted for maximum effect.

Feverfew, *T. parthenium*, a short-lived plant often grown in herb or cottage gardens, is bushy, 30 to 45 centimetres tall, with masses of small, white, daisylike flowers from July to September. Its leaves are bright green and pungent but less divided than those of painted daisy. It often self-seeds. 'White Stars' is compact, to 30 centimetres high, with white, yellow-centred flowers. As 'Golden Ball' flowers lack petals, they appear as golden yellow buttons. 'Aureum' has bright yellow foliage and is effectively used as a contrast with darker-foliaged plants.

Painted daisy prefer full sun or are at risk of flopping; feverfew may be grown in full sun or part shade. The flowers of both attract bees and butterflies and are suitable to use as cut flowers. The plants are toxic to mammals, including people; most insects avoid them. Diseases are rarely a problem. Propagation is by seed or division. The above are hardy through zone 3.

Thalictrum
MEADOW-RUE

Well over 100 species of *Thalictrum* are found across the northern hemisphere, although they are not particularly well known as garden plants—but a few of them should be. *Thalictrum rochebruneanum*, known as lavender mist meadow-rue, is a 2-metre-tall slender plant with lacy blue-tinted foliage reminiscent of columbine or maidenhair fern. During August and September plants produce airy sprays of small, pendant, lavender flowers with a noticeable tuft of yellow stamens. Similar in appearance is *T. delavayi* 'Hewitt's Double', with deep purple, fully double flowers, like miniature pompoms. A little more compact, to 120 centimetres in height, is *T. aquilegiifolium*, which has dense clusters of lavender flowers. 'Black Stockings' has striking black stems. Yellow meadow-rue, *Thalictrum flavum* 'Illuminator', has blue-tinted foliage but lemon yellow, fluffy flower clusters. All of these meadow-rue are ideal for naturalizing in moist open woodlands or wildflower meadows and are appropriate near water features.

If space is limited, try *T. kiusianum*, dwarf meadow-rue, which reaches only 15 centimetres tall. It has maidenhair-like foliage and open airy clusters of lilac flowers. Grown for its foliage rather than its flowers, *T. ichangense* 'Evening Star' has maroon-purple foliage with a central silver star of whitened veins. Forming a clump up to 30 centimetres in height, it is ideal for a moist, partly shaded rockery or border edges.

Meadow-rue prefer full sun to part shade and soil that stays reasonably moist. They have poor tolerance to salt or drought. Pests and diseases are not a problem. The flowers, similar in appearance to those of baby's breath, are suitable as cut flowers. Propagation is by seed or division, but divisions take several years to settle back in. With adequate winter mulching, most should survive to zone 4.

Thalictrum aquilegiifolium

Thymus citriodorus

Thymus
THYME

There are an estimated 350 species of thyme, many which differ only subtly from each other. In Atlantic Canada several species are commonly grown. Culinary thyme, *T. vulgaris*, may reach 30 centimetres in height, while creeping thyme, *T. serpyllum*, is only about 2 centimetres tall. As a group, all thymes are evergreen, with fragrant foliage. They may be mounding in habit like *T. vulgaris* and *T. citriodorus* or creeping like *T. serpyllum* and *T. pseudolanuginosus*. In July and August they produce clusters of small two-lipped flowers that range from white through shades of pink to dark reddish purple. The mounding types may be grown along the edge of a border; the creeping types are popular between stepping stones, as they can tolerate some foot traffic. All are suitable for a rock garden.

Culinary thyme is perhaps the least showy, although *T. pulegioides* and the hybrid *T. X citriodorus*, both commonly called lemon thyme due to their lemony fragrance, are ornamental. Generally, the most common variegated cultivars are

'Silver Queen' and 'Gold Edge', both with pale lilac-pink flowers in July. If allowed to self-seed, they often revert to the all-green-leaved species.

Among the low creeping thymes are three main species. *Thymus praecox* is perhaps the most floriferous and will smother itself in blossoms. It is available in several cultivars: 'Albiflorus' (white), 'Purple Carpet' (mauve-purple), and 'Coccineus' (magenta-red). 'Elfin' is very compact with grey-green leaves and scattered pink flowers. *Thymus serpyllum*, similar to *Thymus praecox*, comes in three main cultivars: 'Albus' (white), 'Magic Carpet' (magenta-pink), and 'Pink Chintz'. For variegated foliage, 'Highland Cream' has white-edged leaves and 'Doone Valley' has gold-tipped foliage. *Thymus doerfleri* 'Bressingham Pink' has fairly hairy foliage. Woolly thyme, *T. pseudolanuginosus*, has very hairy grey-green foliage and pale pink flowers; unlike the other thymes mentioned, it does not have particularly fragrant foliage.

All sun-lovers, the thymes require well-drained soil. They can tolerate drought and poor, gravelly soil; however, excess winter wetness can kill the plant. Typical of most herbs, thyme flowers attract both bees and butterflies. Diseases are rare and most pests, large or small, ignore them. The mounding thymes are hardy to zone 4, the creeping thymes to zone 3.

Thymus citriodorus 'Variegatus'

Tiarella cordifolia

Tiarella
FOAMFLOWER

Of the three species of *Tiarella*, two are from North America, one from Asia. Creeping foamflower, *Tiarella cordifolia*, native to the Maritimes, is a good ground cover in shady locations. The wild form has basal, evergreen, maple-leaf-shaped leaves and spikes of tiny, white to pale pink, star-shaped flowers atop 25-centimetre-tall stems in June. Plants form large mats through the production of stolons. The leaves of the cultivar 'Running Tapestry' have dark, nearly black veins. *Tiarella wherryi*, a runnerless version of *T. cordifolia*, form discrete clumps. It looks much like coral bells, *Heuchera*, and, in fact, has been hybridized with it to create the hybrid X *Heucherella*. Like many *Heuchera*, most of the modern foamflower cultivars are grown for their decorative leaves. Although the cultivars are not as numerous as those in *Heuchera*, more are being produced all the time. Most have varying amounts of black veins and/or vary in the degree of divisions and leaf lobing. These include 'Sugar and Spice', 'Neon Lights', 'Iron Butterfly', 'Cascade Creeper', and 'Black Snowflake', the last with nearly black leaves. 'Candy Striper' has the deepest-cut foliage, while the leaves of 'Crow Feather' take on pink and red tones during the winter. 'Pink Skyrocket' has green leaves but has been selected for its pink blossoms.

X *Heucherella* are also grown for their evergreen foliage. They often have pink flowers similar to those of foamflowers but with the bolder foliage

Heucherella 'Tapestry'

colours of *Heuchera*. 'Sunspot', 'Stoplight', 'Gold Zebra', and 'Mojito' have yellow to chartreuse leaves with red veins. For orange-toned leaves, try 'Sweet Tea', 'Honey Rose', 'Buttered Rum', and 'Brass Lantern'. 'Redstone Falls' has a striking blend of red, gold, orange, and bronze with distinctive dark veins on a trailing plant. 'Solar Eclipse' has nearly black leaves with a green margin.

Tiarella and X *Heucherella* both prefer part shade and evenly moist, acidic soil. They can tolerate full shade but their decorative coloured foliage will be less bright without sunlight. Despite their need for moisture, they do not tolerate excess winter wetness; the soil must be well drained. They are usually grown along the edges of borders but may be used in partly shady rockeries. Diseases are generally not a problem; the main pests are slugs and root weevils. Hares may nibble the leaves. Propagation is by division. Both are hardy to zone 4 but are more reliably evergreen in zone 5 or higher.

Heucherella 'Tapestry'

Tradescantia 'Zwanenburg Blue'

Tradescantia
SPIDERWORT

The genus *Tradescantia* includes about 75 species, found throughout the Americas. The genus was named in honour of John Tradescant (Sr. and Jr.), 17th century botanists and personal gardeners of King Charles I of England. Many *Tradescantia* species are trailing tropicals and well known as houseplants, including Wandering Jew, *T. pallida*.

The hardy garden ornamentals are derived from three main species. The hardiest of these is *T. virginiana*, native to eastern North America from Ontario south to Alabama. The garden spiderworts found in Atlantic Canada are called *T.* X *andersoniana* and are combinations of *T. virginiana*, *T. subaspera*, and *T. ohiensis*. Most spiderworts are upright clumping plants with narrow grass-like foliage and terminal clusters of nearly stemless, three-petalled flowers which reach 3 to 4 centimetres in diameter. Flowers found in the wild are purple-blue, but modern hybrids are available in white and various shades of blue, purple, and pink to nearly red. Individual flowers only last two to three days, but plants produce flowers over several weeks from mid-June to early August. Cultivars reaching about 60 centimetres tall have been on the market for some time and include 'Zwanenburg Blue', 'Rubra' (rose-purple), 'Osprey' (ice blue), and 'Innocence' (white). Newer cultivars have been bred to be 40 to 45 centimetres tall and include 'Concord Grape' (violet-purple), 'Bilberry Ice' (mauve-pink), 'Hawaiian Punch' (bright pink), 'Little Doll' (pale lavender), and 'Red Cloud' (rose-purple). For a strong contrast in foliage and flower colour, try the brilliant yellow-foliaged 'Sweet Kate', with deep purple-blue flowers, or 'Sunshine Charm', with mauve-purple flowers.

Spiderwort prefer full sun and moist, acidic soil. If too shaded or dry, the plants will flop. If this happens, cut the plants back and you may be rewarded with a late summer flush of foliage and early fall blossoms. As Spiderwort will self-seed freely, prompt dead-heading is recommended. Besides the mid-border, they are ideal for cottage gardens, wildflower gardens, and near water features. Pests and diseases are generally not an issue. Propagation is by division. Spiderwort are hardy to zone 4.

Tradescantia 'Osprey'

Tricyrtis formosana 'Dark Beauty'

Tricyrtis
TOAD LILY

All 16 species of *Tricyrtis* are native to eastern Asia. The genus name comes from the Greek words *tri*, three, and *kyrtos*, humped, as the bases of the three outer petals are swollen. As a group, they are woodland plants with heart- to teardrop-shaped leaves positioned alternately along the unbranched stems. Small, usually spotted, lilylike flowers are produced among the upper leaf axils or at the stem ends. Most grow 60 to 90 centimetres tall, but, despite their height, should be placed near the front of a border, where their exotic and intricate flowers can be best appreciated. They are also suitable for woodland settings.

Only a few *Tricyrtis* are suitable for Atlantic Canada. With mid-summer blooms is *T. latifolia*; it grows to 60 centimetres in height and has straw yellow flowers spotted with brown. 'Yellow Sunrise' has pale butter yellow flowers with cinnamon brown spots. *Tricyrtis hirta* often does not bloom until October and into November, if not cut down by frost. It grows to 90 centimetres tall and typically has white flowers heavily spotted with dark purple. 'Miyazaki' has pale pink flowers with darker pink spots. 'Albomarginata' is grown for its cream-edged leaves. *Tricyrtis formosana* is similar, but its spotting is not as pronounced. 'Seiryu' is pale violet-blue with darker purple spots, while 'Dark Beauty' is very heavily spotted in purple. This species' variegated cultivars include 'Gilt Edge', 'Samurai', and 'Autumn Glow'. 'Guilty Pleasure' has all-yellow foliage that may be appreciated irrespective of its mauve-pink flowers. Toad lily hybrids include 'Empress', white with dark purple spots; 'Blue Wonder', with blossoms heavily spotted in purple blue; 'Togen', with lavender-mauve, unspotted flowers; and 'Shirohotogisu', with white flowers. 'Lightning Strike' has cream-streaked leaves.

Tricyrtis 'Shirohotogisu'

Trillium erectum

Toad lilies prefer part shade and evenly moist and organically rich soil. They may be grown in full sun in cool coastal areas. They do not tolerate drought. Diseases are not a problem, but slugs can damage unfurling leaves. Hares generally ignore them, but they may be browsed by deer or moose. Propagation is by division. *Tricyrtis latifolia* and *T. hirta* are both rated for zone 4; *T. formosana* and the hybrids, zone 5.

Trillium

TRILLIUM, WAKEROBIN

The nearly 40 species of *Trillium* are confined to North America and east Asia. All trillium form spreading clumps with unbranched stems topped with a single trifoliate leaf and a solitary three-petalled flower. Heights vary from 15 to 45 centimetres, depending on the species. Bloom time also varies, from late April through June. Four species are native to Atlantic Canada. Nodding trillium, *T. cernuum*, found throughout the region, is perhaps the least showy, with a small nodding white flower. White trillium, *T. grandiflorum*, Ontario's provincial floral emblem, is a rare native species in Atlantic Canada, con-

fined to Nova Scotia. Red trillium, *T. erectum*, and painted trillium, *T. undulatum*, are native in the Maritimes but absent from Newfoundland. Painted trillium is one of the most beautiful but also one of the most difficult trilliums to grow in cultivation; it requires exacting soil conditions that are not generally found in a garden setting. The easiest to grow, and most widely available, are the white and red trillium. White trillium blossoms are among the largest of any trillium and the petals often turn from white to pink as they age. Very expensive but in-demand double forms exist. Western trillium, *T. ovatum*, is similar in appearance to white trillium. Snow trillium, *T. nivale*, has small, early flowers and grey-green leaves. For decorative foliage, try the yellow or red toad trillium, *T. luteum* and *T. sessile* respectively; their small stemless flowers sit atop the leaves, but the foliage is mottled and spotted silver-green. These have fragrant flowers and are the last to bloom of the trilliums, well into June. Although there are many other garden-worthy trilliums, they are generally only available in specialist nurseries.

Trillium are best grown in part shade with soil that is evenly moist, highly organic, and slightly acidic. If the soil is too dry, they may go summer-dormant. Although these woodland treasures may be used in a shady border, they are more commonly planted in woodland or wildflower settings. Diseases are rare, and the main pests are browsing deer or moose. Propagation may be by seed, but these can take two years to germinate; propagation by division is far more popular. Most of the above trillium are hardy to zone 4, but the mottled-leaved types are better suited to zone 5 or higher.

Trillium sessile

Trollius chinensis 'Orange Queen'

Trollius
GLOBEFLOWER

The 30 species of *Trollius* are found in cooler regions of the northern hemisphere. It is closely related to buttercup but more attractive in both flower and form. The Latin name comes from the German *trol*, which means round, referring to the flowers. All globeflowers form a clump of rounded, deeply cut leaves and stems topped with round, 5-centimetre-diameter, white, yellow, or orange flowers in May to early July. Two main species and their hybrids are grown in Atlantic Canada. *Trollius europaeus* 'Superbus' is a heritage plant with semi-double yellow flowers atop 60-centimetre-tall stems. The tallest cultivar, *T. ledebourii* (also known as *T. chinensis*) 'Golden Queen', has deep orange flowers held on 90-centimetre-tall stems. Hybrids include 'Lem-

Trollius europaeus 'Superbus'

on Queen' (60 centimetres, lemon yellow), 'Orange Queen' (70 centimetres, light orange), 'Alabaster' (70 centimetres, butter yellow), 'Cheddar' (70 centimetres, soft cream), and 'New Moon' (60 centimetres, cream-yellow).

Sometimes available in local nurseries is the dwarf globeflower, *T. acaulis* and *T. pumilus*. Flower stems reach a height of 25 centimetres with large, single yellow flowers in May or June. Both are suitable for damp spots in a rock garden.

Globeflower may be grown in full sun to intense shade, although it does not flower well in shade. All types prefer moist, organically rich soil. Even boggy soil is tolerated, but the slightest drought can damage the plants. In addition to being used in a mid-border, they are suited to cottage gardens and near water features. The blossoms are frequented by bees. As the plants are toxic if ingested, they are rarely bothered by any pests. Diseases are also rare, although powdery mildew may be a problem in some areas. Propagation is primarily by division, but species may be grown from seed. It is a very hardy plant, to zone 3.

Verbascum
MULLEIN

Many of the 250 *Verbascum* species are annuals or biennials; a few are short-lived perennials. The common mullein, *V. thapsus*, a European species naturalized throughout Atlantic Canada,

Verbascum nigrum

spike of yellow flowers in the second. Unlike common mullein, silver mullein often produces several spikes of flowers per plant and its blossoms are much larger, up to 2.5 centimetres in diameter. The most spectacular biennial mullein is Greek mullein, *V. olympicum*, which produces a candelabra of yellow spires on stems reaching 2 or more metres. These plants belong at the back of a border. For a smaller garden, nettle-leaved mullein, *V. chaixii*, has hairy grey-green leaves. Its flower stems are shorter, reaching 100 centimetres, but often branching, producing a bolder floral display. The flowers are typically yellow with pink fuzzy stamens, but 'Album' has white flowers. Black mullein, *V. nigrum*, contrary to its common name, is similar to *V. chaixii* in appearance but has all-green leaves.

Showy mullein, *V. phoenicum*, is a short-lived perennial. Suited to a mid-border or cottage garden, it has a basal rosette of wrinkled green leaves from which arise several stems 90 to 120 centimetres in height. The wild species has 2.5-centimetre-diameter purple flowers, but today's cultivars vary from white, through shades of pink and lavender, to deep purple. Hybrid mullein combine *V. phoenicum*, *V. chaixii*, and other similar species. These short-lived perennials resemble showy mullein but come in a greater colour range: yellow, apricot, peach, salmon, and nearly orange. These hybrids often have the pink fuzzy stamens of the *V. chaixii* parent.

Mulleins are sun-lovers and require well-drained soil. Excess winter wetness is an enemy, but dry conditions are well tolerated. All attract bees and make attractive cut flowers. As they are biennials or short-lived perennials, a few seed capsules should be allowed to drop seed to continue the plant's existence. Rabbits, deer, moose, and other pests are generally not a problem, and diseases are rare. All are rated for zone 5, except *V. nigrum*, which is hardy to zone 3.

is a biennial with a bold rosette of white woolly leaves. In the second season a spire arises to 2 or more metres, topped with a dense spike of small yellow flowers in July and August. The plant is too weedy for a border, although it can be attractive in a wildflower garden. Similar but less weedy, silver mullein, *V. bombyciferum*, also biennial, produces a rosette of silver felted leaves in the first season and a 150- to 200-centimetre-tall

Veronica

SPEEDWELL

The genus *Veronica* has about 500 species, several of which are naturalized in Atlantic Canada. There are also several native species in the region. Ornamental garden varieties include low, creeping alpine types as well as taller border species. For the rock-garden enthusiast, many species are available through specialist nurseries but a few of the alpine types are readily available, including 'Georgia Blue', 'Waterperry Blue', *V. aphylla*, *V. pectinata*, *V. repens*, and *V. whitleyi*. These all creep, with small clusters of blue-shaded flowers in June and July. In addition to their being used in rock gardens, they may also be used to cascade over retaining walls or as a ground cover for sunny slopes. Hardiness depends on the species.

Among the low types, creeping speedwell, *V. prostrata*, has several cultivars. Its flowers are in short spikes on stems up to 15 centimetres tall. The wild species have pale lavender-blue flow-ers; cultivars include 'Goldwell' (deep blue), 'Blue Mirror' (medium blue), 'Twilight Lilac™' (lavender-pink), and 'Glacier Blue™' (ice blue). Some have colourful foliage such as 'Trehane', with chartreuse leaves, and 'Aztec Gold', with bright yellow leaves.

For a border, speedwell with narrow spikes of flowers are most commonly grown. The smallest is *V. allionii*, which is less than 15 centimetres tall, with blue spikes. Spiked speedwell, *V. spictata*, and its hybrids are the most popular, with the greatest number of cultivars and widest colour range. The species forms upright clumps with many unbranched stems reaching to 60 centimetres tall. Narrow spikes of violet-blue flowers are produced in July and August. Cultivars include 'Icicle' (50 centimetres tall, white), 'Red Fox' (40 centimetres, deep pink), 'Royal Candles' (30 centimetres, deep blue), 'Baby Doll' (30 centimetres, light pink), 'Giles van Hees' (20 centimetres, hot pink), and 'Blue Carpet' (20 centimetres, deep blue). For decorative foliage, try *V. spicata* ssp. *in-*

Veronica 'Georgia Blue'

cana, whose blue flowers contrast with its silvery foliage. Hybrids with a bushier, more branching habit have been developed: 'Royal Rembrandt' (50 centimetres, medium blue), 'Hocus Pocus' (50 centimetres, violet-blue), 'Purpleicious' (50 centimetres, purple), 'Tickled Pink' (45 centimetres, pink), 'First Love' (30 centimetres, hot pink), and 'Aspire' (20 centimetres, reddish pink). Perhaps the most popular is 'Sunny Border Blue', which won Perennial Plant of the Year™ in 1993. It has deep violet-blue flowers on 45-centimetre-tall plants. 'Purple Explosion' has purple-blue flowers on 45-centimetre-long, multiple-branching stems.

Veronica spicata 'Red Fox'

Tall speedwell, *V. longifolia*, is similar to spiked speedwell but often has clusters of spikes on taller plants. The wild species is a heritage plant with spikes of blue flowers on plants reaching 100 centimetres in height. Several cultivars are more compact: 'Pink Eveline' (60 centimetres, pale pink), 'Eveline' (55 centimetres, purple), 'Candies Candle' (45 centimetres, violet), 'First Lady' (40 centimetres, white), and 'First Glory' (40 centimetres, royal blue). 'Charlotte', a variegated cultivar, has white-edged leaves and white flowers on 75-centimetre-tall plants.

Most of the speedwell prefer full sun and well-drained but evenly moist soil. They can tolerate part shade and some drought but may be vulnerable to powdery mildew under those conditions. The spiked types attract bees and butterflies and are attractive cut flowers. Pests are rarely a problem. Most are hardy to at least zones 4 or 3, if adequately mulched.

Veronicastrum
CULVER'S ROOT

Culver's root, *Veronicastrum virginicum*, native to the eastern US, resembles tall speedwell, *Veronica longifolia*. It differs primarily in having narrow lance-shaped leaves in whorls of three to seven around the stem and in its height of up to 180 centimetres. From July to September, plants produce candelabra-like spikes of white bottlebrush flowers. Cultivars include 'Adoration' (120 centimetres, lilac-pink), 'Erica' (120 centimetres, soft pink), 'Red Arrows' (120 centimetres, magenta), 'Lavender Towers' (120 centimetres, pale lavender-blue), 'Fascination' (120 centimetres, lilac-rose), 'Lilac Karina' (100 centimetres, lavender-mauve), 'Apollo' (100 centimetres, lilac-blue), and 'Cupid' (90 centimetres, lilac-blue).

Veronicastrum sibericum

Culver's root prefers full sun and organically rich, evenly moist soil. It is a plant for the back of a border, a wildflower garden, or a cottage garden. Despite its height, the stems are generally strong enough that staking is not required. It attracts bees and butterflies and makes an attractive cut flower. Pests and diseases are rare. Propagation is by seed for the wild species or division for the cultivars. It is hardy through zone 3.

Vinca
PERIWINKLE, CREEPING MYRTLE

The handful of *Vinca* species are all native to Eurasia. Gardeners in Atlantic Canada grow a single species, *V. minor*, commonly called periwinkle or creeping myrtle, primarily as an evergreen ground cover for dry, shady areas. Plants produce long trailing stems that root as they creep over the soil surface. In May and June, and periodically throughout the summer, solitary, periwinkle blue, 2.5-centimetre-diameter flowers are produced in the leaf axils. The leaves are a shiny deep green and mound to a height of 15 centimetres.

Vinca minor 'Atropurpurea'

Vinca minor 'Alba Variegata'

The flowers are white, in the cultivar 'Alba', or deep purple, in 'Atropurpurea'. 'Double Bowles' is a double-flowered blue cultivar. Several variegated forms are popular in containers or hanging baskets, where they are grown as annuals, but they may also be grown as a perennial in the garden. 'Argenteovariegata' has blue flowers and leaves irregularly edged in white, 'Alba Variegata' has white flowers with irregular yellow edges. More recent variegated cultivars are the blue-flowered 'Ralph Shugert' and the white-flowered 'Evelyn', both of which have evenly white-edged foliage. Perhaps the most striking is 'Illumination', with bright yellow leaves thinly edged in green. It has the typical blue flowers of the species.

Periwinkle may be grown in full sun to full shade. However, in sunny locations, winter sun may burn the foliage if snow cover is not consistent. It prefers evenly moist, humus-rich soil but, once established, tolerates considerable drought. Diseases and pests are not generally a problem.

The main concern is the aggressiveness of the plant; in some regions, it can become invasive. For stabilizing embankments or as a lawn substitute under large trees, however, periwinkle is the best choice. The all-green cultivars are rated for zone 3; the variegated cultivars best in zone 4 or higher.

Vinca minor 'Alba Variegata'

Viola sororia 'Freckles'

Viola
VIOLET

Most of the 500-plus species of *Viola* are native to the north temperate regions, but a few are from tropical regions. Close to 20 species are found wild in Atlantic Canada—the marsh blue violet, *V. cucullata*, is the provincial floral emblem for New Brunswick. From a gardening perspective, the most important *Viola* are pansies. Although these may survive for a second year, and self-seed to maintain themselves in the garden, they are considered annual bedding plants rather than perennials. However, a few truly perennial violets are available and are attractive additions to the garden. Perhaps the most commonly encountered violet is the native woolly blue violet, *V. sororia*; it forms a low mound 20 centimetres tall with basal, heart-shaped leaves and leafless stems that are topped, in May and June, with solitary, 2-centimetre-diameter blossoms. There are two popular cultivars: 'Albiflora', with white flowers; and 'Freckles', whose ice blue flowers have fine, darker blue spotting. This species does not run but can self-seed with abandon. The native marsh blue violet, *V. cucullata*, usually grows in wet areas but can adapt to typical garden settings. It too is a clumper.

Sweet violet, *V. odorata*, produces creeping stolons, resulting in a more matlike habit. Many cultivars in various shades of blue or violet are available, but 'Sulphurea' has apricot flowers; 'Phyllis Dove' and 'Perle Rose' have pink blossoms.

Grown for its purple foliage is *V. conspersa* 'Purpurea', erroneously called *V. labradorica*. This cultivar has violet-blue flowers. It forms a low mound with trailing stems, but unlike the stems of *V. odorata*, these do not root. Downy yellow violet, *V. pubescens*, is a little more upright, with stems up to 30 centimetres in height; Canada violet, *V. canadensis*, is similar but has white flowers with a yellow eye.

The above violets are all suitable for full sun but are more commonly grown in part shade. Classic woodland plants, they are well suited to a wildflower setting or being grown as a ground cover in partly shaded areas. All prefer organically rich soil that stays evenly moist. Slugs may eat the blossoms, but generally insects and diseases are not a problem. Deer and moose ignore them but hares may nibble the leaves and flowers. Propagation is by seed or division. They are all hardy to zone 3.

Viola corsica

GRASS
AND RELATIVES

LEFT AND ABOVE: *Arrhenatherum elatius* var. *bulbosum* 'Variegatum'
PREVIOUS SPREAD: *Festuca glauca*

Arrhenatherum
BULBOUS OAT GRASS

Only one species of bulbous oat grass is grown in Atlantic Canada. Its botanical name is quite a mouthful: *Arrhenatherum elatius* var. *bulbosum* 'Variegatum'. This is a cool-season grass with blades up to 30 centimetres tall and flower stems up to 45 centimetres tall. Plants spread slowly to form a clump, but it is not invasive. It produces small beige seed heads. The variegated foliage of this grass imparts a whitened appearance to the plant when it is viewed from a distance. It is best used as an accent along the edges of a border but, due to its small size, can also be suitable for rockeries.

Like most grasses, it prefers full sun and a well-drained site. It is drought-tolerant once established. If grown in full sun in warmer, inland regions, the plant may brown in mid-summer. If the foliage browns, cut it back hard to allow a new flush of growth. It performs better along cooler coastlines than inland. Few pests or diseases bother this grass. Propagation is by division. It is rated hardy to zone 3.

Calamagrostis
FEATHER REED GRASS

Over 250 species of *Calamagrostis* are found throughout the northern hemisphere, only two of which are popular ornamental grasses in Atlantic Canada. The most popular is a hybrid, *C. X acutiflora*, an upright, clumping grass with leaves reaching 45 to 90 centimetres in height. The flowers, produced in mid-summer, are on stems that reach 120 or more centimetres tall. The spikes are narrow, feathery, and pink-tinted, turning tan in the autumn. The leaves and flowers are stiff enough to last through much of the winter if the snow is not too heavy and wet. The most popular (and tallest) cultivar, 'Karl Foerster', was named Perennial Plant of the Year™ in 2001. This cultivar has all-green leaves and is popular in commercial landscape designs across

Calamagrostis acutiflora 'Karl Foerster'

Calamagrostis brachystricha

Atlantic Canada. Three variegated cultivars have attractive flower heads and foliage: 'Overdam' has white-edged leaves; 'Avalanche' has a white stripe down the middle of each blade; and 'Eldorado' has a yellow central stripe on each blade. All reach 120 centimetres in height when in bloom. The other species often encountered is *C. brachytricha* or Korean feather reed grass; it looks much like 'Karl Foerster', but its flower spikes are wider and fluffier. Use these feather reed grasses toward the back of a border or mass-planted along driveways and foundations.

Feather reed grass, a cool-season grass, does well throughout Atlantic Canada. It prefers full sun and soil that stays evenly moist. It tolerates heavier, wetter soils than most other types of ornamental grasses. Flowers may be used in fresh and dried arrangements. It is rarely bothered by pests or diseases. Plants should be dug and divided every three to four years as they tend to die out in the middle. It is hardy through zone 4 and even into zone 3, if mulched in winter.

Carex
SEDGE

The genus *Carex* has nearly 2,000 species; over 100 are native to Atlantic Canada. *Carex* is Latin for cutter, referring to the sharp leaves and stem edges. Several are grown for their tufted, shiny, green foliage: *C. stricta*, 90 centimetres; *C. muskingumensis*, 50 centimetres; and *C. eburnea*, 30 centimetres. For decorative seed heads, consider *C. grayi*, 90 centimetres, with spiky clubbed flowers, and *C. pendula*, 150 centimetres, with broad leaf blades and nodding clusters of narrow seed heads. *C. elata* 'Bowles Golden', which has brilliant yellow foliage with blades up to 60 centimetres long in a fountainlike arrangement, thrives in wet soil and can be grown as a shallow marginal plant in pools.

From Japan come several *Carex* grown for their variegated broad-bladed foliage. *Carex morrowii* 'Ice Dance', with white-edged leaves, has a mounding habit up to 30 centimetres in height. 'Ice Ballet' has stronger white variegation, while 'Silver Sceptre' has broad white margins and looks nearly white from a distance. 'Aureo-var-

Carex elata 'Bowles Golden'

Carex muskingumensis

iegata' leaves have cream-yellow margins. More dwarf, at 15 centimetres high, is *Carex conica* 'Snowline', which has white-edged leaves. On the taller side, reaching 45 centimetres, is *C. oshimensis*. A popular cultivar is 'Evergold', with cream-yellow leaves edged in green. The recent Evercolor® series includes 'Everest', with white-edged leaves; 'Everoro', green leaves with a central yellow stripe; and 'Everillo', entirely yellow leaves.

Carex conica 'Snowline'

All the sedges mentioned are suitable for the front of shady borders, in woodland gardens, and around water features. They combine well with other shade plants such as ferns, hosta, and astilbe. Most of the above sedges are evergreen.

Sedges may be grown in sun or shade but, in either situation, require soil that stays consistently moist. Pests and diseases are not a problem. Propagation is by seed for species or division for the cultivars. The Japanese species are rated for zone 5, the others primarily for zones 3 and 4.

Chasmanthium
NORTHERN SEA OATS

Northern sea oats, *Chasmanthium latifolium*, native to the eastern and central United States, is a cool-season grass that forms upright clumps

Chasmanthium latifolium

70 to 100 centimetres tall. The leaf blades are relatively short and broad, produced along the length of the stems, which gives the appearance of a dwarf bamboo. Unlike true bamboo, it does not run and is not invasive. In mid- to late summer, plants produce drooping, flattened oatlike panicles of seed clusters on stems reaching 100 to 130 centimetres tall. 'River Mist' has striking white-striped foliage. Use northern sea oats in a mid- to back border, in mass-plantings, or in wildflower or open woodland gardens.

Northern sea oats prefer full sun but tolerate part shade. Although it grows best with even soil moisture, it can tolerate some drought once it is established. The seed heads, fresh or dried, are suitable for use in flower arrangements. Pests and diseases are rare. Propagation is by division or seed. As it is hardy through zone 5, it can only be grown in milder areas of Atlantic Canada.

Deschampsia
HAIR GRASS

Hair grass, as the common name suggests, has very thin leaves and a fine texture. The genus name honours Louis August Deschamps, a 19th-century French surgeon and naturalist. Two ornamental species are grown in Atlantic Canada, *D. caespitosa* and *D. flexuosa*, both forming tidy mounds with upright airy heads of flowers in mid-summer. Two popular cultivars of *D. caespitosa* are 'Gold Dust', with yellow-tinted flowers, and 'Bronze Veil', with bronze-beige flowers. Both reach up to 100 centimetres tall when in bloom. 'Northern Lights', a dwarf cultivar grown for its broader leaves, which are striped pink, white, and deep green, only reaches 20 to 30 centimetres tall and rarely flowers. Unfortunately, the leaves often revert to all-green. *Deschampsia flexuosa* is similar to *D. caespi-*

Deschampia cespitosa

Deschampsia cespitosa 'Northern Lights'

Festuca
BLUE FESCUE GRASS

Blue fescue, *Festuca glauca*, is one of several orna-mental grasses grown for its silver-blue colour. It is the shortest, densest, and finest textured of the blue grasses. Plants forms a dome of narrow, arching, quill-like leaves which reach a height of 20 to 25 centimetres. In early summer they pro-duce narrow brown flowers, which can increase the height of the plant to 45 centimetres. Many gardeners opt to cut off the flowers so that the plants stay mounding and tidy. It is an ideal plant for the edge of a border or pathway and can also be used in a rock garden. If planted 20 centime-tres apart, blue fescue can be used as a ground cover. Cultivars include 'Blue Glow', 'Skinners Blue', and 'Elijah Blue'. In the mildest areas it remains mostly evergreen, but throughout most of Atlantic Canada, this grass turns brown over the winter and requires pruning back to 10 cen-timetres in early spring.

Because blue fescue is a cool-season grass, it grows well in Atlantic Canada's climate. It is a sun-lover and requires a well-drained site. Ex-cess winter wetness can be a problem, but sum-mer drought is tolerated once the plants are es-tablished. Its salt tolerance makes it ideal for a coastal garden. As plants tend to die out in the middle, dividing it is recommended every three to four years. Pests and diseases are not a prob-lem. Propagation is by division. The plant is har-dy to zone 4.

Festuca glauca 'Elijah Blue'

tosa but has slightly broader foliage; its flowers are narrower and arch at their tips. The most popular cultivar is 'Tatra Gold', whose foliage is yellow in spring and becomes more chartreuse as the summer progresses. Hair grass is used as an accent along the front of a border; it may also be used in a rockery or mass-planted as a ground cover. These grasses are evergreen and provide some winter interest to a garden, al-though the flower stems typically collapse after the first snow.

Hair grass, a cool-season species, grows well in Atlantic Canada. *Deschampsia caespitosa* prefers soil that stays evenly moist, while *D. flexuosa* can tolerate drought once it is established. Both are sun-lovers. Pests and diseases are not a problem. Propagation is by division. The former is hardy to zone 3, the latter to zone 4.

Hakenochloa macra 'Aureola'

Hakenochloa
HAKONE GRASS

Hakone grass, *Hakenochloa macra*, is endemic to Japan, where it grows in open woodlands and along rocky cliffs. As a result, it is one of the few grasses that tolerates shade. Plants form graceful mounds of ribbonlike arching leaves 30 to 45 centimetres long. A deciduous species, it completely disappears in winter. It is also late to emerge in spring. Flowers are produced in late summer but are narrow and not very noticeable. Of several cultivars, the most popular is 'Aureola', with yellow-edged leaves, the winner of Perennial Plant of the Year™ in 2009. 'Sunny Delight' is similar but with reverse variegation to 'Aureola'—the leaves are yellow with green edges. 'Albostriata' has white-edged leaves and at 45 centimetres is the tallest and most robust of the cultivars; 'Fubuki™' is a dwarf version of 'Albostriata'. 'All Gold' is relatively small, reaching only 20 centimetres, with entirely golden to chartreuse leaves.

'Nicolas' is green in summer but turns a blend of yellow, orange, and red in autumn. 'Naomi' is yellow-striped but takes on purple tones in autumn. All of these are excellent accent plants for the front of a border, in a rockery, or in a wood-

Hakonechloa macra 'Fubuki'

land garden. It is by far the most desirable ornamental grass for shady and semi-shaded areas.

Hakone grass, a cool-season species that performs best in part shade, tolerates full shade but the plants will be thinner. Full sun is also tolerated if the soil is consistently moist. It is not a grass for droughty conditions, nor will it tolerate too much winter wetness. As it is shallow-rooted and prone to heaving in winter, mulching is recommended. As a woodland plant it thrives in humus-rich soil. Diseases and insect pests are not a problem, but hares relish the new growths. Propagation is by division. Hardy to zone 5, it is only suitable for milder areas of Atlantic Canada.

Helictotrichon sempervirens

Helictotrichon
BLUE OAT GRASS

Blue oat grass is one of several grasses grown for its silvery blue foliage, and perhaps the best blue accent grass for Atlantic Canadian gardens. Only one species is grown in the region, *H. sempervirens*, native to southwestern Europe. Plants form a domed mound of stiff to partly arching leaves which reach 45 centimetres in length. It is similar to blue fescue, but larger. When narrow flower spikes form in July, blue oat grass extends to 90 centimetres in height. Use it toward the front of a border, in a rock garden, or massed as a ground cover.

Helictotrichon sempervirens

Blue oat grass is a cool-season grass that prefers full sun and a well-drained site. Because it is salt-tolerant, it is especially suitable for coastal gardens. Although pests and diseases are not a problem, excess winter wetness can rot the crowns. Once established, it is drought-resistant. It is partly evergreen but requires a thorough trimming in spring. Propagation is by division. Hardy to zone 3, it is suitable throughout much of Atlantic Canada.

Luzula
WOOD RUSH

Several species of *Luzula* are native in Atlantic Canada. The two species occasionally encountered as ornamental garden plants, *L. sylvatica* and *L. nivea*, however, are both European natives. Both are tidy, clumping grasslike plants with relatively broad leaf blades. In mid-summer *L. sylvatica* produce greenish brown flowers and *L. nivea* white flowers. The foliage of both stays evergreen in zone 5 or higher. *L. sylvatica* has two recommended cultivars: 'Marginata' has leaves thinly edged in white, and 'Solar Flare' has attractive chartreuse foliage perfect for brightening up a shady spot. These are some of the few ornamental grasses suitable for shady areas, and they combine well with hosta and astilbe. They deserve to be more widely grown.

Luzula nivea

Wood rush are best grown in full sun to full shade. They require consistently moist soil and grow well in wet soils, lending themselves for use in bog gardens. Although diseases are not a problem, they may be browsed by hares, deer, or moose. Propagation is by seed for the species, division for the cultivars. All are hardy through zone 4.

Miscanthus
MAIDEN GRASS

The maiden grasses are among the most important ornamental grasses grown in North American landscapes. Although many cultivars are available, all have arisen from the species *Miscanthus sinensis*, a native of eastern Asia. As a group, they are clumpers, reaching from 1 to 2.4 metres in height when in bloom. Some are grown for their decorative, pink-tinted, plumed seed heads; others rarely bloom in Atlantic Canada

Miscanthus sinensis 'Purpureus'

189

Miscanthus sinensis 'Silberfeder'

and are grown primarily for their foliage. In fall, the foliage takes on hues of yellow and orange before turning beige in winter. Their leaves and flowers are stiff enough to provide winter interest.

Those grown for decorative seed heads, often called Japanese silver grass, include the silver-plumed 'Gracillimus' (2 metres tall), 'Silberfeder' (2 metres), and 'Yaku-jima' (120 centimetres). 'Malepartus' can also reach 2 metres and has large silver plumes, similar to a pampas grass. It is also the earliest bloomer of the maiden grasses and reliable in cooler areas, where other maiden grasses may not flower. 'Rotsilber' reaches 150 centimetres, with reddish pink flower plumes that later turn silvery. 'Purpurascens' reaches 150 centimetres and its fall foliage becomes a blend of purple, orange, and yellow.

Several maiden grasses are grown for their variegated leaves, in addition to their flowers. One such group has transverse yellow bands across their wide blades. Most popular are 'Zebrinus'

and 'Strictus', both commonly called zebra grass. In ideal conditions, they can reach over 2 metres in height. 'Little Zebra' is a relatively dwarf cultivar reaching 120 centimetres, while 'Gold Bar' has wide yellow bands and can reach 150 centimetres. 'Flamingo' has blades with a central silvery stripe. Its plumes start off reddish pink and then turn coppery later in the season. Those with leaves margined in white include 'Variegatus' at a height of 90 centimetres, 'Silberpfeil' at 120 centimetres, and 'Morning Light' at 180 centimetres. For a visual feast, combine maiden grass with Michaelmas daisies, larger sedums, and purple and/or yellow coneflowers.

Maiden grass is a warm-season grass that requires full sun and well-drained soil, but it will not thrive in dry sites. It is slower to green in the spring than the cool-season grasses but does well with high heat and humidity and performs better in inland locations than along the cooler coasts. Pests and diseases are rare. Propagation is by division. As it is rated hardy to zone 5, it is best used in the milder zones of Atlantic Canada.

LEFT: *Miscanthus sinensis* 'Zebrinus'

Molinia

MOOR GRASS

Only one species of *Molinia*, a cool-season grass native to the damp grasslands of Eurasia, is grown in Atlantic Canada, *M. caerulea*. Several cultivars are available, ranging in height from 75 centimetres to over 2 metres when in bloom. Overall, this is a clumping grass whose leaves create a fountain effect. Narrow bronze-purple flower spikes are produced in August and September. Although the flexible stems are wind-resistant, they promptly flop in winter, providing little winter interest in the garden. As a result, moor grass may be trimmed back in late fall. Plants are slow to establish. 'Moorhexe' is a popular cultivar with dark green leaves and flower stems that reach a height of 75 centimetres. 'Variegata' has leaves edged in cream-white; it also reaches 75 centimetres. The most impressive in terms of height is 'Skyracer', whose tall imposing spikes may exceed 2 metres. The more compact cultivars are best used as accents toward the front of a border, while 'Skyracer' may be used in the back of a border or grown on its own as a specimen. All are suitable for growing around water features.

Molinia 'Skyracer'

Molinia caerulea 'Variegata'

Moor grass, a sun-lover, prefers consistently moist, organically rich, acidic soil. It can tolerate wet soil. All cultivars turn golden in autumn and the flower spikes may be used as cut flowers. Propagation is primarily by division. Pests and diseases arc rare. It is hardy through zone 4.

Panicum
SWITCH GRASS, PANIC GRASS

Most of the 450 species of panic grass are tropical; however, a few do extend into north temperate regions. *Panicum virgatum*, the common switch grass, is the main species grown in Atlantic Canada. It is native from Nova Scotia west to Saskatchewan and south through much of the US. With such a wide natural range, it is not surprising that panic grass exhibits great diversity. The wild form has leaf blades ranging from 40 to 150 centimetres long with airy sprays of pink-tinted flowers atop 150- to 200-centimetre-long stems. Overall, it has a bunching habit.

Perhaps the most popular cultivar is 'Northwind', chosen as Perennial Plant of the Year™ in

Panicum virgatum 'Northwind'

2014. Its upright blades reach 100 to 125 centimetres in height, with flower stems rising to 150 centimetres. The overall habit is narrow, almost columnar. The foliage takes on golden tones in the fall. 'Warrior' is notable for its red fall colour. 'Dacotah' and 'Sunburst' resemble 'Northwind'. 'Cheyenne Sky' is the shortest switch grass, reaching a maximum of 90 centimetres; 'Cloud Nine' is one of the tallest, reaching nearly 2 metres.

Many switch grass cultivars have blades which develop burgundy tips as the season progresses and flowers which are reddish pink when they first open. Among these are 'Haense Herns', 'Shenandoah', 'Red Ribbons', and 'Prairie Fire'. Among blue-foliaged switch grass, 'Heavy Metal' has blades up to 125 centimetres long and 'Prairie Sky' up to 150 centimetres. Both of these are among the most drought-tolerant

Panicum virgatum 'Haense Herns'

Panicum virgatum 'Heavy Metal'

Pennisetum
FOUNTAIN GRASS

Many gardeners are familiar with the annual red-foliaged fountain grass seen in containers and ornamental plantings. Two species of fountain grass may be grown as perennials, however, in the mildest areas of Atlantic Canada: *Pennisetum alopecuroides* and *P. orientale*, both warm-season grasses, with a mounding habit to 45 centimetres in height. In mid-summer plants produce silvery to pink-tinted bottlebrush-like flowers held on 75- to 90-centimetre-tall stems. In autumn, the foliage turns yellow. Among *P. alopecuroides*, the cultivar 'Hameln' is the most popular, with silvery flowers at the ends of 90-centimetre-long stems. Other cultivars include 'Red Head', with grey-pink flowers; 'Moudry', purple-tinted flowers; and 'Desert Plains', red-tipped foliage. Dwarf cultivars which grow to a maximum of 40 centimetres tall include 'Little Bunny' and 'Burgundy Bunny', the latter of which has red-tinted leaves. The most popular *P. orientale* cultivar is 'Karley Rose', reputed to be the hardiest of the fountain grasses. Use fountain grass as an accent toward the front of a border.

switch grasses. Combining the best of the red and blue switch grasses are 'Blood Brothers' and 'Samurai', whose blue-tinted blades develop purplish tips in late summer.

Switch grass prefers full sun and soil that stays reasonably moist. However, once established, it can tolerate some drought. Too organically rich soil or over-fertilizing may cause the plants to become floppy. This warm-season grass may be slower to turn green in spring than a cool-season grass. Use in a mid- to back border, in wildflower gardens, near water features, and even in wet boggy sites. Diseases are uncommon; the most common pests are Japanese beetle and thrips. Propagation is by division. Most are hardy to zone 4, with the exceptions of 'Dacotah' and 'Sunburst', which are considered hardy to zone 3.

Pennisetum alopecuroides 'Hameln'

FAVOURITE PERENNIALS FOR ATLANTIC CANADA

Pennisetum alopecuroides

Fountain grass prefer full sun and sandy soil; avoid heavy wet clays. The seed heads make attractive cut flowers. Diseases are rare and the only pest is likely to be hares. Propagation is by division. Only reliably hardy in zone 6, fountain grass is only suitable for the mildest regions of southern and eastern Nova Scotia. 'Karley Rose' may be hardy to zone 5.

FERNS

Adiantum

MAIDENHAIR FERN

Over 250 species of maidenhair fern are found throughout the world, most of them tropical. Only two are regularly grown in Atlantic Canada—*Adiantum pedatum* and *A. aleuticum*. The northern maidenhair fern, *A. pedatum*, native to Nova Scotia and New Brunswick, forms a loose clump up to 75 centimetres tall. The hand-shaped fronds are matte light green with almost black stems. The compact 'Miss Sharples' reaches a height of only 40 centimetres. Aleutian maidenhair, *A. aleuticum*, native to New-foundland, resembles 'Miss Sharples', reaching 40 to 60 centimetres.

Maidenhair ferns prefer part to full shade and evenly moist soil. In the wild, they often grow in soil overlying limestone; therefore, the addition of lime to the growing area is beneficial. The light green colour and unique frond shape make it an ideal plant for a shady border or for naturalizing under trees. Pests and diseases pose no problems. Propagation is by division. Hardy through zone 3, the northern and Aleutian maidenhairs are suitable to use throughout most of Atlantic Canada.

LEFT AND ABOVE: *Adiantum pedatum* 'Miss Sharples'
PREVIOUS SPREAD: *Adiantum pedatum*

Asplenium scolopendrium

Asplenium
HART'S-TONGUE FERN, SPLEENWORT

Although there are over 700 species of *Asplenium* worldwide, only one is popular as a garden perennial in Atlantic Canada: hart's-tongue fern or *A. scolopendrium*, formerly *Phyllitis scolopendrium*. This fern forms an evergreen vaselike clump with broad, waxy, tongue-shaped, leathery fronds 30 to 45 centimetres long. Cultivars include 'Angustifolia', which has narrow fronds; 'Undulata', wavy-edged fronds; and 'Cristatum', fronds with crested, ruffled tips. Hart's-tongue fern may be grown near the front of a shady border, under trees, in a shaded rockery, or along a foundation. It combines well with hellebores, dead-nettle, and hakone grass.

For a shady rock garden, try ebony spleenwort, *A. trichomanes*, a very lacy fern with narrow, arching fronds with rounded leaflets. It forms a clump about 20 centimetres tall.

These ferns prefer part shade or bright shade with moist but well-drained soil. Excess winter wetness may cause root rot. Ebony spleenwort can tolerate a dry shaded area once it is established. As both species prefer alkaline soil, add lime if the growing area is acidic. Pests and diseases are generally not a problem. Propagation is by division. Both are rated hardy to zone 5.

Asplenium trichomanes

Athyrium
LADY FERN

While about 180 species of lady fern are found throughout the world, only a few are grown as garden ornamentals in Atlantic Canada. The common lady fern, *Athyrium filix-femina*, is native in this region. From a stout crown, it forms a spreading clump of bright green fronds up to 90 centimetres tall. The fronds are deciduous and turn yellow in the fall before they shrivel. The many cultivars differ in frond size and shape. 'Frizelliae' has unique rounded pinnae and narrow fronds rarely exceeding 45 centimetres in length. It goes by the common name "tatting fern". 'Dre's Dagger' has short pointed pinnae that crisscross each other. 'Lady in Red' has red frond stems that contrast sharply with the light green fronds.

Japanese painted fern, *A. niponicum* 'Pictum', is one of the most colourful ferns, forming a 45-centimetre-tall mound with a combination of grey-green and silver-grey fronds, with a contrasting burgundy stem. It was awarded Perenni-

Athyrium felix-femina

al Plant of the Year™ in 2004. 'Burgundy Lace', 'Pewter Lace', 'Silver Falls', and 'Apple Court' vary in their silver or burgundy highlights. 'Ghost' and 'Brandford Beauty' are of hybrid origin and have silver-green fronds. Eared lady fern, *A. otophorum*, grows to 60 centimetres tall with light apple green fronds and maroon stems.

Athyrium nipponicum 'Pictum'

TODD BOLAND

The lady ferns are best grown in part shade with evenly moist soil, but they tolerate deep shade and drier conditions than most ferns. Use them near the front in a shady border, under trees, as a foundation plant on the shady side of a house, or along water features. Insect pests and diseases are not a problem, but hares sometimes eat emerging fronds. Propagation is by division. The common lady fern is hardy to zone 3; the others are rated for zone 4.

Dryopteris
WOOD FERN

About 250 types of wood fern exist; several are native to Atlantic Canada, such as mountain fern, *Dryopteris campyloptera*, and spinulose wood fern, *D. carthusiana*. Any of the native species will do well in a shady garden. As a group, most of the wood ferns form vaselike clumps with trian-

Dryopteris carthusiana

gular to lance-shaped fronds 60 to 150 centimetres long, depending on the species. Some are evergreen; others, deciduous. A surprising number of wood ferns are available commercially. Marginal shield fern, *D. marginalis*, a native, has matte green, evergreen fronds 60 centimetres long. Male fern, *D. filix-mas*, another native, is evergreen, with dark green fronds up to 120 centimetres long. Cultivars of male fern include 'Barnesii', 'Crispa', and 'Linearis'. From Europe comes the golden-scaled male fern, *D. affinis*. 'The King' has large shiny evergreen fronds to 120 centimetres long. Also from Europe is the broad buckler fern, *D. dilatata*, which has semi-evergreen fronds up to 60 centimetres long. The most unusual *Dryopteris* is the autumn fern, *D. erythrosora*. This Japanese species has fronds that are copper-coloured when they emerge, later turning shiny bright green. Its fronds reach just 60 centimetres in length. Autumn fern is late to emerge in spring. Wood ferns make admirable companion plants for Siberian bugloss, astilbe, and hosta.

Dryopteris affinis

Dryopteris erythrosora

The wood ferns noted above tolerate full shade but grow better with part sun. The soil should be highly organic and reasonably moist but not soggy. The shorter species may be used toward the front of a shady border; the taller, farther back. They are ideal as a ground cover in high shade under trees or used in a woodland garden. Pests and diseases are not a problem. Propagation is by division. Most are hardy to zone 3, with the exception of autumn fern, which is rated for zone 5.

Matteuccia
OSTRICH FERN

The sole species of ostrich fern, *Matteuccia struthiopteris*, is found throughout the northern hemisphere, including in Atlantic Canada. The genus name honours Carlo Matteucci, an 18th-century Italian physicist. This is the classic edible fiddlehead fern, a spring delicacy throughout Atlantic Canada. It is perhaps the tallest hardy fern, with sterile fronds approaching 2 metres when grown under ideal conditions. The fronds are bright green, feather-shaped, and upright and arise from a stout crown. The fertile fronds are dark green and turn black in winter; often only 30 to 45 centimetres tall, they can add interest to the winter garden. This fern produces underground stolons, with new plants arising some distance from the parent: provide it with room to run. This running habit may be problematic in a border, where new ferns could sprout in the middle of a clump of nearby perennials; it is probably better in a wildflower or woodland garden or along water features. It combines particularly well with hosta, astilbe, and spring woodland wildflowers.

Ostrich fern are best grown in dappled shade but can tolerate full sun if the soil is consistently moist. The soil should be organically rich and acidic. As with ferns in general, pests and diseases are rare. Propagation is by removing the young plants that arise at the end of the underground stolons. Rated hardy to zone 2, this native fern may be grown throughout most of Atlantic Canada.

Matteuccia struthiopteris

TODD BOLAND

Osmunda cinnamomea

Osmunda
ROYAL, INTERRUPTED, AND CINNAMON FERN

The *Osmunda* ferns are all native to Atlantic Canada. Royal ferns grow along streams, cinnamon ferns in peatlands, and interrupted ferns in damp woodland glades. These adaptable ferns make the move to gardens easily, without the need for wet soil. The cinnamon fern, *O. cinnamomea*, and interrupted fern, *O. claytoniana*, both produce a vaselike arrangement of lance-shaped fronds about 90 to 120 centimetres high. The fronds of cinnamon fern are glossy green; those of interrupted, matte green. Both turn golden yellow in autumn. Cinnamon fern also produce central narrow fronds that, while short-lived, turn a cinnamon red as they release their spores. Royal fern, *O. regalis*, is different: its arch-

ing fronds are divided and triangular in outline, with oval-shaped leaflets. New fronds are coppery maroon when they emerge but turn deep green. All of these ferns are suitable toward the back of a border, in wildflower and woodland gardens, or along water features.

Unlike most ferns, *Osmunda* prefer full sun or at least part sun. However, to survive in full sun, the soil must be consistently moist or the edges of the fronds will turn brown. The soil should also be highly organic and acidic. Pests and diseases are rare. Propagation is by division. As they are native throughout Atlantic Canada, and hardy through zone 3, they may be grown in much of the region.

Osmunda regalis

Polystichum acrostichoides

Polystichum

SHIELD FERN, HOLLY FERN

About 260 species of *Polystichum* are found throughout the world, with nearly half found in China. Closer to home, two garden-worthy species are native to Atlantic Canada: the eastern holly fern, *P. acrostichoides*, is native to shady glades and cliffs throughout the Maritimes; and Braun's holly fern, *P. braunii*, is native across the Atlantic provinces. As a group, the holly ferns are evergreen with glossy fronds. The plant habit is mounding and, depending on the species, they have fronds 30 to 120 centimetres long.

Among the smaller-statured species are the native eastern holly fern, the Japanese tassel fern, *P. polyblepharum*, and Makinoi's holly fern, *P. makinoi*, all with fronds 30 to 60 centimetres long. In the mid-sized range is the soft shield fern, *P.*

setiferum, a species native to Europe. This species has finely dissected fronds up to 70 centimetres long. The cultivar 'Divisilobum' has fronds that are even more finely cut than the species *P. setiferum*, while 'Plumosum' has mosslike fronds. Of similar size is the native Braun's holly fern, whose upright 90-centimetre-tall fronds are held in a vaselike arrangement. The giant in the group is the western sword fern, *P. munitum*, from the Pacific northwest, whose fronds can reach 120 centimetres.

The holly ferns require soil that is organically rich and moist but well drained. Dappled shade is ideal, but they can tolerate fairly deep shade and even full sun if the soil stays reasonably moist. Although they are evergreen, in colder zones the fronds may be tattered by spring and require removal to allow new fronds to expand. Pests and diseases are not a problem. Propagation is by division. Hardiness varies with the species. The two native species are hardy to zone 3. Soft shield fern, Japanese tassel fern, and Makinoi's holly fern are rated for zone 5; western sword fern, zone 6.

Polystichum setiferum

PLANT SELECTOR

Latin Name	Common Name	Blooming Season	Light	Height
Achemilla mollis	lady's mantle	early June to late July	Sun to part shade	45 cm
Achillea millefolium	common yarrow	mid-June to mid-September	Sun	100 cm
Aconitum napellus	monkshood	mid-July to late August	Sun to part shade	120-160 cm
Ajuga reptans	bugleweed	May to mid-June	Sun to shade	15 cm
Alcea rosea	hollyhock	late June to mid-September	Sun	150-200 cm plus
Amsonia tabernaemontana	bluestar	mid-June to end of July	Sun	60-90 cm
Anemone hupehensis	Japanese anemone	mid-August to mid-October	Sun to part shade	120 cm
Anthemis tinctoria	golden marguerite	mid-July to late September	Sun	60-90 cm
Aquilegia vulgaris	columbine	early June to mid-July	Sun to part shade	45-90 cm
Arabis caucasica	rockcress	late April to early June	Sun	20 cm
Armeria maritima	thrift	early June to mid-July	Sun	15-20 cm
Aruncus dioicus	goatsbeard	mid-June to late July	Sun to part shade	150-200 cm
Asclepias tuberosa	butterfly weed	early July to late August	Sun	50-75 cm
Astilbe X arendsii	astilbe	mid-July to early October	Sun to part shade	30-120 cm
Astrantia major	masterwort	mid-June to late August	Sun to part shade	70-90 cm
Aubrieta deltoidea	wall cress	early May to mid-June	Sun	20 cm
Aurinia saxatile	basket of gold	early May to late June	Sun	20-30 cm
Baptisia australis	blue false indigo	mid-June to late July	Sun	90-120 cm
Bergenia X schmidtii	rockfoil	mid-April to mid-June	Sun to part shade	30-60 cm
Brunnera macrophylla	Siberian bugloss	early May to mid-June	Sun to part shade	30-40 cm
Campanula carpatica	carpathian harebell	early June to late July	Sun to part shade	15-30 cm
Campanula glomerata	clustered bellflower	late June to early August	Sun to part shade	30-75 cm
Campanula lactiflora	milky bellflower	mid-July to mid-August	Sun	100-175 cm
Campanula persicifolia	peach-leaved bellflower	mid-July to late October	Sun to part shade	60-100 cm

Scientific Name	Common Name	Bloom Time	Light	Height
Centaurea montana	mountain bluet	early June to early July	Sun to part shade	60-80 cm
Chelone lyonii	pink turtlehead	late August to late October	Sun	90-120 cm
Cimicifuga simplex	bugbane	early September to late October	Sun to part shade	120-200 cm plus
Convallaria majalis	lily-of-the-valley	mid-May to mid-June	Sun to shade	20 cm
Coreopsis verticillata	thread-leaved coreopsis	early July to late August	Sun	60 cm
Crocosmia	montbretia	early August to late September	Sun	90-120 cm
Delphinium elatum	delphinium	early July to mid-August	Sun	120-200 cm
Dianthus plumarius	cottage pinks	mid-June to late July	Sun	15-30 cm
Dicentra eximia	dwarf bleeding-heart	early May to late September	Sun to shade	30-40 cm
Dicentra spectabilis	bleeding-heart	late April to early July	Sun to part shade	90 cm
Dictamnus albus	gasplant	July	Sun	90 cm
Digitalis purpurea	foxglove	mid- June to early-August	Sun to part shade	150-200 cm
Doronicum orientale	leopard's-bane	early May to mid-June	Sun to part shade	45-60 cm
Echinacea purpurea	purple coneflower	mid-July to early October	Sun	75-120 cm
Echinops ritro	globe thistle	early August to early October	Sun	120-200 cm
Epimedium X rubrum	barrenwort	early may to mid-June	Sun to shade	30-60 cm
Erigeron speciosus	fleabane	July to mid-August	Sun	60 cm
Eryngium planum	sea holly	mid-July to late September	Sun	60-90 cm
Euphorbia epithymoides	cushion spurge	early May to late June	Sun	45 cm
Filipendula purpurea	Japanese meadowsweet	mid-July to mid-August	Sun to part shade	75-120 cm
Filipendula rubra	queen-of-the-prairie	mid-July to mid-August	Sun to part shade	200 cm plus
Filipendula ulmaria	queen-of-the-meadow	mid-July to mid-August	Sun to part shade	120 cm
Gaillardia aristata	blanketflower	early July to late October	Sun	30-80 cm
Gentiana asclepiadea	willow gentian	mid-August to late September	Sun to part shade	90 cm
Geranium pratense	meadow cranesbill	late June to late July	Sun to part shade	60-90 cm
Geranium sanguineum	bloody cranesbills	mid-June to late October	Sun to part shade	20-30 cm
Geum chiloense	avens	mid-June to mid-September	Sun to part shade	45 cm
Gypsophila paniculata	baby's breath	early July to mid-September	Sun	100 cm

Latin Name	Common Name	Blooming Season	Light	Height
Helenium autumnale	Helen's flower	mid-August to late October	Sun	50-175 cm
Helianthus X laetiflorus	cheerful sunflower	late July to mid-September	Sun	120-175 cm
Heliopsis helianthoides	false sunflower	late July to late September	Sun	75-150 cm
Helleborus orientalis	hellebore	mid-April to mid-June	Sun to part shade	40-60 cm
Hemerocallis	daylily	mid-June to late September	Sun to part shade	30-120 cm
Heuchera sanguinea	coral bells	early June to late July	Sun	30-45 cm
Hibiscus moscheutos	rose mallow	mid-August to early October	Sun	100-200 cm
Hosta	hosta	mid-July to late September	Sun to shade	15-120 cm
Hylotelephium hybrids	border stonecrop	early August to late October	Sun	60 cm
Iberis sempervirens	perennial candytuft	mid-May to late June	Sun	25 cm
Inula helenium	elecampane	early August to late September	Sun	150 -200 cm plus
Iris ensata	Japanese iris	mid-July to early August	Sun	90-120 cm
Iris siberica	Siberian iris	late June to late July	Sun	90-120 cm
Iris X barbata	bearded iris	late May to late July	Sun	20-120 cm
Kniphofia uvularia	red hot poker	mid-July to mid-September	Sun to shade	120 cm
Lamium maculatum	dead-nettle	early June to late July	Sun to shade	20 cm
Leucanthemum X superbum	shasta daisy	mid-July to mid-September	Sun	35-100 cm
Liatris spicata	blazing-star	late July to late September	Sun	75-100 cm
Ligularia 'The Rocket'	rayflower	mid-July to mid-August	Sun to part shade	150-200 cm plus
Lilium	lily	late June to early October	Sun	30-200 cm plus
Lupinus polyphyllus	lupine	mid-June to late July	Sun	100-120 cm
Lychnis chalcedonica	Maltese-cross	early July to late August	Sun	90-120 cm
Lysimachia punctata	yellow loosestrife	early July to late August	Sun to part shade	100 cm
Malva moschata	musk mallow	early July to mid-September	Sun to part shade	80 cm
Monarda didyma	beebalm	mid-July to early September	Sun	70-120 cm
Nepeta X faassenii	catmint	mid-June to mid-September	Sun	20-75 cm

Scientific name	Common name	Flowering period	Light	Height
Oenothera fruticosa	sundrops	early June to late July	Sun to part shade	45 cm
Paeonia lactiflora	peony	mid-June to late July	Sun	90 cm
Papaver orientale	oriental poppy	early June to late July	Sun	75 cm
Phlox paniculata	garden phlox	late July to early October	Sun	50-120 cm
Phlox subulata	creeping phlox	early May to mid-June	Sun	15 cm
Physostegia virginiana	obedient plant	early August to late September	Sun	50-120 cm
Platycodon grandiflorus	balloonflower	early August to late September	Sun	20-80 cm
Polemonium caeruleum	Jacob's-ladder	early June to late July	Sun to part shade	60-75 cm
Polygonatum X hybridum	Solomon's seal	early May to late June	Sun to shade	120 cm
Primula denticulata	drumstick primrose	mid-April to early June	Sun to part shade	30 cm
Primula japonica	Japanese primrose	mid-June to mid-July	Sun	45-60 cm
Primula X polyanthus	English primrose	late April to mid-June	Sun to part shade	15-20 cm
Pulmonaria	lungwort	mid-April to late June	Sun to shade	30 cm
Pulsatilla vulgaris	pasqueflower	late April to mid-June	Sun	20-45 cm
Rudbeckia fulgida	common coneflower	early August to late October	Sun	30-100 cm
Rudbeckia hirta	black-eyed Susan	early July to late October	Sun	60-90 cm
Salvia X sylvestris	perennial sage	early July to early August	Sun	60-75 cm
Saxifraga X arendsii	mossy saxifrage	early May to mid-June	Sun to part shade	15 cm
Saxifraga X urbium	London pride	mid-May to late June	Sun to shade	20-30 cm
Scabiosa columbaria	pincushion flower	mid-June to early October	Sun	20-45 cm
Sedum species	stonecrop	early July to mid-August	Sun	15-30 cm
Sidalcea hybrids	prairie mallow	mid-July to late September	Sun	60-90 cm
Symphyotrichum novi-belgii	Michaelmas daisy	late August to late October	Sun	30-60 cm
Tanacetum coccineum	painted daisy	mid-July to mid-August	Sun	60-90 cm
Thymus serpyllum	creeping thyme	early July to late August	Sun	15 cm
Trollius hybrids	globeflower	late May to early July	Sun to part shade	60-90 cm
Veronica spicata	spiked speedwell	early July to late August	Sun	20-60 cm
Vinca minor	periwinkle	late April to late June	Sun to shade	15-30 cm

INDEX

PLANTS BY LATIN NAME

INDEX

PLANTS BY COMMON NAME

ACKNOWLEDGEMENTS

I would like to extend my appreciation to the photographers that graciously allowed the use of their photos to fill the gaps in my own image library. They are listed by name in the photo credits below.

Many thanks to Stephanie Porter and Iona Bulgin for their careful attention to the prose of this book.

A special thank-you to graphic designer Todd Manning who combined the text and many photos to create this work of beauty.

Finally I would like to thank Boulder Publications for accepting this book proposal and allowing me to share my love and knowledge of plants and gardening with other Atlantic Canadian gardeners.

PHOTO CREDITS

All plant photographs are by Todd Boland, except those by the following photographers. Sincere thanks to:

Per Aasen: *Helianthus tuberosus*
Sean James: *Convallaria majalis* 'Albostriata'
Panayoti Kelaidis: *Acanthus hungaricus*, *Limonium latifolium*,
   Penstemon digitalis 'Huster Red'
Matt Lavin: *Panicum virgatum* 'Northwind', *Panicum virgatum* 'Heanse Herns'
Bill McLaughlin: *Baptisia* 'Carolina Moonlight'
Forrest and Kim Starr: *Panicum virgatum* 'Heavy Metal'

Todd Boland is the author of *Trees & Shrubs of Newfoundland and Labrador*, *Trees & Shrubs of the Maritimes*, *Wildflowers and Ferns of Newfoundland and Labrador*, *Wildflowers of Nova Scotia*, *Wildflowers of New Brunswick*, and *Wildflowers of Fogo Island and Change Islands*. He is the Horticulturalist at the Memorial University of Newfoundland Botanical Garden.

Boland has written about and lectured on various aspects of horticulture and native plants internationally. He is a founding member of the Newfoundland and Labrador Wildflower Society and an active website volunteer with the North American Rock Garden Society.

Born and raised in St. John's, Newfoundland and Labrador, Boland graduated from Memorial University of Newfoundland with an M.Sc. in Biology and a specialization in Plant Ecology. Alpine and Asian plants are his longstanding outdoor gardening passion; indoors, he maintains an ever-increasing orchid collection. Photography and bird watching occupy any non-gardening downtime.

NOTES

NOTES

NOTES

NOTES

NOTES